CAPEX Excellence

CAPEX Excellence

Optimizing Fixed Asset Investments

Dr Hauke Hansen

Dr Wolfgang Huhn

Mr Olivier Legrand

Dr Daniel Steiners

Dr Thomas Vahlenkamp

A John Wiley and Sons, Ltd., Publication

Published in 2009
Copyright © 2009 John Wiley & Sons Ltd

Registered office
John Wiley & Sons Ltd, The Atrium, Southern Gate, Chichester, West Sussex, PO19 8SQ, United Kingdom

For details of our global editorial offices, for customer services and for information about how to apply for permission to reuse the copyright material in this book please see our website at www.wiley.com

Library of Congress Cataloging-in-Publication Data

CAPEX excellence : optimizing fixed asset investments / Hauke Hansen . . . [et al.].
    p.   cm.
  Includes bibliographical references and index.
  ISBN 978-0-470-77967-5 (cloth)
  1. Capital investments.   I. Hansen, Hauke.
  HG4028.C4C344   2009
  332.63–dc22   2009011962

A catalogue record for this book is available from the British Library.

ISBN 978-0-470-77967-5 (HB)

Typeset in 10/12pt Times by Aptara Inc., New Delhi, India.
Printed in Great Britain by CP1 Antony Rowe, Chippenham, Wiltshire

Contents

Acknowledgements

No book is solely the effort of its authors and this book is certainly no exception. Several people worked closely with us, providing support that was essential to the completion of the book. Therefore a big thank you to:

Andreas Gupper, Franck Temam, Herbert Pohl, Jörg Doege, Juliane Bardt, Marcus Klemm, Olivier Cazeaux, Robin Schlinkert, Sebastian Serfas, Stefan Buchkremer, Thilo Dückert, Thomas Hundertmark, Ute Roelen, and Volker Jacobsen for helping us develop the ideas and the material that led to the chapters in this book.

Colleagues from all around the world who helped us with discussions on specific topics or provided case examples.

Our assistants, Carolin Bindert, Dagmar Krüger, Elif Ebci, Jana Stövesand, and Sabrina Michel, for help in preparing the manuscript and coordinating the flow of paper, e-mails, phone calls and meetings.

Our manuscript editors Ivan Hutnik and Jürgen Raspel for their contributions to the clarity and crispness of many chapters.

The team at John Wiley & Sons, including Karen Weller, Kerry Batcock and Jenny McCall, for their patience and understanding during the manuscript production process.

Finally, we would like to thank our wives, Angela Vockel, Dunja Vahlenkamp, Gesa Hansen, Petra Steiners, and Virginie Legrand, for their kind understanding and persistent support.

About the Authors

Hauke Hansen works as a production manager for ASML in Veldhoven (NL). Prior to his current job he was an Associate Principal in McKinsey's Düsseldorf office. He served high-tech, logistics and telecom companies and supported several multi-billion dollar investment projects. He holds a PhD in physics from the University of Konstanz and was a Fulbright Scholar at the California Institute of Technology.

Wolfgang Huhn is a Director in McKinsey's Frankfurt office. He primarily serves clients in the high-tech industry as well as in energy. Wolfgang is a member of the Business Technology Office where he leads the industrial sector in Europe and he also leads the European Product Development Practice. Prior to joining McKinsey, Wolfgang studied electrical engineering and physics at Aachen and in the UK and obtained his PhD in Physics from the RWTH Aachen. From 1998 to 2000, Wolfgang was the CEO of a VC-backed company.

Olivier Legrand is a Principal in McKinsey's Paris office. He serves clients in the transportation, steel and aluminum industries as well as in consumer goods and energy. Olivier co-leads McKinsey's global capital productivity group. Olivier holds an MBA from Stanford Business School.

Daniel Steiners is an Associate Principal in McKinsey's Düsseldorf office. He serves clients in electric power and chemicals and is a co-leader of McKinsey's European capital productivity group. Daniel received a diploma in business administration from Münster University and a PhD in management accounting from the European Business School in Oestrich-Winkel.

Thomas Vahlenkamp is a Director in McKinsey's Düsseldorf office. He serves clients in the coal, oil, gas, power, and chemicals as well as transportation industries. Thomas is the sector leader of the Energy and Materials Practice in Germany and a member of the leadership group of the European Electric Power and Natural Gas Practice. His educational background is in polymer chemistry. He holds a degree from the Technical University of Aachen (RWTH) and a doctorate from the Max Planck Institute for Polymer Research.

Part I

Why Investments Matter

1

Introduction

1.1 INVESTMENTS: THE FORGOTTEN VALUE LEVER

Much of the current management literature focuses on a limited set of "classical" value levers, such as cost reduction, sales optimization or mergers & acquisitions, thus neglecting another core value lever: capital investments (Capex).

That capital investments receive such limited attention is all the more surprising when one considers just how vitally important they are to the economy as a whole and to business in particular. In 2007, more than \$11.8 trillion was spent on capital investments globally – more than the combined GDP of Japan, China, India, South Korea, and Taiwan (or Germany, France, Italy, Spain and the UK). Not only is the sum invested enormous, but its influence on long-term company performance is critical. Since the early 1990s, asset-heavy companies in the S&P 500 have increased their average return on invested capital by 3.8 %. Our analysis indicates that about half of this increase (48 %) is related to investment activities (Figure 1.1).

Investments are important not only in optimizing the asset structure of a venture but also for enabling the introduction of new products or for introducing structural cost reductions.

Managers know that the value of an investment is not a "given" that results in an inevitable rate of return. A wide range of variables influences the outcome both positively and negatively. Understanding these variables is therefore critical in assessing the likely performance of an investment.

The experiences from a range of capital investment optimization projects show that there is significant value creation potential in optimizing capital investments. Results achieved across a wide range of optimization projects demonstrate this potential to be of the order of 15–40 % of the return on an investment. This value potential arises from three core improvement levers for investments: reductions in the amount of capital invested, acceleration of the production ramp-up, and increases in the operating cash flow during the productive life of an investment (Figure 1.2).

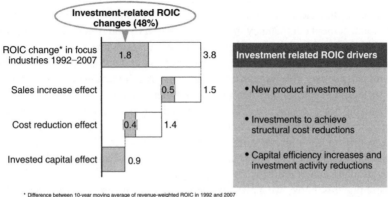

Figure 1.1 Drivers of the increase in ROIC, 1992–2007

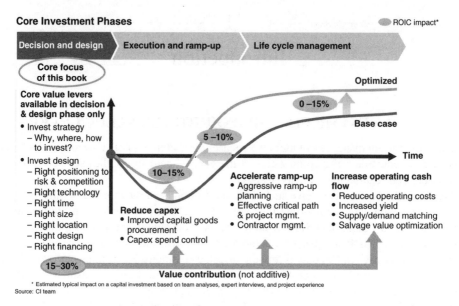

Figure 1.2   Core value levers for optimizing capital investments

1.1.1   The early bird catches the worm

Once a project progresses from the design phase to the execution and ramp-up phase the potential for optimizing the investment narrows, as much of the cash has already been spent or committed. The decision and design phase, therefore, is of critical importance to the performance of any capital investment. This phase provides the largest value creation opportunity for investing companies. The crucial questions managers are faced with in this phase are, of course, "Where, when and how to invest?", "How do we design the investment so as to ensure an optimum return?" and "What is the best way to finance the investment?"

The decisions made in this phase determine the boundary conditions for the business assets – and a significant part of its ROIC – for many years to come. Despite the importance of these decisions, it is rare to find them managed well from the outset. One of the reasons why companies continue to struggle with the design and execution of large capital investments is that their often discrete nature makes it difficult for companies to build up and maintain investment management competency in-house. A second reason is that, despite the wealth and depth of material on financial investment valuation and assessment, there is currently little or no hands-on, practical advice for capital management and optimization written from a top management perspective. To a large extent, managers are left leaning on their own experience, pulling together the best team they can find within their organization.

This surprising lack of practical management advice has been one of the main reasons prompting us to write this book: decision-makers need the best possible advice to aid them in making decisions on large investments. We intend this book to fill this gap and to provide a strategic manual on large fixed capital investments. It has a holistic approach to the topic, one that is both strategic and practical in its perspective.

In researching this book, we have invested a significant amount of time and effort in collecting and analyzing the information that forms the basis of the ideas that shape it. In the course of this work we have made extensive use of the wealth of knowledge and experience

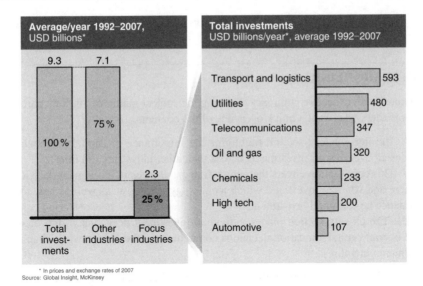

Figure 1.3 Share of investment of the asset-heavy industries under review[1]

present within McKinsey & Company – based on more than 500 capital investment-related engagements for many of the world's leading companies. These efforts have contributed to building up the capital investment practice within McKinsey.

We hope not only that this book will be interesting and readily digestible for the reader but that the ideas within it will serve to sharpen management's focus on the impact capital investments have on the wellbeing and growth of their companies – whether the companies concerned are already leaders in their field, or aspire to become so.

CAPEX Excellence is addressed in particular to the top management of companies which are based in asset-heavy industries – and especially to managers faced with the challenges of making individual or portfolio capital investment decisions and who are responsible for managing these capital assets over their entire asset lifecycle (this includes CEOs and CFOs, as well as senior managers in the business planning, financial, management accounting and control functions). We hope *CAPEX Excellence* will also be of interest to graduate management students, as well as to all those who want to gain a deeper understanding of the core strategic choices companies face when making and implementing large capital investment decisions.

Throughout the book we use many industry-specific examples, focusing in particular on seven asset-heavy industries (our "focus industries"): Utilities, Oil & Gas, Telecommunications, Transportation & Logistics, Chemicals, High Tech, and Automotive. Together, these seven industries account for about 25 % of all global annual investments (Figure 1.3). However, this is not to suggest that we think the book's relevance will be limited to these sectors alone. Other capital intensive industries, such as Steel, Aluminium, or Pulp & Paper, also face very similar challenges, so hopefully the insights here will be relevant to these industries too.

Finally, whatever your particular industry, we hope that, as the reader of this book, you will benefit from our industry and company analyses of what constitutes best practice in capital strategy.

---

[1] The largest contributors to "other industries" are real estate (24 %) and public and social services (17 %) which we do not include as focus industries since they are driven by either private or public players rather than companies.

1.2   A BIRD'S-EYE VIEW OF THE BOOK CONTENT

CHAPTER HIGHLIGHTS

This chapter is an executive summary outlining the subject matter of all three parts of this book for readers who want a quick overview of the contents.

- Part I: The introductory section highlights the importance of capital investments and provides an overview of investments across the globe, industries and time.
- Part II: This core section covers the major strategic choices in investment decision, such as where and when to invest and which technology to choose, as well as how to design and finance large capital investments.
- Part III: The closing section places individual investment decisions within the context of the overall capital allocation decisions companies are faced with when shaping their investment portfolio.

Though we hope most people will choose to read this book from cover to cover, all the chapters have been designed to stand alone, enabling the reader to study any individual chapter independently of the others. To aid the reader, wherever appropriate, we have included references to topics which are covered in more detail elsewhere in the book.

1.2.1   Part I: Why investments matter

The importance and structure of capital investments

In this chapter we examine how investments are a prerequisite for growth and what determines their structure and timing. Today about 20 % of the world's GDP is spent on capital investments. Eight out of the 10 fastest growing economies have investment intensities well above the global average. The correlation between investment and growth is even clearer in the world's emerging economies, which achieve more than twice the average economic growth with almost twice the capital intensity.

Not only is investment critical at the national level but getting investments right at the company level makes an enormous difference to a company's value creation. During the last 10 years roughly half the S&P 500's growth in return on invested capital (ROIC) has been related to investment activity.

Investment patterns vary widely between industries. The most investment-intensive industries are Transport & Logistics, Utilities, Telecommunications, and Oil & Gas, followed by Chemicals, High Tech and Automotive (the industries which are the primary focus of this book).

Investment is also highly cyclical, with a regular pattern of boom followed by bust. We observe that – while unpredictable in specific site and timing – industry cycles are far from random displaying clear cycle frequencies around 5, 10, and 30–40 years.

We conclude Part I with a brief examination of why investment volumes are likely to continue to grow in coming years, despite any short-term economic problems.

1.2.2   Part II: Getting investments right

Part II focuses on the strategic choices that companies and decision makers are faced with when making investment decisions, and provides a number of frameworks and strategies to deal with these challenges.

Chapter 2: Right positioning: Managing an asset's exposure to economic risk

We examine how the degree to which an investment asset is protected against economic risks largely determines its achievable return on investment. The degree of an asset's exposure varies: the lowest levels of exposure are conferred by exclusive access to critical resources or a natural monopoly-type situation; the highest levels are derived from leveraging commercial advantages, such as strong brands or a superior distribution network.

The core of this chapter focuses on the use of an "asset exposure scoring metric". This allows companies to quantify the degree of exposure their investment asset is likely to be subject to. The metric enables the investment to be benchmarked against the expected returns of competitors or other investments.

We close by examining a number of strategies available to companies for managing their asset exposure, looking at how companies create public-private, win-win outcomes, or go "asset light" in highly exposed markets.

Chapter 3: Right technology: How and when to invest in a new technology

Technological innovation is a critical challenge for companies. Though no company can afford to ignore technological developments, switching too early can leave it highly exposed. In this chapter we focus on how companies can determine the right timing for making the transition to a new technology.

We show that the right moment for making such a transition is not, as commonly thought, at the point when the value created by the new technology exceeds that of the existing technology, but at a significantly later point. The exact point depends both on the degree of technological risk as well as the company's appetite for risk.

We show how to determine the optimum switching point and provide an enhanced metric for measuring the value created by investments in new technology.

Chapter 4: Right timing: How cyclicality affects return on investments and what companies can do about it

Cyclicality destroys value and increases the risk of bankruptcy or investment failure. In this chapter we examine the underlying causes of cyclicality in economic systems, how it is driven by imbalances between customer demand and the available production capacity of the market, and show what companies can do to counteract it.

We examine how the time delay between the point at which companies react to differences between supply and demand and that at which these changes actually happen underlies economic cycles. We look at underlying causes of complex cycle patterns and why some cycles are stronger than others, before examining how price sensitivity and company responses to cyclicality can actually aggravate the cycle.

In the final section of this chapter we look at the various options companies have for counteracting cyclicality and how some companies can, in effect, leverage cyclicality to their advantage.

Chapter 5: Right size: Balancing economies and diseconomies of scale

In this chapter we show how defining the optimum size for an investment requires the identification of the investment "sweet spot" – the point at which diseconomies of scale begin to exceed economies of scale.

It is commonly understood that the economics of fixed costs improve with larger production volumes. We enlarge this discussion of scale effects to include, among other issues, a look at technical scaling laws, and how the "chunkiness" of capacity additions impacts higher capacity utilization.

While scale effects are often incorporated into the assessment of large investment projects, diseconomies of scale are almost always neglected. In consequence, companies often underestimate complexity costs, loss of flexibility, and the increasing risks associated with large investments. We show how this leads to a bias favoring assets that are larger than the optimum size.

We suggest a structured approach to assessing diseconomies of scale that takes into account *scale costs* as well as *economic risks* associated with scale increases. We consider a wide range of cost and risk effects, such as increased logistics costs, supply chain limitations, and increased management complexity.

Chapter 6: Right location: Getting the most from government incentives

Government incentives can have a significant impact on the longer-term returns of an investment and are often a major consideration when deciding on an investment's location. Often, however, there is very little transparency about the range of incentives available and the conditions attached to them. In this chapter we shed some light on the various categories and types of incentives that are available.

To help companies identify the incentives that are appropriate to their business case we provide a general framework which classifies the structure of the various investment instruments. We also provide an overview developed through an international screening of the incentives instruments available around the world.

We examine the impact incentives have on the business case in terms of their cash contribution and provide a simple framework to help investors select the appropriate types of incentives.

Chapter 7: Right design: How to make investments lean and flexible

In this chapter we show how lean thinking and principles can be extended from operations into investment design. We illustrate how this can enable investors to carry out the execution of investment projects in a time-efficient and resource-efficient manner, overcoming many of the limitations typically found in production plant design.

This approach, rather than focusing on a single investment, puts in place a standardized "investment system" which enables the company to bring the new capacity to market faster and at lower cost while increasing the asset's flexibility. This flexibility is necessary to cope with changing customer needs and short product lifecycles.

The outline of the investment system includes a look at the technical set of tools and practices, the required management infrastructure, and an outline of the required mindsets and behaviors. We discuss the main elements of a lean investment system in terms of defining the project objectives, design principles, and project targets, and how the design process should be optimized at the macro-, midi- and micro- levels, according to the lean principles established in the design phase.

Chapter 8: Right financing: Shaping the optimal finance portfolio

The composition of the financing portfolio is often critical to the longer-term success of an investment project. In this chapter we discuss how the project's financing can be made cost effective while maintaining the liquidity throughout the early stages of the project necessary to ensure that the repayment schedule can be met.

We examine how banks are currently at an advantage in negotiating finance due to their ability to assess and mitigate risks. This enables them to achieve very high profitability in project finance. Companies can learn much from their approach.

We show the importance of developing a thorough analysis of the likely cash flow curve over the project's lifetime. This will produce a good understanding of the project's assumptions and interdependencies.

We look at how to assess all the project's risks and to quantify their potential impact, identifying which can be mitigated and which cannot. This understanding will give companies an advantage in negotiating the project's finance.

Finally, we take a brief look at the composition of the finance portfolio and how costs can be balanced with repayment flexibility at an adequate level of confidence.

1.2.3   Part III: Right allocation: Managing a company's investment portfolio

Although there is not a one-size-fits-all approach to selecting the right investment portfolio, in the third and final part of this book we develop some guidelines to portfolio development based on the "best practices" of successful companies.

We show how such companies have four common characteristics in their capital allocation approach: 1) the alignment of capital allocation to their strategy; 2) the use of clearly-defined metrics and processes; 3) the adoption of mechanisms to avoid conscious and unconscious distortions in decision making; and 4) processes to ensure close collaboration between the corporate centre and the business units in compiling the investment portfolio.

We discuss how in a multi-divisional company the capital allocation approach is dependent on the role and involvement of the corporate center. In this regard, we illustrate the differences between "strategic architects", "financial holdings", "operators" and "strategic controllers". Taking these differences into account, we propose two different approaches to capital allocation.

TECHNICAL INSERTS

Throughout this book we will include inserts which cover some of the more technical aspects of our work. The content of these inserts will provide more details about the mathematical and analytical background to the results being discussed in the main text. It is not necessary for the reader to understand the content of these inserts in order to be able to follow the line of thought in the main text.

1.3   WHY INVESTMENTS MATTER: THE IMPORTANCE AND STRUCTURE OF CAPITAL INVESTMENTS

CHAPTER HIGHLIGHTS

In this introductory section we provide an overview of the relevance and structure of capital investments at the company, national and global levels. We investigate the drivers of national and company growth, provide a comparative overview of investments across regions and industry sectors and analyze investment behavior over time to reveal the underlying trends and causes of investment cycles.

The intent of this section is to provide the reader with a fact base to serve as a backdrop for the specific strategic choices discussed in the later chapters. Whilst reflecting some of our analytic work on capital investments, in contrast to rest of the book it is largely descriptive in nature.

1.3.1   The relevance of capital investments

Capital investments matter for business for obvious reasons: they are a prerequisite for entering new businesses, fuelling future growth, and allowing sustained production. Beyond this, capital investments are also a main driver of economic performance at the macroeconomic as well as the microeconomic level:

- *Economic growth and investments go hand in hand.* Macro-economic analysis shows a significant correlation (~70 %) between economic growth and investment in the top 30 most significant economies.
- *Investments drive business value creation.* Within the last decade companies have been able to significantly increase their return on invested capital (ROIC). We estimate that for the top companies worldwide (taken from the S&P 500 index) more than half their recent ROIC growth is related to investment activity.
- *Investments drive company growth.* An analysis of 25 of the top companies from the S&P 500 worldwide reveals ~70 % correlation between growth and investment intensity. This connection between investments and long-term company growth is also supported by fundamental microeconomic considerations.

Investments are a core driver of economic growth worldwide

In 2007, a total of more than $11.8 trillion – 23 % of the world's GDP – was spent on investments. When analyzing the changes in GDP for the 30 countries with the largest GDP, we find a correlation of up to 69 % between changes in the GDP growth and the gross fixed capital formation – a surprisingly high correlation given the wealth of factors that influence economic growth (Figure 1.4).

A word of caution is in order, however: investment and growth are rather like the proverbial chicken and egg: it is difficult to distinguish what is cause and what is effect due to the multitude of interdependencies between the two. It is interesting to note, however, that GDP growth precedes investment activity, not the other way around as one might expect. One reason why this might be the case is that a large fraction of a nation's private and public investments is typically spurred by economic growth, rather than the other way around. Also important in

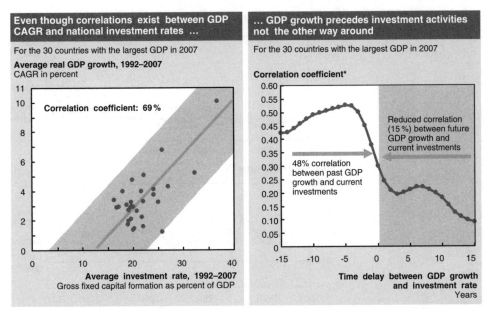

Even though correlations exist between GDP CAGR and national investment rates ...

For the 30 countries with the largest GDP in 2007

Average real GDP growth, 1992–2007
CAGR in percent

Correlation coefficient: 69%

Average investment rate, 1992–2007
Gross fixed capital formation as percent of GDP

... GDP growth precedes investment activities not the other way around

For the 30 countries with the largest GDP in 2007

Correlation coefficient*

Reduced correlation (15%) between future GDP growth and current investments

48% correlation between past GDP growth and current investments

Time delay between GDP growth and investment rate
Years

* Correlations of 5-year moving averages of investment rates and time-delayed real GDP growth between 1972 and 2005
Source: Global Insight, McKinsey

Figure 1.4   Correlation between GDP growth and investment rate

explaining this phenomenon is the tendency to invest pro-cyclically – an effect that we will investigate further in Chapter 4.

Regardless of whether it is the rate of economic growth that drives the level of investment or vice versa, the observed correlation is a clear indication of how closely economic growth is linked to investments – be they private or public in nature.

Investments are a core driver behind recent ROIC increases

Over the past 20 years we have observed a paradigm shift in how companies are run: the maximization of profits is no longer regarded as their key target. Value creation has taken over as the core metric of company success. Companies create value by investing capital at rates of return above their cost of capital. While value has been advocated by economists for a long time, it has only found widespread application in recent years, supported by the advent of modern spreadsheet applications. Return on invested capital (ROIC), together with other value metrics such as economic value added (EVA) and net present value (NPV), is now used widely as a value creation metric both by companies and by company analysts.

This new focus on ROIC appears to have had a significant impact on performance in that there has been a substantial increase in the ROIC achieved by top companies over the past 15 years. The median ROIC of S&P 500 companies rose strongly in the period 1992 to 2006, rising from 11% to 26% (Figure 1.5). This is all the more remarkable since the recent ROIC increase has not been accompanied by an increased rate of growth in sales. Sales growth has remained within its historical band during the last decade (ignoring the excursion around the year 2000).

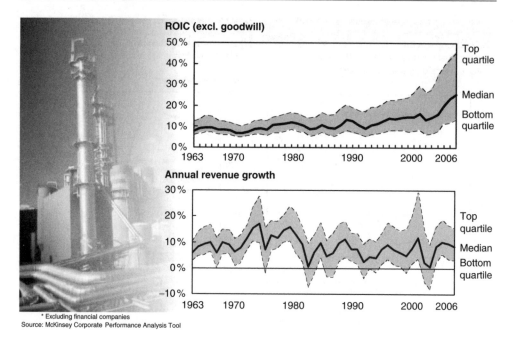

* Excluding financial companies
Source: McKinsey Corporate Performance Analysis Tool

Figure 1.5 ROIC and revenue growth rates in the S&P 500, 1963–2006

The recent increase in ROIC growth also seemed relatively robust until recently. Even the dot.com meltdown at the turn of the millennium only slowed ROIC growth temporarily, before it gained renewed momentum in 2002. This ROIC increase has been helped in part by the structural changes that have taken place in the composition of the S&P 500, which now favours less capital intensive industries in the tertiary sector, such as services and IT. However, after separating these less capital intensive industries from the more capital intensive ones, we find that only a third of the recent ROIC increase is associated with structural changes. Roughly two thirds of the total increase (3.8 %) arises from ROIC increases within capital intensive industries, such as utilities, telecommunications, transport and logistics, oil & gas, chemicals, automotive, and high tech (summarized as "focus industries" in Figure 1.6).

Capital investments have been a major driver of this increased value creation. We estimate that 48 % of the recent non-structural ROIC increase is investment related. This can be broken down further (see Figure 1.7). One quarter of the increase is driven directly by reductions in the level of invested capital relative to net profits. This increase in capital efficiency is fuelled in part by the increased awareness of value metrics, such as ROIC, and in part by the de-capitalization that took place in the mid- and late-1990s through the increased use of "capital light" approaches, including the new leasing approaches of airlines and restructuring in the utilities sector.

The other three-quarters of the recent increase in ROIC derives from the growth in corporate profitability. This enhanced profitability is driven both by increased sales and by cost reductions, with both drivers providing almost equal value contributions. This is interesting, since many executives seem to resort to cost reduction efforts rather than sales enhancement programs as the primary lever for increasing company performance.

Δ ROIC*; Percentage points

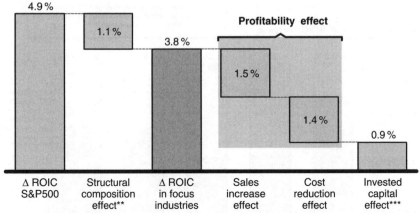

* Difference between 10-year moving average of revenue-weighted ROIC in 1992 and 2007
** Due to structural composition of S&P 500 index, which also contains asset-light industries like Services and IT that naturally
   have a higher ROIC than the asset-heavy focus industries; excludes financial companies
*** Invested capital growth below NOPLAT growth, leading to a relative decrease in invested capital
Source: CPC calculation, MCPAT, McKinsey analysis

Figure 1.6   Components of the ROIC increase between 1992 and 2007

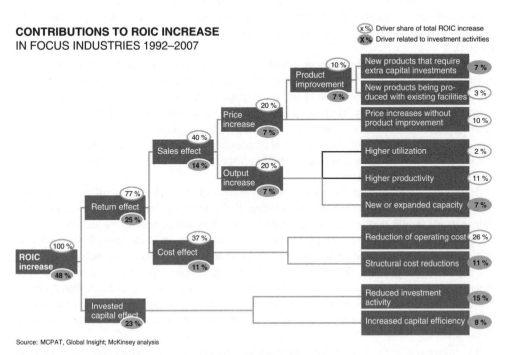

Source: MCPAT, Global Insight; McKinsey analysis

Figure 1.7   Drivers of ROIC increase and investment contribution

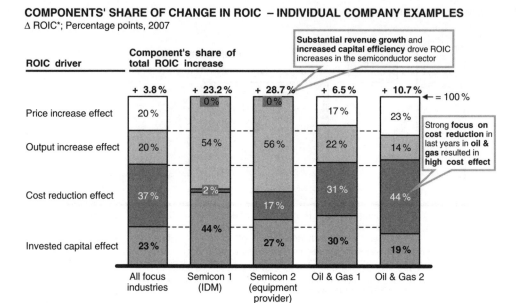

COMPONENTS' SHARE OF CHANGE IN ROIC – INDIVIDUAL COMPANY EXAMPLES
Δ ROIC*; Percentage points, 2007

Figure 1.8   Individual ROIC drivers are influenced by industry- and company-specific factors

Not all profitability enhancements require new capital investments. Often, however, fresh investments do go hand-in-hand with sales enhancement or cost reduction programs. We estimate that sales or cost-related investments contribute 26 % to the ROIC increase out of the total 48 %.

Looking at this general picture at a higher level of granularity reveals a somewhat more textured pattern. From investigating individual companies in a variety of industry sectors it is clear that the specific combination of factors responsible for the overall ROIC increase differs substantially from industry to industry and company to company (see Figure 1.8). Whereas leading semiconductor companies have achieved ROIC increases between 20–30 %, based mainly on higher output volumes as well as increased capital efficiency, leading companies in the oil and gas industry have largely resorted to price increases and cost reductions to achieve ROIC gains between 5–10 %.

If we look at a greater level of detail, even in industries in which the overall picture appears fairly uniform, there can nevertheless be substantial differences at the individual company level. For instance, while two leading companies in the semiconductor industry achieved similar ROIC increases overall and both companies realized half the increase through sales growth, with a large contribution from increased capital efficiency, there were nonetheless significant differences between them. While in the case of the equipment provider cost reduction played a substantial role in achieving these gains, this was not the case for the integrated device manufacturer. We see a similar pattern in the oil and gas sector, where the contribution from cost reductions and capital efficiency gains once again varies significantly between companies.

In summary, over the past 15 years, companies have been able to significantly increase their value creation through higher returns on their investments. Since only the smaller part of this increase can be attributed to changes in the industry structure, the greater part appears to result from how companies have adjusted their own behavior, with investments playing a major role in achieving the increase.

Company success relies on capital investments

Given how important investment is for growth overall, is this also true at individual company level? To answer this, we need to look at the nature of company growth. If a company intends to grow it has two avenues by which to do so: it can either expand its revenues through acquisitions (inorganic growth) or by selling more goods (organic growth). The delivery of most goods requires some level of investment upfront, no matter how the investment is used, whether this is to install a new production line for a car manufacturer or to extend an airline's plane fleet. It is therefore reasonable to expect some degree of correlation between the revenue growth and the capital expenditure of a company. This correlation is likely to be far from perfect, however, due to the numerous other factors that affect company growth, such as the impact of business cycles, changes in customer preferences and – most importantly – acquisitions. Nevertheless, with 50–65 % of M&A activities reported to fail to deliver on expectations (depending on the time period analyzed)[2], investments are likely to add significantly more value and in a predictable manner. A recent growth decomposition analysis by McKinsey has shown that 69 % of large companies' revenue growth on average is due to organic growth, the remaining 31 % being delivered by inorganic growth through M&A activities.[3]

There is a further challenge in establishing the nature of this relationship, however. Even if we were to assume the absolute dependence of growth upon investment (which we do not), it would be expected that the spread, timing and impact of the many small and large investments that a company makes over many years, all of which affect its growth in any one given year, would blur the picture significantly and make any correlation harder to establish. Indeed, when we analyzed 25 out of the top 50 companies worldwide[4] for the period 1988–2005, the period for which capital expenditure and revenue figures are available, this is what we found: the data show a considerable amount of spread. However, we also found a clear correlation, of up to 69 %, between revenue growth and investment intensity (Figure 1.9).

This correlation takes time to unfold, however. Typically, before the full impact of the investment can be seen in a company's results, a period of between six and 10 years needs to elapse. One of the main reasons for this delay is the lead time between the start of an investment and its production ramp-up. For example, the time that elapses from the initial investment of a new semiconductor fabrication plant (a "fab") to that at which the investment reaches full production, is of the order of 3–4 years. The most productive years in the life of a semiconductor fab will be 5–10 years after the start of production. It can therefore reasonably be expected that in most cases there will be a delay between the time an investment is made and when the impact of that investment shows up in company growth.

This presents the CEO with a number of difficult questions. The average CEO tenure has declined significantly in recent years, dropping from around nine to six years. This makes managing investments more problematic, as the CEO is unlikely to witness the full benefits of the investments they are responsible for. Neither do CEOs any longer have the luxury

---

[2] Dobbs et al. (2007).
[3] Viguerie, Smit, and Baghai (2007).
[4] Taken from the S&P 500 index.

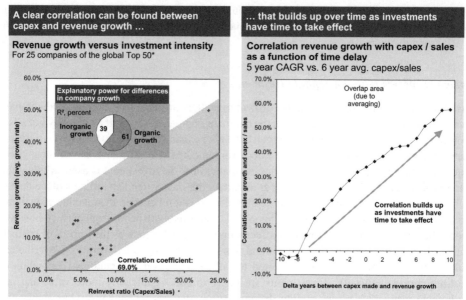

Figure 1.9   Correlation between investment and revenue growth

of sequencing consolidation and growth in the companies they manage, moving through a consolidation phase before fostering future growth. Due to the likelihood that their time in the role will be limited, there is now an imperative for them to launch growth programs at the outset. Only in this manner are they able to demonstrate the benefits of their actions while they are still in charge.

Basic microeconomics asserts the conclusion that higher investment rates support increased growth for a simple reason: A higher reinvestment rate allows faster output growth. If the investing company is able to sell the additional output in the market the investment will enable revenue growth in the future, which in turn will raise value creation if the company is able to reach an acceptable level of profitability on the additional production volume.

1.3.2   The structure of capital investments

Having looked at the fundamental relevance of investments to economic success, we will now examine how the structure of investment varies across geographical locations, across industries and over time.

A geographical perspective

Looking at the geographical distribution of investments worldwide, it is clear that there are significant differences in the pattern of investments between different regions, countries, and industries. The question we will attempt to answer here is whether these differences have a significant impact on the development of the various economies.

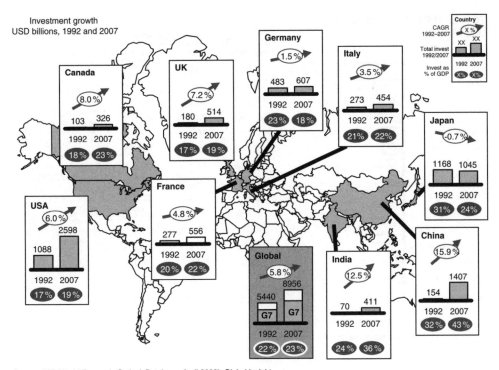

Source: IMF (World Economic Outlook Database, April 2008), Global Insight

Figure 1.10   G7, India, China and global investment growth, USD billions,1992–2007

It seems natural to start from a top-down global perspective of investments (see Figures 1.10 and 1.11). Global investments are still driven largely by the seven biggest economies, which account for more than 60 % of the total fixed capital formation (whereas all of Africa accounts for only 2 %). Overall, Asia is gaining ground, outpacing the growth of Europe and the Americas. We will take a somewhat closer look at the anatomy of Asian growth later; suffice to say for the moment that despite the increasing importance of the emerging Asian economies, such as China and India, almost three quarters of the recent ROIC increase has been realized in the developed economies rather than in the emerging ones.

Taking a look at the list of the top investor countries (Figure 1.11) we are not surprised to observe that the US is still in the lead, even increasing its investment intensity slightly, rising from 17 % in 1992 to 19 % in 2007. In second place, China has taken the position formerly held by Japan. China has fuelled its rapid economic expansion (achieving 13.5 % average GDP growth in the period 1992–2007) through a record investment intensity, which rose from an already extremely high level of 32 % in 1992 to a staggering 43 % in 2007.

Despite the economic crisis in the second half of the 1990s, Japan, in third place, has maintained a comparatively high investment level of 24 % in 2007, well above the global average. While for the US and China increased investment was turned into economic growth, for Japan it was not. Nevertheless, based on this high investment intensity, Japan continues to maintain a leading position in new technology. Germany, in fourth place, achieved a high level of investment connected to its reunification in the early 1990s. Since then it has seen its investment intensity drop, falling behind that of the US and its European neighbours,

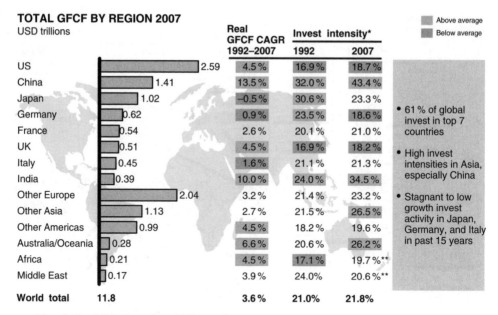

TOTAL GFCF BY REGION 2007
USD trillions

	USD trillions	Real GFCF CAGR 1992–2007	Invest intensity* 1992	Invest intensity* 2007
US	2.59	4.5%	16.9%	18.7%
China	1.41	13.5%	32.0%	43.4%
Japan	1.02	–0.5%	30.6%	23.3%
Germany	0.62	0.9%	23.5%	18.6%
France	0.54	2.6%	20.1%	21.0%
UK	0.51	4.5%	16.9%	18.2%
Italy	0.45	1.6%	21.1%	21.3%
India	0.39	10.0%	24.0%	34.5%
Other Europe	2.04	3.2%	21.4%	23.2%
Other Asia	1.13	2.7%	21.5%	26.5%
Other Americas	0.99	4.5%	18.2%	19.6%
Australia/Oceania	0.28	6.6%	20.6%	26.2%
Africa	0.21	4.5%	17.1%	19.7%**
Middle East	0.17	3.9%	24.0%	20.6%**
World total	**11.8**	**3.6%**	**21.0%**	**21.8%**

Above average
Below average

- 61% of global invest in top 7 countries
- High invest intensities in Asia, especially China
- Stagnant to low growth invest activity in Japan, Germany, and Italy in past 15 years

* Gross fixed capital formation as share of GDP
** 2006
Source: Global Insight, UN Statistics Division, McKinsey

GDP AND INVESTMENT STATISTICS FOR TOP GROWTH COUNTRIES*
Percent

Above average

	Real GDP CAGR 1992–2007	Share of global GDP 2007	Average GFCF/GDP
China	10.1	6.0	37
Ireland	6.9	0.5	21
UAE	6.9	0.4	25
India	6.8	2.1	26
Kuwait	6.5	0.2	25
Singapore	6.5	0.3	31
Malaysia	5.9	0.3	29
South Korea	5.2	1.8	32
Taiwan	5.1	0.7	22
Chile	5.0	0.3	22
World	**3.1**	**100**	**21**

* Above 0.2% of global GDP
Source: Global Insight, UN Statistics Division, McKinsey

Figure 1.11   Global overview of investments (GFCF – Gross Fixed Capital Formation)

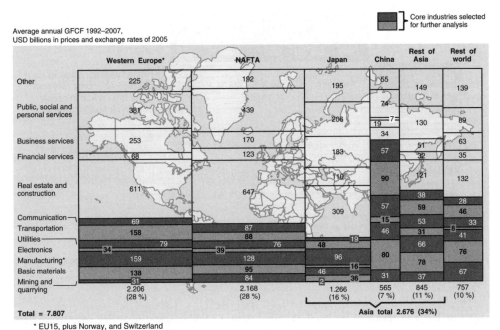

Figure 1.12 Global investment map

such as France and Italy. There are several reasons for this decline, including the increase in consumptive expenses in the eastern part of the country and reduced economic growth rates.

When the countries of the world are ranked in order of their growth during the period 1992–2007, rather than in terms of their absolute investments, we find that in all of the top 10 fastest-growing countries that this strong growth is connected to an investment level well above the global average. Three of the top 10 (China, Singapore, Korea) have fuelled their growth with an investment intensity above 30 % (Figure 1.11).

To obtain a more comprehensive overview of investments worldwide we have created a global investment map by region and industry (Figure 1.12). A quick comparison of the data reveals that Asia has become the largest investment region, accounting for 34 % of global investments. NAFTA and Western Europe[5] together contribute 56 % of total investments globally and are characterized by a similar investment pattern, although Western Europe and Japan invest more in manufacturing than does NAFTA, which invests more in the service sector.

Overall we find that the level of investments in emerging economies – starting from a lower base – is outpacing that of established economies (Figure 1.13). The emerging economies are growing twice as fast as the established ones, an evolution enabled by an investment intensity which is 50 % higher.

While this overall trend is not unexpected, it is interesting to take stock of some of the details that exemplify the links between economic growth and investments. In Asia, China is

[5] EU 15 plus Norway and Switzerland.

USD trillions	Real GDP*			Capital intensity**		(XX%) GDP selected/GDP global
	1992	CAGR	2007	1992	2007	
1 Emerging economies (Asia w/o Japan)	3.4 (10%)	5.5%	5.8 (13%)	24%	34%	• Higher capital needs to develop economy (almost twice the capital intensity of established economies)
vs.						
2 Established economies (US, EU, Japan)	23.6 (69%)	2.4%	33.9 (62%)	22%	20%	• Are the established economies falling behind?
World	34.3	2.9%	54.4	21%	22%	

* In prices and exchange rates of 2007
** Gross fixed capital formation as share of GDP
Source: Global Insight, McKinsey

Figure 1.13 Differences in capital intensity between the emerging and established economies

ahead of India in terms of its level of investment. China's capital intensity rose from 32% in 1992 to an astounding 43% in 2007. During the same period, India was able to raise its former investment level of 24% up to 34% in 2007, also well above the global average. But while China's GDP more than quadrupled in the period 1992–2007, India achieved just half this rate of growth, raising its GDP by 165%. Nevertheless, India has been able to accelerate its growth rate from annually 5% to 9% in the recent past.

In the established economies, although the US and the EU 15 displayed an almost identical level of investment in the period 1992–2007 ($1.9 trillion a year in the US compared to $2.1 trillion per year for the EU 15), the US has grown its investments at almost twice the rate of the EU 15 (at a CAGR of 4.5% compared to 2.7%). This goes hand-in-hand with the faster economic growth of the US.

At the overall level, the structure of investments in the US and Europe still show substantial commonality – in contrast, say, to that of the less developed economies. However, in the US there is nonetheless a perceptible shift from manufacturing towards electronics and real estate and housing that is not so apparent in Europe. In Europe, especially in Germany, a significantly greater share of investments go into manufacturing. Europe also invests more in business services, including accountancy and financial advice, while in the US the level of public sector investments is higher, reflecting the higher level of commitment to defense expenditure. At a more granular level, the US and Europe should not be considered monolithic blocs, of course. In Europe, for example, both Ireland and the UK have achieved above-average economic growth. In both cases this has gone hand-in-hand with increased investment intensity.

To summarize: during a period that has witnessed increasing economic integration across national boundaries, when outsourcing and off-shoring have become widely practiced in an increasingly global economy, there are nevertheless still significant differences in the investment structures of the world's largest economies, not only between regions but also within regions. In this complex landscape, where to invest remains a crucial question for companies.

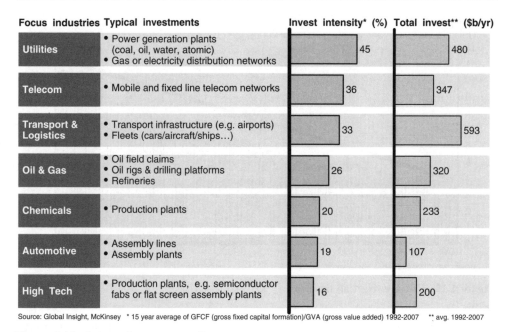

Focus industries	Typical investments	Invest intensity* (%)	Total invest** ($b/yr)
Utilities	• Power generation plants (coal, oil, water, atomic) • Gas or electricity distribution networks	45	480
Telecom	• Mobile and fixed line telecom networks	36	347
Transport & Logistics	• Transport infrastructure (e.g. airports) • Fleets (cars/aircraft/ships...)	33	593
Oil & Gas	• Oil field claims • Oil rigs & drilling platforms • Refineries	26	320
Chemicals	• Production plants	20	233
Automotive	• Assembly lines • Assembly plants	19	107
High Tech	• Production plants, e.g. semiconductor fabs or flat screen assembly plants	16	200

Source: Global Insight, McKinsey * 15 year average of GFCF (gross fixed capital formation)/GVA (gross value added) 1992-2007 ** avg. 1992-2007

Figure 1.14   Industry investment profiles

Investment profiles across industries

We have identified seven industries that show a combination of high investment intensities and high levels of total investments (see Figure 1.14)[6]. We will draw upon these industries throughout this book for examples that illustrate the investment challenges and solution approaches.

The type, intensity and total investment volume vary widely between these focus industries. Whereas investments in utilities, such as power generation and water supply, are driven by fairly predictable increases in long-term demand or regulatory changes, investments in the high-tech sector are driven by sudden changes in technology and the highly cyclical nature of the markets. Overall, during the period 1992–2007, the investment intensity in utilities was the highest of the industries studied (45 %), whereas the highest total investment was in transport and logistics (an average of $593 billion per year).

1.3.3 Time dependence of capital investments

Looking at the overall pattern of global investments from the 1970s onwards we see a cyclical pattern not unlike that of the global economic cycle. Looking a little closer, we observe that a typical investment upturn lasts for about 5–8 years, followed by a period of stagnation of about three years (Figure 1.15). Of course, there are many variations to this pattern. There were longer upturns during the periods 1983–1990 and 1992–2000, with a shorter period of stagnation in between.

---

[6] And are not of a private or public nature such as real estate or public and social investments

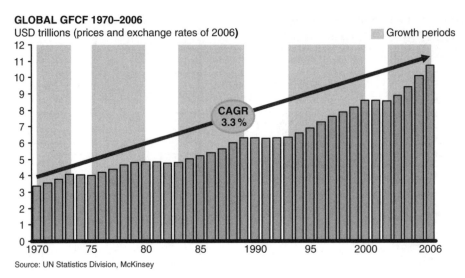

Source: UN Statistics Division, McKinsey

Figure 1.15   Global investments timeline

Even though this periodic behavior is not inevitable, after a prolonged phase of growth, any adverse economic incident is more likely to start a slowdown. The latest upturn started in 2002. Since we started writing this book, we have started to see the beginnings of another economic slowdown, in this case triggered by the subprime debt crisis in the US.

This is not to suggest that all economies follow the same cycle. Distinct differences between regions become visible when we look at national economies (see, for instance, Figure 1.16).

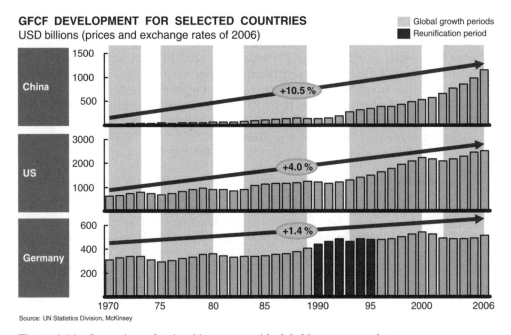

Source: UN Statistics Division, McKinsey

Figure 1.16   Comparison of national investment with global investment cycles

As already pointed out, while the US grew its investments at a solid CAGR of 4.0 % during the period 1970–2006, Germany, in contrast, saw only a meager growth of 1.4 % a year during the same period. As a result, the US has more-or-less tripled its total investment volume over the last 30 years, whereas Germany has only increased its investments by ∼40 %. Starting from a very low level, China's investment volume has grown to exceed $1100 billion, making it the world's second biggest investing nation.

Common sense suggests that the GDP fluctuations cannot be predicted from historical data – and rightly so. All the time correlations are quickly blurred by the incoherence of actions of individuals responding to such information in the deals they make. This leaves little room for arbitrage that could potentially exploit historical patterns. However, this does not mean that there is no structure to economic evolution. Quite the contrary: for instance, the frequency distribution of US GDP trends show characteristic cycle patterns.

- The **classical economic cycle** centers on a cycle frequency of **10 years**. These cycles are connected to the ebb and flow of investments, which are themselves a response to the ups and downs of the economy. They were first observed and described by Clement Juglar in the middle of the 19th century.
- A second, **shorter, five-year cycle** accompanies this 10-year cycle. It is partly driven by aggressive investment cycles in fast-growing industries such as semiconductors but is fuelled mainly by inventory fluctuations. It was first characterized by Joseph Kitchin in 1923.
- **Megacycles of 25–45 years** complete the picture. These megacycles are a superposition of infrastructure investment cycles that exhibit frequencies of up to 25 years (as described by Nobel Laureate Simon Kuznet in 1930) and "grand supercycles" or Kondratieff waves of 45–60 years (first identified by Nikolai Kondratieff in the 1920s).

We have applied the method of wavelet transforms to derive the frequency spectrum of economic cycles from the observed timelines. For an overview of this method we refer the interested reader to Appendix 1.1 at the end of this chapter.

A greater understanding of the texture and nature of these cycles can be gained by looking at individual industries. While the cycle of the electronics industry is dominated by a five-year peak, a pronounced 10-year peak governs the economic cycles in the chemical industry. The utilities industry is more complex in this respect, however, and is characterized by a mix of short, four-year fluctuations and a broad spectrum of longer-term frequency components. Overall this is not surprising, considering the differences in the underlying businesses of the two industries, such as the rapid succession of product generations in the electronics industry versus the extended lifetime of utility assets (of 20–30 years and longer). The pattern in the utilities industry is also influenced by overhaul cycles of between two and four years.

A pressing question for many business leaders in the present economic climate is: how is investment evolution at the industry level linked to that of the economy as a whole? In order to investigate this question we have compared investment growth at the industry level to that of the growth of the economy as a whole over a period of more than 30 years. This analysis reveals a clear but far from perfect correlation of 60 %. The fact that both timelines seem to be linked is not unexpected. It is reasonable to assume, for instance, that public and private investment budgets are managed, at least in part, in proportion to the total available budget. However, further examination shows that the investment timeline amplifies the various ups and downs of the GDP: changes in investment growth are more than three times as pronounced as those in GDP growth. This is true both in the established economies as well as in the emerging ones.

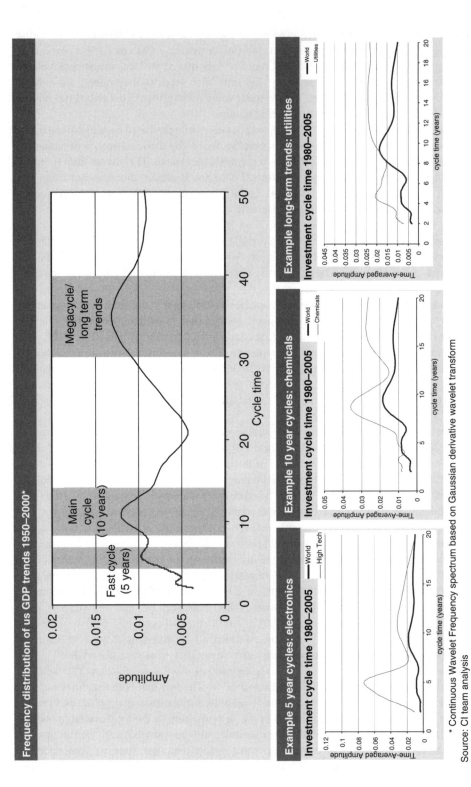

* Continuous Wavelet Frequency spectrum based on Gaussian derivative wavelet transform

Source: CI team analysis

Figure 1.17 Wavelet analysis of the overall and industry investment timelines

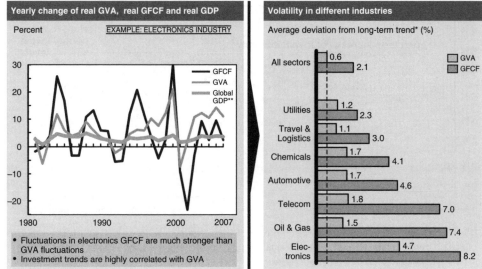

Figure 1.18 Investment (GFCF – Gross Fixed Capital Formation) volatility compared to industry value add (Gross Value Add = Revenues – Cost of Goods) and GDP volatility

Figure 1.18 depicts the value added and investment volatilities overall, as well as that for a selection of industry sectors. The investment (GFCF) volatility across all sectors is 3.5 times higher than that of the gross value added (GVA) measured over a 20-year period from 1985–2005. This amplification effect is even more pronounced if we look at individual industries. The volatility of the electronics industry's GVA is almost eight times that of the economy as a whole; the investment volatility in the electronics industry is even higher, at 14 times that of the economy. This volatility can have drastic economic consequences. One laminate producer,[7] for example, which serves the electronics industry, encountered an 80 % revenue drop during 2001–2002 due to buffer effects along its value chain. Thus, if the economy sneezes, the electronic industry catches a cold and the electronics investments goods sector is likely to suffer from severe pneumonia.

Company investments tend to show a similar pattern of amplification. Companies often experience difficulties in reducing costs sufficiently quickly to align themselves with the cycle so, instead of cutting costs, they tend to postpone or abstain from investing during downturns, since it is often easier for them to reduce investments than to reduce recurring costs. Typically, therefore, investments tend to follow cash availability and react more strongly to market fluctuations than revenues.

We will examine the underlying forces behind the cyclical aspects of investments in more detail in Chapter 4.

---

[7] Laminate producers manufacture the laminate plates used in the fabrication of printed circuit boards. Typically, a laminate consists of one or more layers of epoxy resin and metal fused together by pressure and/or heat.

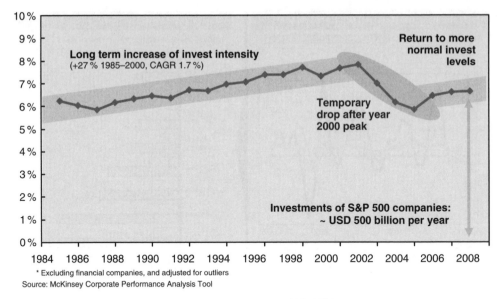

* Excluding financial companies, and adjusted for outliers
Source: McKinsey Corporate Performance Analysis Tool

Figure 1.19 Capex levels of the Fortune 50 companies, 1998–2009

1.3.4 The future of capital investments

Despite the present economic situation, there are a number of reasons why we believe investment levels will continue to increase in the longer term. A look at the history of the capital
expenditure of the Fortune 50 companies reveals increasing investment intensity over the
period 1984–2000. However, there was a significant drop in overall investment levels during
the downturn of 2001–04. This investment gap will need to be compensated for by increased
investments at some point in the future (Figure 1.19).

Some factors that are expected to drive this investment growth are:

- The increased need for **replacement investments** in countries such as Germany and Japan,
  which have recently fallen behind in their long-term average investment intensity. In
  addition, in certain industry sectors, such as utilities, a large proportion of the generation
  capacity will need to be renewed at some point in the near future in order to meet increased
  environmental standards and/or enhanced efficiency. Within the utility sector alone, OECD
  and IEA estimates suggest that approximately €11 500 billion will need to be invested
  globally in the areas of power generation, transmission and distribution during the period
  2006–30.[8]
- The **ramp-up of the emerging economies** in Asia. The accelerated growth in the rapidly
  growing economies of countries such as China has already led to a significant increase in
  fixed capital formation. We expect this trend to continue in the coming years.
- The continued trend of **globalization**, which is leading to a rebalancing of industrial
  capacities at the international level. This will continue to go hand-in-hand with further
  investments, both in the countries that take over production as well as in the countries that
  are off-shoring operations in order to rededicate their productive assets to new tasks.

---

[8] World Energy Outlook 2007, OECD/IEA.

A final example of why there will be a continuing need for increased investment levels in the coming years comes from what is maybe a less obvious source – the demand produced by global warming and the need to reduce CO_2 emissions in order to control the greenhouse effect. The sums involved in putting these problems right will be enormous. One source, the International Agency for Energy (IEA), estimates that \$45 trillion will be required in investments by 2050 in order to stop global warming.

Investments have always been a core driver and enabler of economic growth. We expect them to continue to be so in the future.

1.4 SUMMARY

The first part of this book has painted a broad picture of the important role investments play for economic success at the aggregate, industry and business levels. We have seen how investment varies by industry and geography, and how the level of investment is subject to significant variation over the course of the business cycle. In Part II of this book we will focus on trying to decipher some of the underlying determinants of whether an investment is likely to be a success or a failure. These chapters seek to provide the reader with a good understanding of the most important aspects that determine whether or not a company is able to get its investment right – in terms of managing an assets exposure to competition and risk, the right choice of technology, its timing, size, location, design, and financing.

APPENDIX 1.1: WAVELET ANALYSIS: EXTRACTING FREQUENCY INFORMATION FROM INVESTMENT TIMELINES

Any timeline can be decomposed into the frequency components it contains. Consider, for example, a piece of music played by an orchestra. Each note corresponds to a certain frequency. However, the total recording (the entire piece) contains a mix of all the notes played by the individual instruments. A frequency analysis can identify the different frequencies (notes) present in this timeline and is, therefore, very helpful in separating out the individual frequency contributions. A graphic equalizer makes use of this effect by influencing only certain frequency segments, amplifying them or reducing them to influence the balance of the bass or treble components of a song.

Fourier transformations are widely used in engineering and science to obtain frequency transforms of time data. However, to yield useful results Fourier transforms require stationary sine-oscillation components with a fixed-phase relation (coherent signals) to be present. In order to perform a frequency analysis for non-stationary (incoherent) oscillations, the Fourier transforms need to be replaced with so called "wavelet" transforms. In this case a "mother wavelet" of finite duration is used to analyze the time data.

Figure 1.20 provides an example of such a wavelet transform where the sampling wavelet is an oscillation with time delays – or a "wave package" – in the form of a Gaussian derivative. The timeline under consideration is a simple sine wave of a fixed frequency but disturbed by a number of delays scattered over time. The resulting overall frequency distribution clearly shows the core frequency despite this disturbance. It also shows that the distribution tail travels across a range of frequencies. The full transformation result reveals the frequency components along the x-axis and the time information along the y-axis. The delay periods in the timeline show up as gaps in the spectrum.

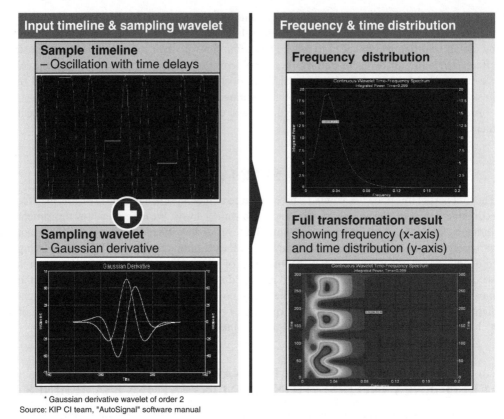

* Gaussian derivative wavelet of order 2
Source: KIP CI team, "AutoSignal" software manual

Figure 1.20   An example of a simple wavelet analysis on a sine wave with interrupts causing phase delays

Economic timelines, while often demonstrating cyclical features, cannot be represented as stationary oscillations. Therefore, wavelet transforms need to be used to extract meaningful frequency information from the time data. Although economic evolution is highly unpredictable, such an analysis is able to reveal the presence of dominant frequency regimes that govern the evolution of the economy (as typified by Juglar, Kitchin or Kuznet/Kondratieff waves).

Figure 1.21 provides an example of a wavelet analysis of GFCF development in the communications sector in the period 1980–2005. The changes in communications investments have been largely in line with the overall patterns of GFCF apart from the boom and bust involved with licensing 3G Universal Mobile Telecom System (UMTS) around the year 2000. The overall frequency transform shows two major frequency components to be present:

- A stable 10-year cycle that is visible across the whole period. This is a reflection of the overall economic and investment cycles.
- A shorter 5-year cycle with a pronounced peak around 2001. This peak is a reflection of the excursion of the industry into UMTS. While this peak does not reflect a regular pattern in the communications industry, it may well reflect the characteristic response times in the mobile segment of the industry (of around five years' duration).

FREQUENCY ANALYSIS* OF COMMUNICATIONS GFCF CYCLES (1980–2005)

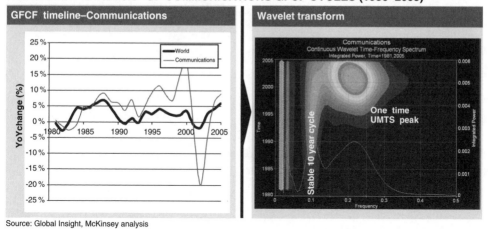

Source: Global Insight, McKinsey analysis

Figure 1.21   Wavelet analysis of the investment timeline in the communications industry

This analysis shows that wavelet transforms can be a powerful tool for identifying and analyzing cyclical economic patterns and can uncover the underlying characteristics of an economic system at both the microeconomic and macroeconomic levels.

REFERENCES

Dobbs, R., Goedhart, M., and Suonio, H. (2007). Are companies getting better at M&A? *McKinsey on Finance*, Winter, pp. 7–10.
Viguerie, P., Smit, S., and Baghai, M. (2007) *The Granularity of Growth*. Marshall Cavendish.

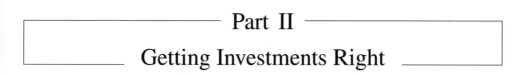

Part II
Getting Investments Right

2

Right Positioning: Managing an Asset's Exposure to Economic Risk

CHAPTER HIGHLIGHTS

The degree to which an investment asset is exposed to economic risks to a large extent determines what return on investment (ROIC) it can achieve. In this chapter we:

- see that there are five distinct levels to limit asset exposure, ranging from commercial protection achieved through a strong market position or brand, all the way to a "natural" monopoly situation, in which one or more companies operate in a market largely devoid of competition;
- construct a set of metrics for scoring asset exposure that allows the degree of exposure to be quantified. This tool can also be used to assess the ROIC of an investment, as well as for benchmarking the predicted returns against that of competitors or other industries;
- examine how companies have developed strategies to manage the degree of their exposure successfully, such as creating public-private, win-win situations or going "asset light" in highly exposed markets.

2.1 PREFACE

The purpose of this chapter is **not** to call for increased protectionism. On the contrary, we advocate open competition under fair market conditions. Open competition is the main driving force behind progress in product and process developments. Fair market conditions ensure that suppliers receive appropriate compensation for the value they add and that customers are not charged excessive prices for the goods they buy.

2.2 ASSET EXPOSURE DETERMINES THE ACHIEVABLE RETURN ON AN INVESTMENT

From a company's perspective, a large capital investment can be considered as a bet on future demand. By investing, companies take an economic risk in order to increase their future cash flow. Companies will only invest if they believe that they can realize a sufficient return on their investment to cover their initial investment costs and the risk they bear and to make a reasonable profit.

While there are many internal factors in a company that influence the return on an investment – such as the timing and execution of the investment and the product's performance and quality, as well as whether its operation is reliable and efficient – it is external factors, in terms of the asset's exposure to economic risk and competition, that concerns managers most. The reason for this is that while these factors can have a very strong influence on the

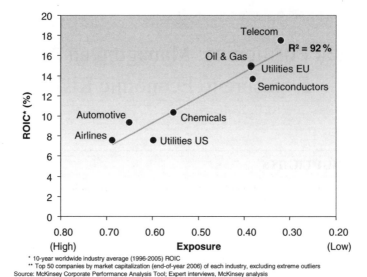

Figure 2.1 Correlation between exposure level and return on invested capital (ROIC)

asset's economic performance, managers often have only limited means to control them. It is the exposure to these external factors that this chapter focuses on.

The level of exposure to economic risk and the degree of competition determines, to a substantial degree, the return that is achievable for any given investment asset. Clearly, a fully protected asset, i.e. one in a monopoly situation, can reasonably be expected to yield higher returns than a commodity product exposed to a highly competitive market. However, though this is commonly understood there is surprisingly little quantitative research into the effects of different levels of exposure on returns.

To correct this, and to test the correlation of investment returns to asset exposure, we have defined a metric for scoring the level of economic exposure (to be explained in more detail later in this chapter). This metric shows that in the case of asset-heavy industries there is indeed, as might be expected, a clear correlation between the return on the capital invested and the level of exposure of the asset (see Figure 2.1). What is more surprising is that there is such a high degree of consistency in this relationship that this tool has a powerful predictive capability in forecasting the return on an investment.

TECHNICAL INSERT

Definition asset exposure

In the context of this chapter we use the term "asset exposure" to describe an investment's exposure to economic risk and competition. An asset's exposure to risk and competition can be reduced by a number of factors, ranging from the case where the company that owns the asset has a strong market position as a result of private or public legal protection (such as Intellectual Property rights) to that of a natural monopoly situation.

Managing an asset's exposure enables a company to raise its chances for generating the continuous and stable cash flows necessary to ensure sufficient return on that investment.

We believe that companies and managers may profit in two ways from a more systematic approach to measure asset exposure.

Firstly, a systematic approach to measure asset exposure can allow companies to develop strategies to influence the degree of protection provided to an asset. Doing so can raise the chances for a high-risk, long-term investment being able to yield a sufficient return to cover the investment costs and risks. This could turn an otherwise unviable investment into a feasible one.

Secondly, companies can compare the predicted returns for their investment against those achieved elsewhere for assets that have a similar degree of exposure to economic risk and competition. Managers can thereby get an independent reading of whether the ROIC levels they have assumed for the investment proposal will be realistic or not. The remainder of this chapter is organized into three main sections:

- A framework for the various degrees of exposure. We use real-life examples to illustrate the different exposure reduction mechanisms.
- A simple metric by which to measure exposure based on a set of predefined criteria. We show results from applying the exposure metric to various industry sectors, individual segments and companies and discuss the application of the exposure metric as a benchmarking tool.
- Strategies by which to actively manage commercial exposure. We provide an overview of the approaches and examples of strategies that have successfully been applied to manage asset exposure.

2.3   FIVE LEVELS OF PROTECTION DETERMINE THE ASSET EXPOSURE

Managing asset exposure by putting in place protective mechanisms is not a new idea. In most capital-intensive industries, protective mechanisms of some sort are in place. The different protective mechanisms give rise to varying degrees of exposure. We have classified these various mechanisms into five distinct levels of asset exposure (see Figure 2.2).

The five categories range from the lowest level of exposure, that of a natural monopoly situation (which confers little or no exposure to competition), to the highest level, in which there is no protection at all and companies are therefore subject to full competition.

It is important to realize that even in seemingly unrestricted markets some mechanisms of protection are often still in place. For instance, supermarkets, which sell everything from food to fast-moving consumer goods, typically conduct their business in a highly competitive environment. They can, nonetheless, reduce their exposure. They do so by using market share as a means to "bundle" purchasing. This helps them achieve lower prices for the goods they procure, while the high volumes also give them greater efficiencies in their network of distribution stores. All this confers some level of competitive advantage – and, therefore, reduces the exposure of individual assets.

Between these two extremes there are three other levels of exposure. The second lowest level of asset exposure is public protection, resulting from government actions such as, for example, licensing (e.g. 3G/UMTS telecommunications licenses) or mining claims. Next is private legal protection, which refers to rights that can be enforced in a court of law (e.g. patents and exclusivity contracts). This is followed by commercial protection, the weakest

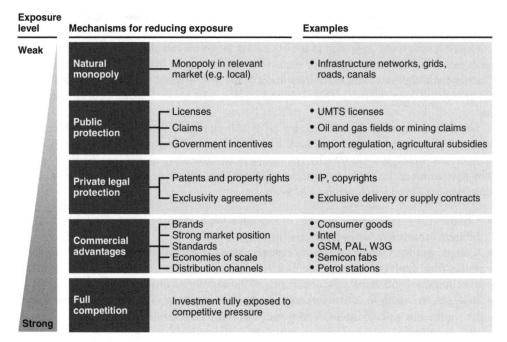

Figure 2.2   Asset exposure levels and associated exposure reducing mechanisms

safeguard, which entails the creation of barriers to market entry through commercial action, e.g. in the form of strong brands or strong market share.

Let's consider a few examples from various industries to illustrate the different protective mechanisms.

The Panama Canal is an example of a highly profitable **natural monopoly** yielding more than €1 billion net cash inflow for the Panamanian authorities annually and achieving an annual revenue growth of above 40 % (we return to this example in more detail below).

Government incentives (e.g. subsidies, finance support, or tax relief) act as a form of **public protection** and as such often play an important role in decisions about where to build a factory, especially in industries such as semiconductors and chemicals. In the automotive industry, which has faced a good deal of scrutiny, a variety of public protection mechanisms are still in place, although their importance is decreasing as the result of World Trade Organization (WTO) agreements. In consequence, public protection mechanisms for car manufacturers are mainly provided at the regional rather than at the national level, through mechanisms such as tariffs, quotas, or import bans. Quite often the forms of public protection are not direct. Shanghai, for example, enforces regulation that ensures all taxis are purchased from a single car manufacturer. There are a few exceptions in which national protection does still play an important role, as in the case of Hyundai, which still receives preferential treatment from the Korean government in its home market.

Patents are frequently used as private legal protection in the chemicals and pharmaceuticals industries. For example, Merck protects its leading market position in liquid crystals through several key patents. Basell, the world's largest producer of polypropylene and advanced polyolefin products, has established process patents that extract license fees for its special methods of producing certain polymers.

Commercial protection is used frequently in a number of industries. For example, Intel has achieved very solid commercial protection by building and defending its extremely strong market position through branding, technology leadership and privileged customer relationships. Likewise, BMW and Mercedes have invested heavily in building a superior brand positioning, which can be viewed as a protection for their business.

Companies that find themselves in a situation of **full exposure** often decide to follow "asset-light" strategies. For instance, in semiconductors, an increasing number of companies have switched to fabrication-light or fabrication-free production to avoid the prohibitively high investment costs required to establish a state-of-the-art semiconductor fabrication plant.

In the following section we employ these categories of exposure level to construct a simple metric by which to measure asset exposure.

2.4   A SIMPLE SCORING METRIC TO MEASURE ASSET EXPOSURE

So far we have highlighted the role asset exposure plays in the expected return on an investment and have discussed the five levels of asset exposure. In order to turn these notions into a useful tool for judging the viability of an investment, we have derived a metric to quantify the degree of exposure that an individual investment is subject to.

The asset exposure metric acts as a diagnostic tool which can be used to compare asset exposure across investments, locations, companies, or industries. Its primary purpose is to quantify an asset's exposure to economic risk in the business case. It therefore paves the way to make a comparison of exposure levels for different investments and provides the ability to correlate asset exposure to measures of economic success, such as the ROIC. The metric can also be used to benchmark the ROIC expected from an investment. We will return to this notion later in this chapter.

The exposure metric is a criteria-based scoring assessment that uses the five exposure levels discussed above. For each level of exposure a number of criteria have been derived by which to judge the degree of exposure at that level.

For each criterion a score is given for the asset, company or sector under consideration ranging from 0 ("full exposure, no protection") to 1 ("no exposure, full protection"). The criteria are then weighted and the results totalled to obtain the overall score for the level (ranging from 0 to 1). The results for the exposure levels are then multiplied with each other to obtain the total asset exposure score.

The scoring sheet underlying the metric is simple to use and easy to adapt to a company's individual needs. It should be stressed that the exposure metric does involve a degree of subjectivity in scoring the individual criteria. Nevertheless, because of the metric's structure and the rigorous definitions that are used, we have found variations to be within acceptable limits. The results have been shown to be reproducible when scored by different experts.

Since the assessment criteria form the heart of the exposure metric we will provide a short overview of each of the four criteria. We hope this will provide a useful starting point for managers who wish to develop or refine an asset exposure strategy. (For the reader interested in the more technical aspects of the criteria, this information can be found in the technical insert below.)

Natural monopoly: Four criteria are used to assess an asset's protection through natural monopoly mechanisms:

- The first criterion checks the degree to which the company does or does not control *unique assets*. Examples of such assets are special geographic locations, such as the Suez or Panama Canals, or exclusive claims to natural resources, such as oil reserves or diamond mines.
- The second criterion is whether *high entry barriers* are present in the market. We take the size of the initial investment for entering a market as an indication of this, such as for establishing mobile network infrastructure, in combination with low marginal costs.
- The third criterion is that of the distinctive nature of *product properties*, i.e. that products are interchangeable rather than differentiated and no real substitutes are available.
- The *number of players* in the market is the last criterion applied. The fact that only few players are present, or that one player owns the lion's share of the market volume, is a clear indication of the presence of a quasi-monopolistic situation.

Lastly we test whether *regulatory adjustments* are in place to reduce monopoly power. This information is used to obtain the final exposure value for natural monopoly protection.

Public protection: There are four criteria to judge the level of public protection:

- Are *state licenses, concessions or claims* in use?
- Does the government impose *health, safety or environmental (HSE) regulations*?
- Are there *government trade restrictions* in the market?
- Do companies receive *government subsidies* for their investments and, if they do, to what degree?

Private legal protection: Four criteria are used to assess whether private legal protection is present.

- Does the company hold key *product patents*?
- Does the company benefit from substantial competitive advantages due to *process patents*?
- Does the company hold *other key property rights*, such as trademarks or copyrights?
- Does the company have *exclusive or long-term contractual agreements* with key suppliers or customers?

Commercial protection: Four criteria are used to assess whether a company has commercial protection:

- Is it a leading player in its market, possessing a *high revenue market share*?
- Has it been able to build a competitive marketing advantage through *priority access* to certain or all *distribution channels*, or by establishing a *strong brand*?
- Does it benefit from financial advantages due either to significant *entry or exit barriers* as a consequence of high upfront investments, or the presence of substantial economies of scale, or exit limitations resulting from long-term commercial, financial or labour obligations, or due to *structural cost advantages*, such as privileged access to supplies, a depreciated asset base or significantly higher productivity?
- Has it been able to build competitive advantage through *technology leadership*?
- Has it been able to establish formal or de facto *industry standards*?

Figure 2.3 reproduces the overall scoring sheet including an overview of the criteria.

Summary scores	Low exposure situation (score = 0.0)	High exposure situation (score = 1.0)		Exposure score
Natural monopoly subtype	Natural monopoly is in place and monopoly power is not subjected to regulation or existing regulation is not effective	No monopolistic characteristics present or monopoly power effectively controlled by regulation		0.95
Public protection subtype	Very high degree of public protection	No relevant public protection mechanisms in effect		0.82
Private legal protection subtype	Very high degree of private protection	No relevant private protection mechanisms in effect		0.63
Commercial protection subtype	Effective commercial protection in place	Full exposure to commercial risk and competition		0.43
Total exposure level		Averaging exponent	4	**0.68**

Detailed scores	Example for low exposure (Indicator score = 0.0)	Example for high exposure (Indicator score = 1.0)	Weight	Score

Natural monopoly exposure

Indicators			Weight	Indicator score
Unique assets	Company has exclusive access to or ownership of unique assets (infrastructure, raw material, ...)	Company does not own unique assets (infrastructure, raw material, ...) that are vital to produce or offer products in the market	1	1.00
Network effects	Company cash flow and value creation grow more than linearly with size. Size is a dominant factor determining competitiveness in the market and size synergies can be leveraged.	Company cash flow and value creation does not grow more than linearly with size. Size is not a dominant factor determining competitiveness in the market or size synergies cannot be leveraged.	0.50	1.00
Marginal costs	Marginal costs are very low compared to initial investment	Marginal costs are high compared to initial investment	0.25	0.70
Initial investment hurdle	Initial investment is very high and effectively prevents new players from entering the market	Initial investment is low and does not provide a relevant market entry hurdle	0.25	0.90
Product standardization	Product is standardized. Almost exclusively standardized type(s) of products present in the market	Product is differentiated. High product diversity present in the market	0.25	1.00
Substitute availability	No real substitutes are available to the customers	Substitutes are readily available to the customers	0.25	1.00
Number of players	Only 1 major player in the market	Many players in the market, no dominant player	2	1.00
Preliminary exposure level for nat		Averaging exponent	2	0.95
Regulatory adjustment	No regulation in place to control monopoly power	Regulation reduces monopoly power considerably		0.00
Natural monopoly exposure level				**0.95**

Public protection

Indicators			Weight	Indicator score
Licenses required	Market players need a state license or claim, and only a small number is issued effectively limiting the number of market participants. Alternatively: Licenses are required, available in sufficient number but prohibitively expensive.	Market players do not need a state license or claim, or licenses and claims are not limited in number. License / claim price is low.	2	1.00
Health-Safety-Environmental (HSE) regulation	Government imposes strict regulations for health, safety, or environmental issues	Government does not impose regulations regarding health, safety, or environment or existing EHS regulations are not enforced	1	0.80
Trade restrictions	Market is fully protected by governmental trade restrictions (e.g., import regulations)	No governmental trade restrictions exist in market	2	1.00
Government subsidies	Company's investments are fully covered by state subsidies	Company does not receive subsidies for its investment	1	0.85
Public exposure level		Averaging exponent	2	**0.82**

Private legal protection

Indicators			Weight	Indicator score
Product patents	Company holds exclusive key product patents and patent protection is effectively enforced	Company does not hold key product patents or patent protection is not enforced	2	1.00
Process patents	Company holds exclusive process patents leading to substantial competitive advantages	Company does not hold relevant process patents conveying competitive advantages	1	1.00
Other IP ownership	Company has other key intellectual property rights, like trademarks or copyrights that are effective enforced	Company has no key intellectual property rights, (trademarks, copyrights, ...) or IP rights are not enforced	1	0.40
Exclusive contracts	Exclusive or long-term contractual agreements with key suppliers or customers are in place and provide a strong competitive advantage	No exclusive or long-term contracts with key suppliers/customers are in place or existing contracts do not provide a competitive advantage	2	1.00
Private legal exposure level		Averaging exponent	2	**0.63**

Commercial exposure

Indicators			Weight	Indicator score
Market share	Company is a dominant market player with a very high (volume) market share	Company has an insignificant share of the total market volume (revenues)	3	0.40
Distribution channels	Company has exclusive control of relevant distribution channels providing a strong competitive advantage	Equal access to all relevant distribution channels for market participants	2	0.70
Strong brands	Company has several strong brands	Company has not branded its products or branding is not relevant in this market	1	0.85
Up-front investment	Prohibitively high up-front investment are required to be competitive in this market	Up-front investments are low and do not play a relevant role. New market entries are common.	2	0.90
Economies of scale	Economies of scale significantly affect the asset or company competitiveness. Large players or assets dominate the market.	Assets have no relevant economies of scale, fixed costs are low	1	0.65
Exit barriers	Exit barriers effectively prevent exit of market participant or closing down of assets. Market exits are infrequent.	No market or asset exit barriers exist or existing barriers are ineffective	1	0.85
Structural cost advantage	Company has a decisive structural cost advantage vs competitors or substitute products e.g. through unrivaled productivity	No structural cost advantage (or cost disadvantage)	2	1.00
Technology leadership	Company has a decisive competitive edge vs competitors or competing substitutes due to superior technology	No technology lead or technology follower or technology not a relevant competitive factor	2	0.40
Industry standards	Company's products are de-facto established market standards. The vast majority of products in the market comply with this standard	Company's products are not standardized. High product diversity in present in the market	1	0.95
Commercial exposure level		Averaging exponent	8	**0.43**

Figure 2.3 Scoring overview to measure asset exposure

TECHNICAL INSERT

Considerations in constructing the asset exposure metric

This section provides information for the reader who is interested in understanding more detail about the technicalities underlying the working of the asset exposure metric but is not required to follow the fuller flow of arguments in the rest of the chapter.

The total asset exposure level is determined in a three-step approach:

1. The first step, as mentioned in the main text, is to provide a score for each individual criterion, ranging from 0 ("No exposure, full protection") to 1 ("Full exposure, no protection").
2. Combine all the criteria scores for each exposure level in a weighted average score. We use a generalized geometric mean to calculate the weighted average score using the formula:

$$E_M = \sqrt[K]{E_{M,1}^{k1} \cdot E_{M,2}^{k2} \cdot \ldots \cdot E_{M,n}^{kn}}$$

where M is the exposure level (i.e. 1 = nat. monopoly, 2 = public protection, 3 = private legal protection, and 4 = commercial protection), $E_{M,1\ldots n}$ is the exposure score for the criterion x of level M, $k1 \ldots n$ are the criteria weight factors and K is the averaging exponent ($1 < K < k1 + \ldots + kn$) (see also Figure 2.4).

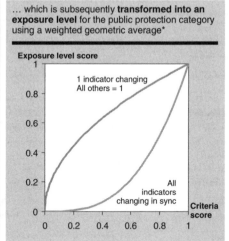

* $E_M = \sqrt[K]{E_{M,1}^{k1} \cdot E_{M,2}^{k2} \cdots E_{M,n}^{kn}}$ with EM denoting the weighted average level score, EM,x the individual criteria scores, k1...n the weight factors and K the averaging exponent
** Measure of exposure ranges from 0 (no exposure, i.e., full protection) to 1 (full exposure, i.e., no protection)
Source: McKinsey analysis

Figure 2.4 Calculation of exposure level score from individual criteria scores

This formula has been chosen to achieve the following behavior:

- If full protection (exposure = 0) is provided for any one criterion then the total exposure value is also full protection, no matter what the other values are.
- The combination of all exposure scores results in a value ranging from 0 to 1.

- The combination of several partial protections scores ($E_{M,x} < 1$) results in a higher degree of protection, i.e. the level of protection accumulates.
- Weight factors are used to give individual scores a higher or lower contribution to the overall score, reflecting their differing degrees of relevance. The weight factors can be adjusted by the user if required.
- The averaging exponent corrects for overlaps between the individual criteria and compensates for the different number of criteria used at each exposure level. This has the effect of averaging the level of protection where the criteria scores deviate significantly from each other. The averaging exponent used in the exposure metric is the best match to expert expectations.

For the natural monopoly exposure level some adaptation to this general approach has been made in order to accommodate several specific considerations:

- Criteria 2 to 5 are first averaged arithmetically before calculating the total score. This is done because only the combination of the individual scores can be considered to be a reliable indication of natural monopoly tendencies, i.e. a good indication of monopoly type protection would include product standardization, coupled with limited availability of substitutes, high entry barriers, and low marginal costs.
- In some circumstances, governments can counteract monopolistic tendencies by regulatory measures, such as placing limitations on market share, price regulation, or regulating access to critical resources such as a transportation networks or power distribution grids. To reflect this, we apply a regulatory correction factor that reduces the degree of protection when such regulations are present.

3. The total exposure score E is calculated as a geometrically averaged score of the individual scores, i.e.

$$E = \sqrt[4]{E_1 \cdot E_2 \cdot E_3 \cdot E_4}$$

with $E_{1\ldots4}$ denoting the four exposure scores for the levels of "natural monopoly", "public protection", "private legal protection" and "commercial protection".

Figure 2.5 shows a simplified, illustrative example of the application of the exposure metric in comparing the exposure of three hypothetical companies from the pharmaceutical industry. All three companies experience the same level of natural monopoly and public protection since, though they all operate in the same market, they each offer different products to tackle the same disease. Companies A and B, however, hold product patents that decrease their degree of exposure, while company C offers a generic variant that has no patent protection. Furthermore, company A is the clear market leader. Its dominant market position further reduces its degree of exposure as compared to its two competitors.

When carrying out this scoring procedure, certain issues have to be kept in mind. Firstly, the approach includes a certain degree of subjectivity (as when scoring the indicators for each category of exposure). This cannot be avoided completely but is best addressed by an expert team reviewing all the measurements in relation to each other. This will help ensure consistency in judgment. Secondly, although we have carefully tested this metric in a number of circumstances, there has been no full scientific calibration of the metric to achieve optimum fit with observed ROIC levels. It is possible that the parameters employed to calculate the exposure levels might therefore not be optimal. Despite these limitations, we believe the asset exposure metric will prove a valuable tool for managers in helping them to measure and sharpen their assessment of their company's asset exposure to economic risk and competition.

Example from the pharmaceutical market   FOR ILLUSTRATION ONLY

Situation
- 3 companies operate in the pharmaceutical market with different products that tackle the same disease
- Companies A and B both have patents, company C produces a generic drug
- Company A is the market leader, companies B and C are of the same size, but smaller than A

Protection type	Exposure			Comments
	Company A	Company B	Company C	
Natural monopoly	1.00	1.00	1.00	No natural monopoly protection exists
Public protection	0.75	0.75	0.75	All players have a protection level of 25 %, as they receive similar government subsidies
Private legal protection	0.33	0.33	1.0	Companies A and B have limited exposure due to their patents, company C has full exposure
Commercial protection	0.2	0.8	0.8	Company A as a clear market leader has a commercial advantage
Total level of exposure	0.13	0.26	0.76	Company A has the lowest exposure (13 %) of all market players (i.e. the highest protection)

* Measure of exposure ranges from 0 (no exposure, i.e., full protection) to 1 (full exposure, i.e., no protection)
Source: McKinsey analysis

Figure 2.5   Application example of the asset exposure metric from the pharmaceutical industry

2.5   QUANTITATIVE ASSET EXPOSURE ANALYSIS SHOWS HIGH CORRELATION WITH ROIC AT ALL LEVELS

Despite its simple construction the exposure metric can be used to compare asset exposure in a broad range of situations:

- across industry sectors;
- across industry segments within a sector;
- between individual companies within a sector;
- across geographic locations;
- for a company's different investments, especially where these occur in different business units.

In this section we give examples of the results from applying the metric across a range of industry sectors, segments, and individual companies. We will briefly touch upon the influence of geographic locations. Data on individual investment opportunities are usually considered by companies to be highly confidential. As a result, there is little reliable data for the individual investment level. In consequence, we do not show any analysis for individual investments here.

A major geographical influence on the overall exposure level – government incentives – is discussed in more detail in Chapter 6 "Right Location", where we provide a comparison of the structure and level of government incentives in various geographical locations.

Across industry sectors: We have already seen that companies in industries with a relatively low exposure level, such as oil & gas and telecommunications, obtain considerably higher returns on invested capital than those in industries with high exposure levels, such as the automotive and airlines (see Figure 2.1). Furthermore, this analysis also highlights some geographic differences due to the different regulatory conditions, for example, between utilities in Europe (which have had a low exposure and high ROIC in the past) to those in the US (which have a high exposure and low ROIC).

It is interesting to turn this analysis around. If industries with lower exposure are able to realize a higher ROIC, does this go hand-in-hand with higher investment intensity (capital expenditure divided by sales)? One would expect that companies in protected situations would be able to invest more than less-protected companies. The reduced level of exposure gives them the security to invest without the fear that they will not be able to recover their initial investments and with the certainty that they will be able to achieve a reasonable rate of return on their assets. Our analysis across industries confirms that there is indeed a good correlation between the asset exposure level and capital expenditure (per sales unit) in asset heavy industries (Figure 2.6).

As an example, consider the case of California, which was the first US state to pioneer utility deregulation in 1996. The electrical power supply shortage that occurred in California during 2000 and 2001 was, at least in part, a reflection of the reduced level of capital investment resulting from regulatory changes that gave companies an increased level of exposure to risk. The California power crisis highlights a dilemma for governments and companies that walk the fine line between striving to achieve a competitive market and the need to create boundary conditions which provide adequate comfort to ensure there is a sufficient level of investment.

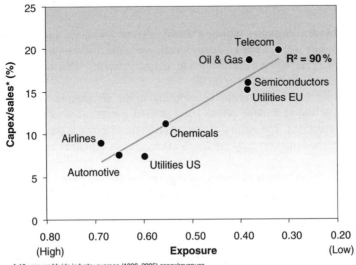

* 10-year worldwide industry average (1996–2005) capex/revenues
** Top 50 companies by market capitalization (end-of-year 2006) of each industry, excluding extreme outliers
Source: McKinsey Corporate Performance Analysis Tool; Expert interviews, McKinsey analysis

Figure 2.6 Correlation ROIC vs. capex intensity for capital heavy industries**

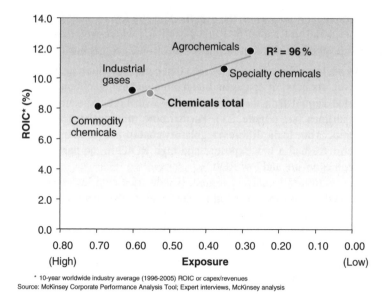

Figure 2.7   Correlation ROIC vs. asset exposure for chemical industry segments

Between industry sectors: The asset exposure level not only varies between industries and geographic locations but also by sub-sector within an industry. Commodity chemical companies, for example, experience a lower degree of protection relative to companies that produce fertilizer or specialty chemicals, which are often protected by patents. This is reflected in the average return on invested capital. While commodity players worldwide have realized a 10-year average ROIC of 8.1 % (in 1995–2004), agrochemicals achieved 11.8 % (see Figure 2.7).

Between individual companies within a sector: Figure 2.8 shows an example of the application of the exposure metric at the company level in the semiconductor industry. The individual companies in this example have been scored by industry experts. This again results in a highly significant correlation of the order of 90 %.

The primary mechanism for reducing exposure in the semiconductor industry is private legal protection achieved through product and process patents (and other means of intellectual property protection). The ability of this mechanism to provide product differentiation is somewhat diminished, however, by the frequent changes of alliances and partnerships within the industry.

In this industry, both natural monopoly and public protection play a lesser role in reducing exposure in the industry, although market segment leaders such as Intel, Samsung and TSMC tend to profit as a result of their market share and size.

Private commercial protection has a variety of roles to play. Technology leadership, for instance, plays a very significant role in this highly innovative industry. The high investment costs entailed in each new technology development form an effective entry barrier. Branding has also been applied successfully by companies such as Intel or Sony, providing them with competitive advantages. Another important form of commercial protection is high market share at the segment level. This can enable companies to achieve a positive ROIC across the

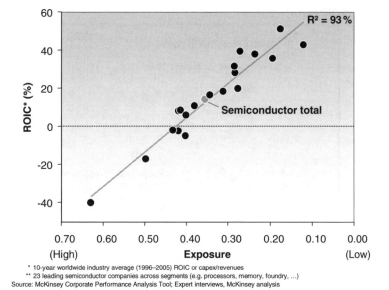

Figure 2.8   Correlation ROIC vs. asset exposure for semiconductor companies**

entire economic cycle. For example, Intel, with its strong market position and strong brand, achieves a higher return on invested capital than AMD.

2.5.1   Using exposure level analysis for benchmarking

The asset exposure metric is primarily a diagnostic tool for assessing and comparing the exposure a company faces to economic risk and competition, as well as its sources of protection. The asset exposure metric's true power is revealed, however, once it is combined with a measure of capital returns, such as the ROIC. Once this is done, it gains additional value as a benchmarking tool.

Many companies struggle to define appropriate expectations for the overall returns on their investments, especially if these investments are made by several different business units acting in several different markets. Often only a general target ROIC is set for all the proposed investments based on the corporate cost of capital (WACC[1]). One reason why this is the case is that business leadership can be overwhelmed by the sheer amount of data presented to them when business units are making their business cases proposals especially if this forms part of a regular annual budgetary cycle. For large investments it is often highly challenging to judge whether the targeted return on investment is realistic or not.

The asset exposure metric can help in these situations by providing an independent benchmark to judge the viability or performance level of a proposed or existing asset. In particular, it may be helpful in the following ways:

---

[1] Weighted average cost of capital.

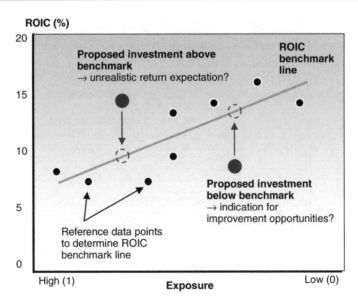

Figure 2.9   Usage of exposure level as a benchmarking tool

- as a **means to judge whether the ROIC** (or NPV[2]) stated in the business case for a proposed investment is unambitious, realistic, or overly optimistic;
- to provide an **independent confirmation of the estimated WACC level**, and establish a means to differentiate the WACC levels for each of the various investment proposals which will operate under different levels of asset exposure;
- as an **asset performance benchmarking tool**, to compare the targeted or actual performance of an asset with other assets in the same company or with competing companies in the same industry.

Figure 2.9 illustrates the approach for using the asset exposure measure as a means to cross-check investment proposals. In the first step, a ROIC benchmarking line is established by determining the exposure and ROIC levels for a number of assets or companies operating under different exposure conditions. The various investment proposals can now be compared to this benchmarking line to establish where their targeted ROIC lies in relation to the benchmark line, given each asset's exposure level. This can provide opportunities to improve the return on the individual investment or can provide evidence to challenge overly optimistic assumptions.

Once the underlying reasons for any deviation from the benchmark line have been fully understood, and any potential flaws corrected, this also gives the company the opportunity to optimize the potential return on their investment by investigating the options for reducing the level of exposure for their asset. This is the topic of the final section of this chapter.

---

[2] The calculated NPV of an investment is often highly dependent on the WACC used. The asset exposure measure allows the provision of an independent cross-check that does not depend on the specific cost and return assumptions as taken in the business case.

2.6   STRATEGIES TO REDUCE ASSET EXPOSURE

So far we have seen that the level of asset exposure plays an important role in determining the level of return for an investment and how the asset exposure measure can be used as a tool to benchmark assets against each other. Until now, we have considered the level of exposure largely as a given. Clearly, however, if there is a high correlation between asset exposure and return, managing the level of exposure can be a strong value lever for companies to enhance the returns for their asset.

In this section we provide an overview of the strategies that companies have applied successfully to manage their level of exposure. Protective measures often lead to a lack of transparency in markets and do not allow market access for all (potential) market participants. This, in turn, can lead to inflated prices for customers. However, it is a fact that there is a wide range of protection mechanisms in existence in many different industries and in many geographical locations – and making use of these protection mechanisms is currently accepted as part of fair business conduct. For example, it is generally accepted that a pharmaceutical company, a medical device company or an information content provider have the right to protect their products by patents, copyrights or other forms of intellectual property (IP) protection in order to compensate them for the expense they have incurred in developing their products. Conversely, product piracy or the selling of unlicensed copies of IP-protected products is recognized as a danger to fair trade and is illegal under international trade laws.

In this section we will discuss the various strategies companies have applied successfully to manage the level of exposure for their assets. In some cases this has made an investment possible which otherwise would not have been viable. Figure 2.10 provides an overview of the strategies used and how they fit with the differing circumstances.

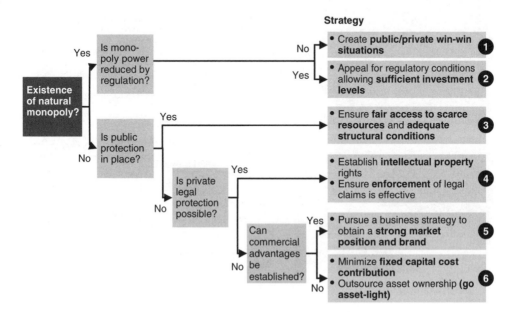

Figure 2.10   Strategies to reduce asset exposure

2.6.1 Strategy 1: Create public-private, win-win situations in natural monopoly environments

Most industries with tendencies to "natural monopoly" are usually subject to regulation, as is the case in the utilities and telecommunications industries. Often they were in the past subject to direct ownership by the government, as is true in Europe of institutions such as postal services or airlines. Privately-owned natural monopolies only survive if the state has an interest in keeping them alive and if international bodies accept their existence. This is usually only the case either if the state itself is the monopolist or if a state's interest is congruent with that of the monopolist's. Companies operating successfully in natural monopoly environments are able to do so because they manage to create or shape a win-win situation which benefits both the public and private interests.

One approach to achieving this is to establish **public-private partnerships** that maximize the benefits for both partners, ensuring an alignment of interest between the state and the company. The Panama Canal Authority, for example, operates a natural monopoly in a partnership with the national government of Panama and has managed to create a win-win situation both for itself and for the Republic of Panama (see Figure 2.11). It is a highly profitable organization that allows the government to extract around $500 million in fees each year. In October 2006, the Panama Canal Authority, in partnership with the national government of Panama, decided to invest $5 billion by 2015 to enlarge the canal and reinforce its competitiveness in world trade and transport, thereby renewing its monopoly status and future earnings.

Another reason for the persistence of monopolies is that they can be perceived to yield benefits for the economy and society as a whole. This can be the case for utilities, for

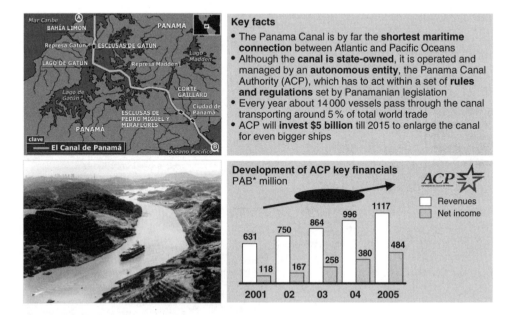

Key facts
- The Panama Canal is by far the **shortest maritime connection** between Atlantic and Pacific Oceans
- Although the **canal is state-owned**, it is operated and managed by an **autonomous entity**, the Panama Canal Authority (ACP), which has to act within a set of **rules and regulations** set by Panamanian legislation
- Every year about 14 000 vessels pass through the canal transporting around 5 % of total world trade
- ACP will **invest $5 billion** till 2015 to enlarge the canal for even bigger ships

Development of ACP key financials
PAB* million

Revenues
Net income

631 / 118   750 / 167   864 / 258   996 / 380   1117 / 484
2001   02   03   04   2005

* Panamanian Balboa (PAB); PAB 1 ≈ $1.03 (Oanda.com)
Source: NA R&I; Autoridad del Canal de Panama (ACP); McKinsey analysis

Figure 2.11 The Panama Canal as an example of a successful natural monopoly

instance, as they ensure the provision of clean water or electricity. Another reason may be that duplicating costly infrastructure to facilitate competition, as in the case of telecommunication infrastructure or a railway network, is seen as wasteful expenditure that will significantly raise costs for customers. In such cases the regulators need to make certain that they can put in place efficient systems to ensure that the costs and benefits are distributed fairly. Examples of where such considerations play an important role are in the provision of access rights to power distribution or transport networks. In these cases, a fair sharing of costs and benefits could mean that if access is granted to multiple users then these users need to participate in the costs for establishing and maintaining the necessary infrastructure.

2.6.2   Strategy 2: Foster regulatory conditions that enable sufficient investment levels

Companies operating in a regulated environment need to make sure that the regulators understand what is needed to ensure a sustainable level of investments (e.g. in infrastructure). In capital-intensive sectors, the regulation needs to encourage the necessary investments by, for example, using metrics based on ROIC, or by ensuring that tenders include a requirement for investment.

Companies can apply various approaches to achieve this. Firstly, they can make the regulator aware of any actual or predicted adverse effects of regulatory interventions (including planned regulation that has yet to be enforced). Utilities and telecom companies, for instance, are in constant discussion with the regulatory authorities to ensure that the regulator creates the right conditions to enable continued and sustainable investment.

A second approach is for companies to promote voluntary industry commitments to tackle potential problems before they become subject to regulatory intervention. For example, in 2001 German transmission and distribution operators agreed on a joint industry standard to calculate fees they charge to third parties for using electricity grids. In 2005, this voluntary agreement was transformed into a law.

Thirdly, companies can take active discussion one step further and seek to as a partner to the regulatory bodies in shaping the regulatory conditions.

In this case it can be difficult to define rules that reflect the interests of companies, the state and customers in a manner that balances the risks and returns in a fair way.

2.6.3   Strategy 3: Create the right structural conditions and ensure fair access to scarce resources

Companies without monopoly position can seek public protection, working with the state to put in place structural conditions that ensure fair access to scarce resources.

In many sectors, the government regulates access to scarce resources (e.g. as in the case of UMTS/3G licenses), restricts trade (e.g. import tariffs), provides investment incentives (e.g. tax exemptions), or sets minimum requirements (e.g. regulations on health, safety, and environmental conditions). These regulations can reduce the level of exposure. For example, in a country that regulates access to 3G frequency bands, a company that secures a 3G license obtains a certain level of protection because those that do not have such a license cannot enter the market. This does not mean that such licenses have unlimited value, however. In order to avoid paying excessive amounts for resources sold by the government companies need to determine the fair value for these resources and to point out to the government the potential consequences for investments in overpricing them.

The auction of UMTS/3G licenses in Germany provides an example of the negative impact of high prices. Despite the fact that the licenses provided protection for the mobile phone operators by limiting the number of players in the market, the high prices paid for the UMTS/3G licenses led to a substantial decline and delay of investment in mobile communication infrastructure in the period 2001—05.

Government incentives can also have a positive effect in encouraging the creation of regional clusters. This requires ensuring that these incentives produce the right structural conditions for investment. Germany's "Silicon Saxony" is a good example of the successful creation of such a regional cluster (see also Chapter 6, especially Figure 6.3). Silicon Saxony was the result of the state government's program of effective monetary incentives and structural benefits, in combination with access to the right human resources and the provision of the special status conferred on high-tech companies' investments within the state. These incentives were sufficient to encourage investments of several billion euros in the area, thereby securing thousands of jobs in the creation of what has become one of the leading semiconductor clusters in Europe.

2.6.4   Strategy 4: Establish protection for intellectual property

Companies that are unable to obtain sufficient public protection can use mechanisms for private legal protection to secure their intellectual property (e.g. through patents, copyright, or exclusivity agreements).

One approach in using legal protection is to acquire a set of key **patents**, thereby effectively excluding competitors from making a quick copy of a specific product. Basell, for instance, has established key process patents on its special method of producing certain polymers. As its competitors also use this superior method of production, Basell is in the position to extract license fees.

Another option is to put in place safeguards against competition by obtaining a large share of the patents (many of which will in themselves be of only medium importance) in a particular area. For instance, Merck KGaA has successfully used patent protection strategies in its liquid crystal business, in which it achieved a ROCE of around 50 % in 2004, by making a concerted effort to acquire as many relevant technology patents as possible (see Figure 2.12).

2.6.5   Strategy 5: Achieve a strong commercial position

Companies without sufficient public or private legal protection can only resort to the normal competitive practices and commercial actions to limit the exposure of their fixed assets as, for example, by obtaining a leading market position, establishing strong brands, or gaining preferential access to distribution channels.

Companies which are successful in developing a strong market position typically focus on achieving distinctiveness in terms of their technology, quality or cost leadership. This is particularly important in capital-intensive businesses with significant scale advantages. Intel, for example, has continuously built up its position through fresh investment in new generation chips. Its high volume and large market share of 80—85 % create an entry barrier for potential new market entrants and keep competitors at a distance. Together with its aggressive marketing techniques, these commercial advantages enable Intel to reduce its asset exposure (Figure 2.13).

Another successful approach in developing commercial protection is to establish a **technological standard**. This is an effective means for reducing exposure for market leaders as they

Liquid crystals	Liquid crystals (LCs) are used for a variety of purposes, from simplest displays in watches, calculators, or mobile phones to high-quality graphics in portable media devices, notebooks, PC monitors, and large television sets

MERCK

Merck is clear market leader

Merck gains leading position

Merck enters the LC market

- Research started in the **1960s**
- Merck **only a small player** among several other companies (e.g. Hoffmann-LaRoche, Siemens, Kodak, 3M, etc.)
- **Merck realized** very early **the future value** and importance of liquid crystal technology and **started acquiring** key technology **patents** from others

- **Acquiring technology** from players wanting to exit the market
- **Raising entry barriers** by securing application technologies with patents
- Spending considerable amounts on **R&D** to further improve their portfolio
- **Closely cooperating** with equipment suppliers and customers

- Market amounted to about **$1 billion** in 2004 with expected annual **growth rates of 10–15 %**
- Today, **Merck is the leading supplier** of liquid crystal components and liquid crystal mixtures with a **share of sales of nearly 70 %**
- Merck **continues to increase its position as market leader** in liquid crystals and achieved a **ROCE of more than 50 %** on LCs in 2004

New technology – same game?	Merck seems to have identified a **new technology** with excellent prospects, the emerging **OLED** signage and lighting market. During the last years, **Merck has acquired several OLED business divisions** from other companies and **secured various key patents and licenses** in order to be the leader in design, development, and manufacture of OLED materials

Source: McKinsey Chemicals practice; SRI

Figure 2.12   Merck KGaA's use of patents to protect its liquid crystal business

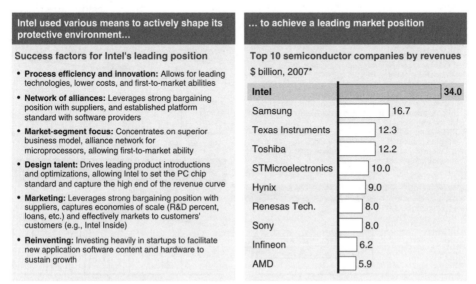

Intel used various means to actively shape its protective environment...	... to achieve a leading market position

Success factors for Intel's leading position

- **Process efficiency and innovation:** Allows for leading technologies, lower costs, and first-to-market abilities
- **Network of alliances:** Leverages strong bargaining position with suppliers, and established platform standard with software providers
- **Market-segment focus:** Concentrates on superior business model, alliance network for microprocessors, allowing first-to-market ability
- **Design talent:** Drives leading product introductions and optimizations, allowing Intel to set the PC chip standard and capture the high end of the revenue curve
- **Marketing:** Leverages strong bargaining position with suppliers, captures economies of scale (R&D percent, loans, etc.) and effectively markets to customers' customers (e.g., Intel Inside)
- **Reinventing:** Investing heavily in startups to facilitate new application software content and hardware to sustain growth

Top 10 semiconductor companies by revenues
$ billion, 2007*

Intel	34.0
Samsung	16.7
Texas Instruments	12.3
Toshiba	12.2
STMicroelectronics	10.0
Hynix	9.0
Renesas Tech.	8.0
Sony	8.0
Infineon	6.2
AMD	5.9

* iSupply Semiconductor Market Share
Source: McKinsey High-Tech practice

Figure 2.13   Intel as an example for successful commercial protection

are in a position to dominate the market and establish their technology as the standard for the entire market. Microsoft is the classic example of this approach. It has been able to establish its operating system and office software packages as a de facto standard and this has, as a result, enabled it to occupy a privileged market position.

Commercial advantages offer the lowest level of protection, because a company's market position can change rapidly. Unfettered competition means that companies with a strong market position are forced to constantly watch their competitors' actions and be ready to defend their market position each and every day.

2.6.6 Strategy 6: Minimize fixed capital costs or outsource asset ownership (go "asset light")

Companies operating in a fully exposed environment often have to take actions to reduce the risks associated with their exposure to full market competition.

One approach that companies have used in this situation is to minimize the contribution of fixed capital costs by making investments as cost effective as possible. This is achieved by reducing the level of their investments, either by investing in a smaller portfolio or by reducing the size of individual investments. To develop a smaller portfolio without harming profitability requires better focus for the remaining investments, for example, by making only those investments that lead to structural cost advantages. A number of companies limit the size of their individual investments. Honda, for example, reduces its exposure and investment risk by building small-scale production sites. However, whenever they establish a new site they

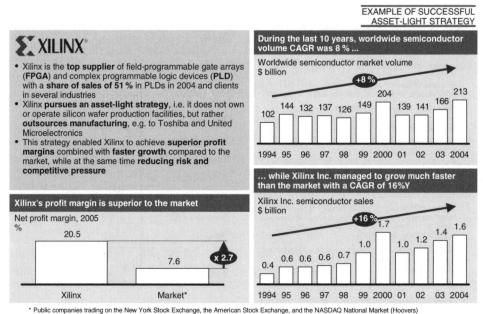

Figure 2.14   Xilinx as an example of a successful asset-light strategy

make sure that it has sufficient built-in flexibility to allow for any future capacity expansions that may be required, so the company can meet the changing demands of the market.

A more radical approach is to reduce asset exposure by outsourcing the ownership of the asset (that is, to go **"asset-light"**) or by transferring the capital investment risk to other players (e.g. by employing asset specialists). For example, Xilinx, currently the market leader in programmable logic devices, was the first semiconductor company to tackle the high competitive pressures of the industry by establishing a fabrication-less production model. Going asset-light in this way reduced its risks considerably (see Figure 2.14). In this approach, Xilinx kept major value-adding activities such as chip design, distribution, and managing customer relationships in-house while outsourcing the highly capital intensive chip production. This outsourcing of fixed production assets has given rise to the advent of manufacturing specialists, semiconductor foundries such as TSMC or Hynix, which carry out chip fabrication for their fab-less customers.

This completes our discussion about the different levels of asset exposure and the various strategies for managing this risk.

2.7 SUMMARY

In this chapter we have discussed how the right positioning of an asset may determine its economic success to a large degree. We see a clear link between the degree an asset is exposed to competition and economic risk and the return on invested capital (ROIC) that an asset is able to achieve. With the asset exposure metric we have derived a scoring method that allows companies to assess their asset exposure level or to provide an independent benchmarking tool for investment business cases.

While many of the economic boundary conditions determining an asset's exposure cannot readily be changed, several case examples illustrate that companies can follow a number of strategies to create a more favourable environment for their investments and improve their economic performance. In fact, much of the subsequent chapters of this book are dedicated to describing in more detail which strategies companies can apply to get investments "right".

3

Right Technology: How to Optimize Innovation Timing and Risks

---

CHAPTER HIGHLIGHTS

When faced with the choice of whether or not to invest into a new technology a critical challenge for companies is to determine the right time to make a technology transition. In this chapter we:

- show that, while striving to understand the opportunities offered by a new technology, companies should keep a close watch on their currently employed technologies to determine the right switching point. A careful evaluation of the remaining value of the existing assets based on the established technology may call for a somewhat later point in time for the investment into the new technology;
- illustrate how the optimum time to make a switch from an old to a new technology can be determined by assessing the company NPV as a function of possible switching times;
- examine how the optimum switching time depends on risk posture. Innovations carry risk – uncertainties due to limited knowledge about the new technology as well as inherent uncertainties such as market development or customer behavior. The inherent risk will influence the optimum switching point depending on a company's risk posture: Companies which have reason to be risk tolerant can make a transition earlier than companies with a reason to be risk averse.

3.1 CAPITAL INVESTMENTS IN TECHNOLOGY INNOVATION

New technologies can have a major influence on investment decisions. Many investments are primarily motivated by the need to introduce a new technology into the production process or the product itself. Making the right decision about the technology investment can therefore be of the utmost importance. The choice of technology can ensure the competitiveness of an operation for years ahead, whereas not making the right investment at the right point in time can lead to the longer-term failure of a company.

New technologies can significantly complicate investment decisions for capital goods. This is particularly the case for certain types of technology. Whereas new product technologies are usually driven by R&D investments in improvements of the functionality of their products (e.g. in the next generation of software, the use of new materials for certain parts, or new designs), these are not investments in the narrow sense, as they are not asset-heavy and therefore do not significantly impact the balance sheet. Process innovations, on the other hand, very often involve investment in sophisticated new equipment and frequently have a highly visible impact on the balance sheet. In this chapter we concentrate on the latter category – focusing on innovations that affect capital goods, as in the acquisition of new production equipment.

The semiconductor industry provides a quintessential example of the investment decisions associated with new technology. First of all, Moore's law[1] requires the industry to invest in the next generation of technology every 18 months. This forces the frontrunners in the semiconductor industry to basically replace their complete pool of equipment once every three years. As this technology investment has been forced on the industry pretty much as if Moore's law were a physical law, the industry's investment decisions are very much simplified. It is not a question of whether or not to invest in new equipment for a next generation process, but of which technology to invest in, i.e. which etching process equipment, how large the fabrication unit should be, and what level of automation should be used.

Even more interesting are questions regarding the timing of technology investment decisions. Periodically the industry sees a major shift in overall productivity, as in the transition from 200 mm to 300 mm wafer size, or one that has a major impact on product performance, such as that from copper to aluminum. These investment decisions reveal the full complexity of the decision process in the industry. When is the right point in time to make the transition?

Being too early can lead to unnecessarily high investment costs, or the loss of productivity and production through the immaturity of the technology. An investment made much too early can run the risk that the inherent technological challenges cannot be mastered at all, and thus could lead to the complete write-off of the investment. Being too late, on the other hand, can carry the risk that competitors will gain an advantage in being able to produce at substantially lower costs for significant periods of time, or that – by getting further along the learning curve for the new technology – they will develop a long-term competitive advantage. There is also the risk that competitors will file patents that can later prove a major obstacle to any company moving at a slower pace.

The decisions remain just as complicated when one is dealing with investments that do not shape the industry but which nevertheless can still drive long-term competitive advantage or disadvantage. When is the right time to invest in the next generation IT architecture for an ERP or supply-chain management system? When is the right time to invest – and what is the right level of investment – to significantly upgrade a product development process through the introduction of a product lifecycle management system? When we invest in a new automotive assembly line, should we use the most modern laser welding technology or should we stay with the well-established point welding method? In building a new combined-cycle power plant, should we invest in the most sophisticated dual-combustion gas turbine, which promises a significant step-up in overall efficiency, or should we stay with well-established and fully-tested gas turbines? Whatever answers are given to these questions, the companies concerned will have to live with their investment decisions for many years to come, as they cannot easily be reversed once the investments are committed.

Surprisingly, although decisions about investments in new technology are extremely risky and complex, very often business leaders fall back to relying on gut feeling or experience. Sometimes non-business criteria also come into play – especially such concerns as prestige

---

[1] Moore's law states that the performance of semiconductor chips – measured as the number of transistors per chip – effectively doubles every two years. In essence, Moore's law is an economic law, since IC manufacturers have to respond to the forecasted technological progress if they are to remain competitive. Rewritten in economic terms, Moore's law implies that the cost per transistor drops by approximately 37 % per year. A company standing still for one year will therefore be at an almost 40 % cost disadvantage in comparison to its competitors (though less so in products that are not at the leading-edge, such as automotive controllers).

or the ambition to be the first to establish a latest generation factory ("real men have real fabs").

In the face of technological risks that can be mitigated to some extent but which cannot be fully avoided, the question that needs answering is, how can a company invest optimally? How can they avoid investing too early or too late – and too much or too little?

3.1.1 Technology analysis

Though it might sound trivial, the first priority in making a technology choice is to identify whether there is a technological opportunity or not. Much has been written about the S-curve of technological progress. Most of this work has been stimulated by the intriguing fact that companies continue to invest very large sums in mature technologies, failing to recognize that a new technology has much greater potential and will produce a significantly improved performance per invested R&D dollar. Often such new technology goes unnoticed by the established companies which continue to invest in an obsolete technology, whereas the young upstarts spot its potential.

It is therefore vital to understand the basic trends and drivers of innovation. The key is to understand the theoretical limits of a technology, extrapolating from past learning curves and trajectories of performance improvement. At the heart of this challenge is the necessity for choosing the right performance parameters in assessing the relevance of a particular technology's progress.

To reflect on and illustrate the challenges posed by technological innovation we consider two examples.

Gas turbine technology provides an interesting example that shows how even shared perceptions may be deceiving. From the point of view of thermodynamics, dual-combustion gas turbines – using a second combustion chamber to make better use of the chemical energy stored in the gas – offer the opportunity to deliver higher efficiency compared to a single-combustion turbine. So should a utility invest in this new technology? At the end of the 1990s, many utilities answered this question in the positive. It then transpired that this technology was not yet mature – we will come back to this question when we talk about risk. More relevant in the evaluation of the technological opportunity, however, is the fact that the traditional technology was still progressing and so was able to catch up with the advantages de facto delivered by the new technology. It did so through a combination of increasing the combustion temperature, using more sophisticated materials in the construction of the turbine blades, and by introducing steam cooling. As the traditional technology was inherently cheaper due to the lower internal pressures in the turbine, it yielded lower lifecycle electricity generation costs for the utility. So in spite of the higher theoretical efficiency of the new technology, the established technology was actually the better investment choice at the end of the 1990s.

Semiconductors provide another good example of the challenges resulting from technological innovation. It has been repeatedly predicted that the use of traditional **optical lithography** in semiconductor production – an optical technology to imprint nanometer-scale features on a semiconductor wafer – will necessarily come to an end due to diffraction effects (even using the high end of the blue spectrum). The reason for this is that the structures that have to be projected onto the wafers are significantly smaller in size than the wave lengths of the light used in the lithography machines (called steppers or scanners, since they step from one chip on the wafer to the next and scan the exposure light across a chip). Optical resolution is conventionally limited by the wave length of light.[2] As a result, a number of alternative light sources have been proposed, e.g. soft X-rays called extreme ultraviolet radiation (EUV). In reality, however, over many years and even right up until now, engineers have been able to tweak the established technology and introduce twists, enabling them to still work with visible light. If a semiconductor manufacturer or an equipment producer had embarked on EUV lithography when it was first proposed, this would have proved to have been a catastrophic investment. At some point, however, it is likely that EUV will take over and companies which failed to acquire the required know-how may not be able to catch up quickly enough to avoid losing market share.

Let us now turn to possible methods to quantitatively support an investment decision for a new technology.

The examples show that it is not sufficient to just look at the net present value (NPV)[3] of a new technology, which might or might not be positive at some point of time. Nor is it sufficient to simply compare the NPV of the new technology with that of the old – as often done in economic practice. Rather, to obtain an optimum NPV and investment timing for a technology transition, the total path NPV – i.e. the NPV generated by assuming that the old technology is employed up to the transition point and the new technology from this point onward – should be calculated as a function of the switching time. With switching time we denote the point in time an economic decision is made to transition to a new technology. Note that before such a technology decision can take effect, a realization time is needed before a company is able to use the chosen new technology to produce goods that are sellable in the market. We suggest calling this path NPV the **Switch NPV**. The point where this Switch NPV reaches its maximum is the point where a technology transition decision creates the most value – the optimum time to decide to switch (Figure 3.1).

While the concept of a Switch NPV might at first sound somewhat theoretical, the underlying concept is nevertheless quite simple. To identify the most favorable timing for switching to a new technology, in addition to making an NPV calculation, it is also necessary to understand the likely trajectories for the development of the new technology in relation to that of the old technology. This will reveal the optimum point at which to make the switch.

Let us use the concept of the switch NPV of a technology investment to give a more analytical answer to the following two questions:

- What is the right timing for the investment?
- What is the right amount of investment?

First, an NPV is calculated for a technology investment at a certain point in time. This reflects all the necessary ingredients relevant for its success: the cashflows from the customers that purchase the product, the cost of operations, cashflows paid out for equipment, construction, testing, and modifications, etc. Let us assume that the NPV is positive. Should the company go ahead with the investment? Despite the positive NPV, the answer is: not necessarily.

---

[2] Advanced optical techniques such as off-axis illumination or the use of optical polarization allow modern scanner producers to progress beyond the classical limit by a factor of three. However, with these techniques, it becomes increasingly cumbersome to reach ever lower resolutions.

[3] NPV is the sum of all the present values of an investment's future net cash flows (i.e. each cash inflow or outflow is discounted at today's monetary value) minus the initial investment outlay. If the result is positive, the investment is expected to add value to the company.

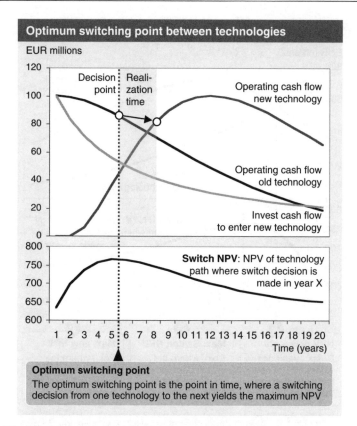

Figure 3.1   The right point in time for a technology transition

The company now needs to test the alternatives. What is the NPV if the investment is made one or two years later? The NPV is a function of time of the investment-start and will therefore show a maximum return on investment at some specific point in time. The NPV will be lower than the optimum if the investment is made before the markets are ready, or if the cost of technology is still too high, or the cost of operating it is still too high. Investments made at a point in time after the maximum NPV for the new technology has been reached will probably encounter market prices that are already on the downturn. As a result, the company will not be able to obtain the full benefit of the technology, and will only capture part of the technology lifecycle before it has to once more reinvest in new equipment because the present technology has reached the end of its useful life.

So should the company invest at the point of the maximum NPV? Once again, the answer is not necessarily. The right answer depends on the NPV of its current technological solution. It is very rare that a company invests in a new technology in a field in which it has had no previous activity. Typically, an investment case will be put together for a company that already has ongoing operations and a portfolio of implemented technologies (e.g. cutting, welding, coating, combustion, etc.). Many of these will be replaced, at least in part, by the new technology.

For example, upgrading a coal-fired power plant will require replacing installed equipment. Even investing in a completely new power plant produces a decision of whether to opt for existing (proven) technologies or for new technology. So the potential for the further development of the existing solution should always be considered in the decision process.

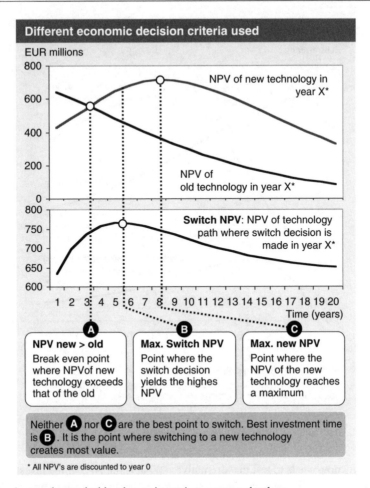

Figure 3.2 Approaches to decide when to invest into a new technology

The NPV of the existing solution gives an indication of the remaining value of the technology from a specific point in time onward. Even at the point in time where the NPV of the new technology reaches its maximum, the NPV of the existing technology might still have a strong positive value contribution, as it requires little reinvestment, is raising cashflows from its products, and requires relatively little cash outlay to maintain its operations.

A proper decsision criterion therefore needs to take into account the perspective of the old and new technology as well as the investment costs to transition between the two. The Switch NPV takes these effects into account to calculate the effective economic value of a technology transition as a function of the decision point. In this way it allows to determine the optimum switching point in time: It is the point in time where the Switch NPV reaches its maximum (Figure 3.2).[4]

---

[4] In calculating the Switch NPV it may be necessary to consider fade-out times for the old and ramp-up times for the new technology. For example, if the old technology is run in parallel to the old for a number of years the resulting NPV will contain contributions from the old technology path during this time.

The reader should be aware that many textbooks or companies at this point do not consider the impact of the switching time in their economic business case assessments. In our experience often the simple criterion "NPV new technology > NPV old technology" is considered sufficient to decide whether or not to invest into a new technology. Other companies use the criterion "maximize NPV of the new technology" which disregards the remaining value potential of the old technology as well as the required realization times to move to the new technology. While in some cases – such as at negligible realization times and transition costs – this is reasonable; in most cases the time dimension cannot be neglected and the "Maximum Switch NPV" criterion will yield better economic results.

TECHNICAL INSERT

Comparison of NPV and switch NPV

A simple example illustrates how using the standard textbook approach (NPV new technology > NPV old technology) may be misleading and does not ensure capturing the optimum value from a technology transition. Key assumptions of the example are:

- A company has the choice between two technologies. The old technology is currently in use. An innovative technology is now available. Only one technology can be used at the same time.
- The old technology decays consistently, leading to a continuous decline of cash flows over the years
- The new technology requires substantial initial investment (200 EUR millions in total, thereof 150 EUR millions (= 75 %) in first year) in the first two years
- The new technology leads to increased cash inflows during the first years and declines much later than the old technology, leading to a slower decrease of cash flows in later years.
- The company uses an 8% discount rate to calculate net present value.

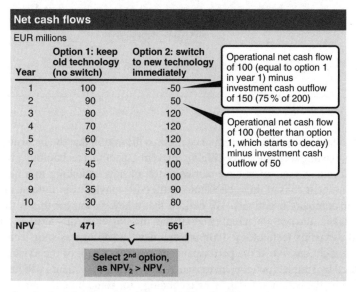

Figure 3.3 Standard textbook approach for switching decision

We assume that the company can switch from the old to the new technology at any point in time. The initial cash outflow for starting the new technology declines over time (15 % per year), due to general technological advancement, reduced risks, cheaper components, etc.

Figure 3.3 compares the cash flows of the company if it keeps the old technology with the cash flow if it decides to switch to the new technology. Since the NPV to transition now is higher than to stick to the old technology it seems advisable to switch now.

Figure 3.4 however illustrates that the best decision is option 3 (switch after year 2) as it has the highest NPV. The reader should keep in mind that there are of course further options for switching time (e.g. after year 1, 3, 5, 6) in addition to options 3 (year 2) and 4 (year 4).

In order to maximize the value of technology innovation, the company must find the most favorable switching time. Choosing the option with the most favorable switching time is equivalent to determining the point in time where the Switch NPV reaches its maximum.

Net cash flows

EUR millions

Year	Option 1: keep old technology (no switch)	Option 2: switch to new technology immediately	Option 3*: switch after year 2	Option 4*: switch after year 4
1	100	−50	100	100
2	90	50	90	90
3	80	120	12	80
4	70	120	84	70
5	60	120	120	42
6	50	100	100	74
7	45	100	100	100
8	40	100	100	100
9	35	90	90	90
10	30	80	80	80
NPV	471 <	561 <	626 >	598

Select 3rd option,
which has highest NPV

Figure 3.4   Technology transition decision based on Switch NPV

At the end of this section let us return once more to the notion that the inclusion of the value potential of an existing technology is a highly relevent aspect in a technology switch decision. With hindsight, many executives have stories to tell of how switching to a new technology at the wrong moment caused them enormous extra cost, maybe even influencing the market position of the company negatively. We believe that a key reason for this is that very often they have not taken into account a highly significant missing element – a sound analysis of the potential of the existing technology. Jumping to a new technology as soon as it arrives often may not be the right answer. If the performance and cost position of the existing technology can be upgraded by simple, low-cost investments, then these investments will have a very high return and change the equation for the new technology for some time to come.

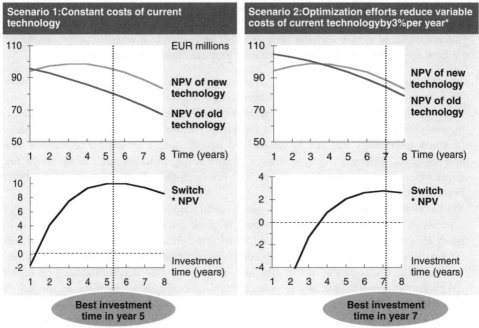

Figure 3.5   Approaches to decide when to invest into a new technology

Consider, for example, the case of a private investor who needs to reduce CO_2 emissions in electricity generation in line with regulation. In the absence of subsidies, the company may well decide to invest in upgrading their existing coal-fired power plants, as the amount of CO_2 reduced per euro invested in the current plants will exceed by far the amount that could be abated through investments in wind power or solar technologies. Similar results can be seen on the manufacturing floor. The results of applying lean management principles to the operation of existing manufacturing equipment, for instance, often by far exceeds the impact of an investment in new technology.

Figure 3.5 illustrates how productivity gains for an existing technology may offset the optimum transition point for a new technology.

3.1.2   Assess risks

The deterministic evaluation of a technology is in many cases just the first step. Finding the optimal point in time for investing into new technology will also require a proper understanding of the risks involved. In addition to the normal project risks that every investment into new assets faces, investments in new technologies pose some additional challenges due to the fact that there are innovation risks that cannot be managed away but are true uncertainties at the moment of decision taking.

We have become so used to new technologies working as expected that we are surprised when problems occur that cannot be removed quickly and which lead to a major delay of a project or even to its complete failure. But these risks exist even if they very often come in more subtle forms, e.g. failure to reach the anticipated cost position of a new manufacturing technology.

Companies faced with a decision about whether and when to invest into new technologies can follow a six-step approach to optimize their expected return on investment:

1. **Identify major sources of risk** such as, for example, market, technology, or financial risks. We will discuss major risk types applicable to new technology investments below.
2. **Distinguish predictable risks from inherent risks.** Predictable risks can be managed away by analysis or research. Examples are the yield, process time or technical performance of a new technology that can be determined by investing a reasonable amount of time and resources. Inherent risks are derived from true uncertainties such as exchange rate developments or operational hazards such as fire or earthquakes that cannot be predicted beyond a statistical level.
3. **Try to resolve predictable risks.** How many of the predictable risks can be resolved often depends on the resources and – most often – the time available before a decision has to be taken. However, the investments may well be worth the effort if they provide a company with information not readily available to their competitors or financial institutions. Based on their better-informed assessment of the situation, investments that would otherwise be highly risky may become feasible at a reasonable level of confidence, providing a competitive advantage or options to save on insurance or high interest rates by taking on risks yourself.
4. **Assess and quantify the remaining risks** taking into account risk mitigation actions.
5. **Decide on your risk posture**, i.e. how much risk you are willing to take. A company trying to capture a first mover advantage may accept a higher risk level than a technology follower playing on cost leadership.
6. **Determine the viablility and the optimum switching time** for a technology investment based on the results of the risk assessment and your risk posture.

The main point we are driving for in this section is that the optimum switching point from an old to a new technology will depend on the risk associated with an investment. As an example, a telecommunication company we know delayed its investment into a 3G network infrastructure for several years based upon its assessment of market risks. It feared that 3G applications were not sufficiently mature and customers were not ready to pay for the enhanced services. A proper risk analysis enables an educated decision about an optimum switching point under risk.

Figure 3.6 further illustrates how risk can affect the possible and optimum timing of a technology transition.

In the following we will first introduce the major types of risks faced by companies making a technology investment decision and then outline how the consideration of these risks affects the assessment of the optimum switching point.

General technology risks: If it were possible to analyze statistically the time management spends discussing issues when making an investment decision, our hypothesis is that the various technology-driven risks would win by several lengths. Technology risk categories include:

- **Business and market risk:** The technology the company is investing in allows it to create a specific functionality for the product or a certain amount of volume. If the market does not require this feature, or does not require the overall volume, the well-established technology

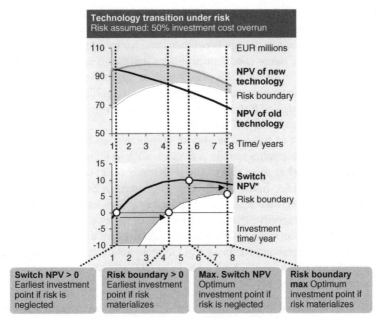

Figure 3.6   How risk may affect the timing of a technology transition

would have been a much better choice. The huge investment the telecom industry has made in acquiring UMTS licenses is the most prominent example of this risk category.

- **Technology application risk:** Is it going to work? We are so used to celebrating technological success that we sometimes underestimate the real technological challenges. The technology might not ever deliver the required cost position or might only do so at a point in time when it is already obsolete. The German highway truck toll pricing system did not work by the required date and operations were delayed by more than a year. Similarly, the new gas turbine technology which makes use of intermediate combustion did not achieve the required availability in its early years.
- **Operational risk:** Often, once the investment has been made, it can turn out that the operating cost is much higher than anticipated, thus killing the benefit the technology originally was expected to have. If, for instance, an IT investment does not achieve its

Table 3.1   Risk types

General technology risks	• Business and market risk
	• Technology application risk
	• Operational risk
	• Project risk
	• Financial risk
	• Political, environmental or legal risk
Risks specific to new technologies	• Learning curve risk
	• Market demand risk
	• Testing and implementation risks

promised performance improvement in its service provision, this can only be compensated for, for example, by increasing the number of people employed in the call center. Thus, the performance deficit of the technology is compensated for by added labor.

- **Project risks:** There are many causes of problems that can delay the realization of a new technology investment for a significant period such as unprofessional project management or supplier delays. For example, suppliers might run into problems producing a particular component which, although of little value in itself, can nevertheless have a major impact in delaying the overall implementation schedule.
- **Financial risk:** The cost of the new facility or equipment can be significantly higher than anticipated, sometimes for rather mundane reasons, such as increasing raw material prices.
- **Political, environmental or legal risks:** The investment could face unexpected intellectual property or regulatory risks. In the rapidly changing arena of environmental legislation, in particular, it could be the case that new environmental legislation is enforced during the course of the investment process, thus raising the cost of the investment significantly or even making it obsolete. The current CO_2 abatement discussion, for example, has certainly made the planned lignite powerplant investments in Germany much more challenging economically, as lignite-based plants emit a high amount of CO_2 per kWh when compared to other power generation technologies.

Risks specific to new technologies: By definition, if the investment includes a new technology, many of the inherent risks cannot be fully mitigated or tested. Here are a few examples of the types of risks specific to new technologies:

- **Learning curve risk:** The cost-position of new technology often benefits from experience, as the learning curve improves its productivity over time. This means that a company can only establish a final-cost position following an appropriate amount of experience with the technology actually in production. The slope of the learning curve and the company's final cost position cannot be predicted deterministically, therefore. In consequence, the investment decision relies on an assessment of the technology's potential and not on a mathematically precise calculation. There is risk inherent in this situation. On the other hand, delaying the investment until the technology has matured can put the company at a long-term competitive disadvantage, as competitors benefit from an early investment and are able to get further along the learning curve.
- **Market demand risk:** Markets very often pay a premium to the first mover that is able to bring a particular functionality to the market. Following in their footsteps or being late to market can mean that the profit pool is already distributed and so the investment will never reach break-even point. Customer adoption rates are inherently difficult to predict. If they are slow, then the premium to be first mover is wasted and a fast-follower strategy can be far more value creating.
- **Testing and implementation risks:** Often, when new technology is first implemented it has only been tested in smaller pilot applications. Whether it will work at the actual production size is often a question of experience and judgment – and the outcome can sometimes bring nasty surprises.

  Very often there are limits to the efficacy of testing. For instance, a technology may have so many features that it is impossible to test them all in every combination in the amount of time that is available. Another major risk arises from the requirement for long-term durability: Are the materials going to last? Very often the lifetime of a technology is so large that it is impossible to carry out real-time tests of the components' durability. A gas turbine, for example, will be in operation for 15 to 20 years. For evident reasons it can only be tested under full load for a few hours prior to being built into the power plant. Some components are expected to last even longer. Concrete, for example, is required to last as much as 50 or even 100 years. What the implications will be of upgrading the material, e.g. by using a new polymer, will not be clear until it has served out its life. Acclerated lifetime tests only partially solve this problem as they cannot completely model the real wear and stress over lifetime.

While the functionality of a component, e.g. its insulation properties or elasticity parameters, can be tested fairly easily, it is often not possible to fully test whether the polymer will encounter significant durability problems after 25 or 30 years in real-life conditions. Extrapolating the long-term durability and performance of a technology from the data that are available is therefore a technology risk that is hard to fully mitigate.

3.1.3 Mitigating technology risks

Many technology risks are inherent and cannot be avoided. However, this is not to suggest that nothing can be done to counteract them. Management therefore needs to ask itself the following questions:

- How can the financial impact of these risks be minimized?
- What impact do the risks have on the investment's timing, size and aggressiveness?
- Can the company be compensated for bearing the risks?

While risks cannot be avoided, in most cases they can be quantified using risk measures such as Value-at-Risk[5] (VAR), the "expected loss" for a specified risk. The expected loss is the product of the probability of a certain risk multiplied by its impact on the overall cashflow of the investment and, thus, on the investment NPV. A number of tools for quantifying risks are readily available and are used regularly in the banking world for calculating risk-adjusted returns and the requirements for risk capital. In an industry environment, such tools are not used nearly as frequently, judgment and gut-feeling commonly substituting for them. Our belief is that a systematic and quantitative approach that includes the quantification of risks in an investment decision can produce substantial financial benefits.

The first step in quantifying the risks is to develop an understanding of the major risk drivers. These need to be disaggregated using a causal tree to show their logical relationship and their impact on the total cashflow. Though the necessary experience and data to produce a causal tree are usually available within the company, often it is not put to this use. The correlations between the individual risks need to be dealt with quantitatively (e.g. using a model or simulation) to systematically calculate their probabilities and impact on a project.

Switch NPV and risk: The quantification of risks using such metrics as "expected loss" or "value at risk" provides an interesting extension to the concept of Switch NPV. The risk exposure of the company investing in a new technology will vary over time. Typically, the level of risk exposure will go down the longer the investment is postponed. At the point in time where the Switch NPV reaches its maximum, the risk exposure may still be fairly high. This allows the management team to make an informed decision, taking into account the following alternative responses:

---

[5] Value-at-Risk (VaR) is a risk measure commonly used by investment banks and risk managers that specifies the expected risk at a given confidence level. In the simplest terms it may be estimated as the economic costs if a risk occurs times the probability the risk will realize.

- **Postpone the investment and accept a lower Switch NPV.** This option trades the lower Switch NPV for a lower risk exposure. This is a good strategy when the first mover advantage is not significant, as in these circumstances it is advantageous that competitors should bear the larger part of the technology risk as they will not be able to create significant entry barriers by being further along the learning curve.
- **Find mitigating measures for risk.** This option enables the company to stick to the investment point indicated by the maximum Switch NPV. Such measures can be quite diverse. Suppliers and partners could be forced to bear part of the risk, for example. Alternatively, the aggressiveness of the investment can be reduced by spreading out the total investment amount over time.
- **Define the company's tolerance for risk.** Defining the level of risk that the company is willing to take sets the boundary conditions for the investment decision. Figure 3.7 shows the situation which a company is confronted with when seeking ways to reduce its risk exposure in return for a lower Switch NPV. The plot sketches the characteristics of the investment while it is postponed: the risk typically decreases whereas the Switch NPV will peak at some point and then decrease. A company has a certain range of Switch NPV and risk which it will be comfortable with which is schematically shaded in Figure 3.6. Only those investment points within the defined risk exposure threshold need be taken into account. If the point of maximum NPV (here: year 5) lies outside this threshold, the company has the three options described above: postpone the investment until year 7 when the risk has become bearable; find mitigating measures which result in lowering the curve such that the risk in year 5 is already bearable; or delineate the tolerance for risk which means increasing the area of bearable risk.

Nevertheless however much a company might try to mitigate risks, some investment risk will remain. Companies therefore need to start by acknowledging that certain risks in a technology investment cannot be removed by hard work or better analysis. These risks have to be treated as determinants of the overall profitability, in a similar manner to the overall cost position or the total cost of investment for the technology itself.

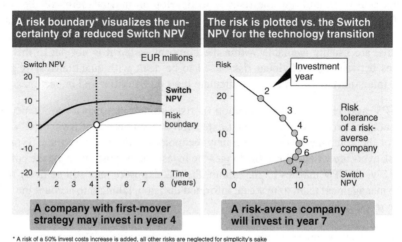

* A risk of a 50% invest costs increase is added, all other risks are neglected for simplicity's sake

Figure 3.7   Trade-off between Switch NPV and risk

It is critical that companies develop a quantified understanding of how the various risk drivers impact the profitability of a technology investment. It is all the more suprising that many do not do so currently since those that finance them certainly do quantify the risks. Banks have shown that they can – albeit not always do as the recent credit crisis has shown – make large project financing very profitable by developing a systematic understanding of the risk drivers, quantifying the overall risk exposure, and then finding mitigation measures. We believe that there is a lot to learn from this approach.

3.2   SUMMARY

In summary we have argued that finding the right time to invest into a new technology is one of the key challenges for managers faced with the challenge to make a technology transition. Using Switch NPV calculations as well as a thorough consideration of the risks associated with a new technology will help managers to make a more informed decision about the proper time for a technology transition and decreases the likelihood of wasting money by jumping too soon or too late.

4

Right Timing: How Cyclicality Affects Return on Investments and What Companies Can Do About It

CHAPTER HIGHLIGHTS

In this chapter we discuss the influence of cyclicality on company success, the underlying forces that drive cyclicality and the means companies have at their disposal to cope with cyclicality. The chapter is structured into the following sections:

- **How cyclicality destroys value** provides an introduction to the detrimental influence business cycles have on company value creation.
- **Industry drivers of cyclicality** takes a closer look at four main drivers of cyclicality, demonstrating their impact on the ethylene industry as an example based on an economic cyclicality simulation.
- **Developing an economic model of cyclicality** shows how basic economic cycles can be derived from first principles, identifying core parameters that drive cyclicality.
- **Measures to cope with cyclicality** discusses the means companies have at their disposal to deal with cyclicality, providing a number of case examples that show how companies have applied them.

4.1 HOW CYCLICALITY DESTROYS VALUE

Economic cycles not only create great problems for those responsible for making investment decisions but also may play havoc with profits. During the manufacture of a typical chemical commodity product, for example, 70–75 % of the operating margin is generated during upturns which last for only 30 % of the cycle.[1] Similarly cyclicality has a major impact on the value creation of airplane manufacturers. Using a standard measure of returns – the spread of the aggregate return (ROIC) versus the cost of capital (WACC) – this industry achieved returns of 4.4 % above WACC in the upturn of 1996–2000 but only 0.3 % in the following downturn of 2001–04.[2] Airlines fared even worse; the industry's spread being negative throughout the cycle, reaching a "high" of -1.6 % in the upturn compared to -5.5 % in the trough.

Cyclicality plays a major role in a wide range of capital-intensive industries, such as electronics, oil & gas utilities, automotive, communications, and travel & logistics. These industries exhibit highly cyclical behavior in terms of prices, investments and capital returns. For instance, the commodity chemicals industry has seen two cycles since 1980 with investment

---

[1] Paul Butler, Robert Berendes and Brian Elliott (2001). Cyclicality: Trying to Manage the Unmanageable. In: F. Budde et al. (Eds) *Value Creation*. Wiley-VCH.

[2] Corporate Performance Center, McKinsey analysis, 2005.

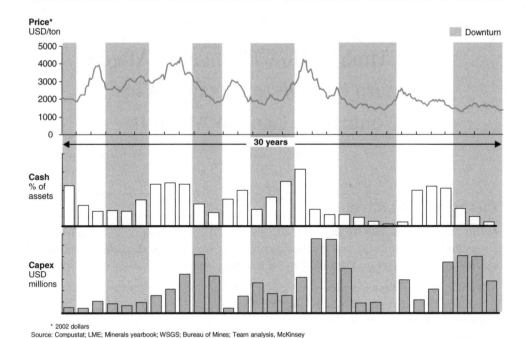

* 2002 dollars
Source: Compustat; LME; Minerals yearbook; WSGS; Bureau of Mines; Team analysis, McKinsey

Figure 4.1 Cyclicality in the mining industry – investments follow cash availability

peaks trailing capital return peaks by two years. Mining is another prime example of an industry that suffers from cyclicality, exhibiting significant and periodic variations in price, cash availability and capital expenditure levels (Figure 4.1). This example also shows that investments typically follow cash availability with a time delay of 3–5 years. Decision makers tend to approve new capex when their cash balance allows them to do so.

On a qualitative basis, the mechanisms that cause cyclicality are well understood: high prices, high capacity utilization and low stocks give rise to excess cash that can either be given back to shareholders or reinvested. Cash availability paired with optimistic forecasts, driven by "peak-cycle euphoria", lead to a pro-cyclical investment boom across an industry. Following this investment wave, new capacities added by several competitors hit the market in parallel. These new capacities start to squeeze out older ones, which are partly or fully depreciated and are ready to compete with the new ones at cash or even at variable cash cost. Hence, the price declines. External fluctuations and intrinsic market properties, such as high price volatility, aggravate the situation and lead to even more pronounced cycles.

In practice, this vicious cycle has led to dramatic value destruction in capital-intensive industries over many decades. Individual companies and even entire industries have shown a negative spread between their returns and their cost of capital over the long term. For instance, it is only when one looks at the very long term – over two to three cycles – that the returns of the pulp & paper and base chemicals industries are at all close to their cost of capital (Figure 4.2). Even though the recent period of strong worldwide growth changed this pattern temporarily, current events indicate that the cyclical nature of the business will continue to challenge sustainable margins and return on investment.

All these examples support one point: cyclicality destroys value in a wide range of industries. Although it is unrealistic to believe that companies can fully eliminate cyclicality, they can

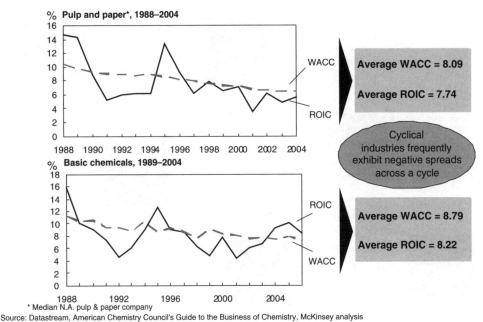

Figure 4.2   Pulp and paper industry performance – ROIC vs. WACC

better manage its impact if the decision makers understand (a) the drivers of cyclicality, and (b) the measures to potentially mitigate its worst effects.

In the remainder of this chapter we analyze the nature of the drivers of cyclicality and discuss the countermeasures that companies have at their disposal to mitigate the risks associated with them.

4.2   INDUSTRY DRIVERS OF CYCLICALITY

In this section we take a closer look at how cyclicality affects companies in cyclical industries. We outline the underlying mechanisms and use a simple empirical simulation to uncover some core drivers of cyclicality. We focus on the industry drivers of cyclicality that can be influenced by companies, rather than on the macroeconomic factors such as demand sensitivity or material supply costs, which often are out of management's control.

Figure 4.3 depicts a simple model of cyclicality at the industry level that links basic market parameters (supply, demand, and price) to the investment behaviour of companies. This creates a feedback loop with four steps:

1. Supply and demand determine the price and capacity utilization of an industry segment.
2. Price and utilization levels determine a company's cash flow.
3. The company determines its investments (or capacity reductions) based on cash availability and its forecast of future economic developments.
4. After the capacity adaptations are realized they affect the supply available to the market, completing the feedback loop.

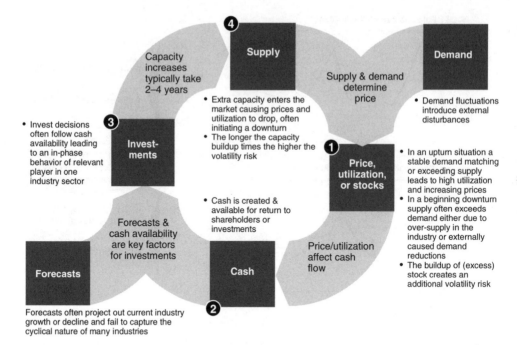

Figure 4.3   The feedback loop giving rise to economic cycles

This cyclicality loop can be observed clearly in the semiconductor industry, which is characterized by cycles with a duration of about five years (Figure 4.4). The industry has experienced a rollercoaster ride of upturns and downturns over a number of decades, which has left only the most successful companies unscarred, the less successful ones dropping out at or soon after the bottom of each trough. The market cycle typical of the semiconductor industry plays out by completing two complete runs through the four steps of our feedback loop. A rising market leads to increasing prices and high utilization. This earns the semiconductor companies plenty of cash. Based on a combination of optimistic forecasts and the "iron fist" of Moore's law, which dictates rapid technological innovation, they use this cash to invest in new capacity. Once the new capacity comes on line – often with several companies bringing in new plant at largely the same time – the sector's total capacity exceeds customer demand. This gives rise to a softening in prices. The resulting stringent cash constraints then lead to conservative capital spending and so little new capacity is added until the next new technology or economic upturn leads to prices firming once more. Once this happens, the cycle begins anew.

We will now look in greater depth at the characteristics of economic cycles, using a specific example – the ethylene industry[3] – to illustrate the discussion.

Ethylene is a basic chemical which is used to manufacture plastics such as polyethylene, as well as other products such as antifreeze and synthetic fibers. It is the single largest product derived from naphtha, a light gasoline-like fraction of crude oil. Globally, there are more than

---

[3] It is not the intention of the model to fully reflect ethylene production but to use this industry as an example to illustrate the major effects of the cycle.

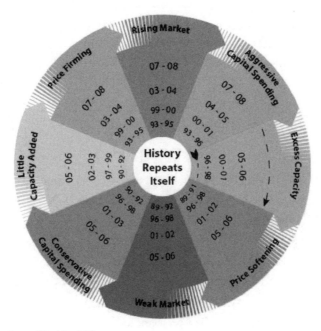

Source: IC Insights 2005

Figure 4.4   Economic cycles in the semiconductor industry. Source: IC Insights 2005

two dozen ethylene producers with a market share greater than one percent; the largest of these has a market share of 4 %. Ethylene prices are highly cyclical and much more so than those of its feedstock naphtha (Figure 4.5).

A look at the investment behavior of the industry shows that sudden upturns in the profit margins of the industry usually trigger new investments. For instance, when margins were high in 1988, three new crackers were announced in the US. In the next upturn during the following year, four more were announced. The same thing happened in each of the upturns in 1995, 1997 and 1999.

We have deployed a simple economic simulation that follows the cycle feedback loop as described above (Figure 4.3) to model the ethylene industry. While the model itself is not industry specific we have used the basic parameters of the ethylene industry to feed the necessary model parameters and to cross check results against the empirical behavior observed in this industry. In this simulation of the ethylene market we have assumed that there are five players, each of which has an equal initial market share of 20 %. The modeling is done in four basic steps (see Figure 4.6) that are repeated for each year of the simulation:

1. Each company in our model pursues yearly investments based on its economic situation, i.e. its cash availability. We assume an investment cash flow profile based on the investments typical of this industry – in our specific example, that for an ethylene plant. Positive cash flows from the investments are generated only after a delay, once the additional capacity becomes operational and supplies goods to the market. Each investment has a predefined useful life, after which the capacity is removed from the market.

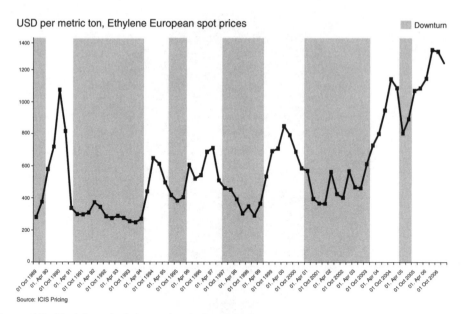

Figure 4.5   Naphtha and ethylene prices in $ per metric ton

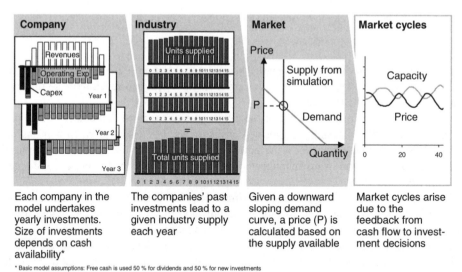

Figure 4.6   Empirical model assumptions

2. Past investments lead to a given production capacity and supply for each company per year. The supplies from all the companies are aggregated to yield the total available supply in the market.[4]

---

[4] Utilization effects have been taken into account but will not be discussed further here.

Table 4.1   Assumptions in base case example

Production volume	1 million tons/year per $1 billion investment (scalable)
Operating costs	$300 per ton capacity (including raw materials)
Capacity investment lead time	2 years
Lifetime	Operating life of 20 years
Investments	Refreshment investment of 10 % every 5 years
Terminal value	None
New investment	70 % of available cash
Dividend	10 % of available cash
Demand	220 million tons, annual market growth of 2 %
Price per ton	$5 (demand – supply)/million tons

3. A market price is calculated based on the total supply using a downward-sloping supply-price-curve, i.e. assuming a decreasing price with increasing supply. The slope of the demand curve is given by the price elasticity to demand typical for this market.
4. Each company generates revenues based on its supply to the market, the price determined by the market and its costs, based on its asset structure from past investments. The resulting cash flow is partially returned to stakeholders and partially reinvested into new assets. The feedback between available cash and investment decisions leads to cyclical behavior in the market.

Several parameters, such as the investment timing, the price elasticity and market demand changes, as well as company investment behavior, can be modified in this model in order to test their impact on the market evolution.

Table 4.1 summarizes the major assumptions of the ethylene industry model.

Using this model, we will now take a closer look at four of the major drivers of cyclicality:

1. The impact of investment lead times.
2. Slow-to-no market growth.
3. High price sensitivity.
4. Investment timing with respect to the cycle.

4.2.1   Impact of investment lead times

Production plants which are large in size relative to the overall demand drive cyclicality in two ways. Both of these effects ensure their production is not synchronized with demand. Firstly, large-scale plants typically take a considerable time to construct. This leads to prolonged periods of under-capacity and high margins while the new capacity is under construction. Secondly, once the large plants come on line, their additional capacity creates conditions of oversupply, and so prices plummet.

The overall impact of these large plants on the industry is to make the industry cycles both longer and harsher. This impact is related directly to the lead time in their construction. This can be illustrated by our model (see Figure 4.7). In the base case, the plant's construction has a lead time of two years. This gives rise to a cycle of moderate amplitude with a cycle time of around eight years. Increasing the construction lead time to three years greatly magnifies the amplitude of the price swings and lengthens the cycle period to around 14 years. In scenario 2, the lead time is shortened to one year. This has the impact of eliminating the cycle altogether.

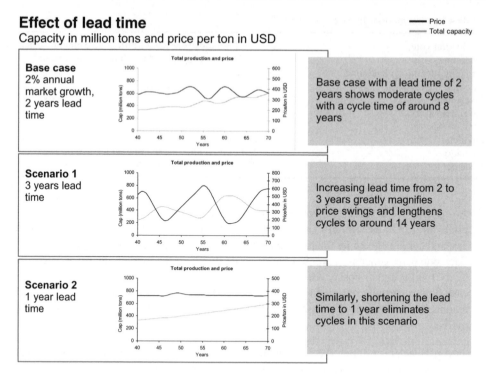

Figure 4.7   Effects of increasing or reducing lead times (after an initialization period)

4.2.2   Slow-to-no market growth

Market conditions also have a big impact on the absorption of additional capacity. In a fast-growing market, the increasing demand will ensure that new production capacity can be absorbed quickly, even if the addition is large relative to the overall demand. The story is quite different in a stagnating or declining market due to the fact that it often is more difficult to take out capacity from the market than to add new capacities. Companies are often reluctant to close assets in the hope that they will be able to make them profitable again at some point in the future. The release of the workforce, as well as other obligations, can also effectively prevent or delay capacity shutdowns.

Figure 4.8 illustrates this link between market growth, new capacity, and cyclicality. In the base case, under conditions of slowly growing demand, the market is able to absorb some level of capacity addition. However, this still results in a degree of overcapacity for a number of years, thereby creating a cycle of moderate amplitude. In scenario 3, we assume an annual market growth of 4 %. As expected, capacity additions in excess of customer demand are absorbed quickly in this scenario and cyclicality is reduced significantly. In scenario 4, we model the effects of stagnant or declining demand. In this scenario, overcapacity can lead to long phases of low prices, resulting in low levels of investment, until age finally removes the old capacity.

4.2.3   High price sensitivity

In circumstances where prices are highly sensitive to changes in supply or demand, any divergence from the economic equilibrium is likely to initiate a swing in the investment cycle.

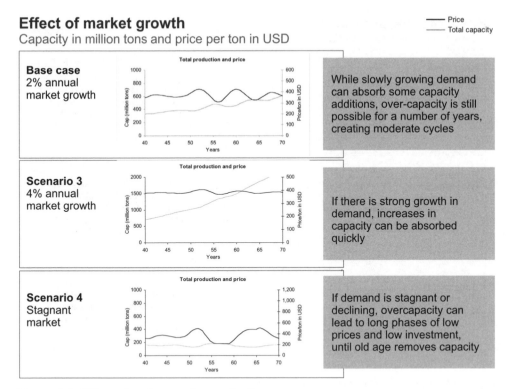

Effect of market growth
Capacity in million tons and price per ton in USD

Base case
2% annual
market growth

While slowly growing demand can absorb some capacity additions, over-capacity is still possible for a number of years, creating moderate cycles

Scenario 3
4% annual
market growth

If there is strong growth in demand, increases in capacity can be absorbed quickly

Scenario 4
Stagnant
market

If demand is stagnant or declining, overcapacity can lead to long phases of low prices and low investment, until old age removes capacity

Figure 4.8   Effects of market growth on cyclicality

Under these conditions, a supply shortage will lead to hefty price rises, making overinvestment more likely.

In the base case of our model, even moderate price fluctuations are sufficient to create significant swings in cash flows, investment, and thus capacity (Figure 4.9). In scenario 5, the model's price sensitivity is increased by 20 %. This leads to an unstable situation, where positive feedback creates an ever-increasing price-cycle amplitude. In scenario 6, we decrease the price sensitivity by 20 %. This eliminates the cycle altogether and lets capacity rise steadily in line with demand.

4.2.4   Investment timing with respect to the cycle

Investment timing is another important driver of cyclicality, as it determines if and when incremental capacity is added during the cycle. In the base case of our model, the investment behavior of the industry follows cash availability, i.e. all five companies invest in new assets when they are making high profits (Figure 4.10). This implies that all the companies invest more or less at the same time, when prices are high. As a result, new capacity from all these companies will enter the market at largely the same time, creating a situation of oversupply. In consequence prices decline. This behavior leads to price and capacity cycles. In scenario 7, in a change in behavior, a single player makes its investments based on market growth and not on cash availability. This leads to a visible reduction in the amplitude of the cycles. In

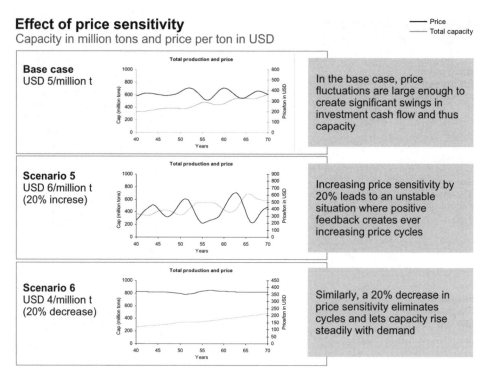

Figure 4.9   Effects of price sensitivity on cyclicality

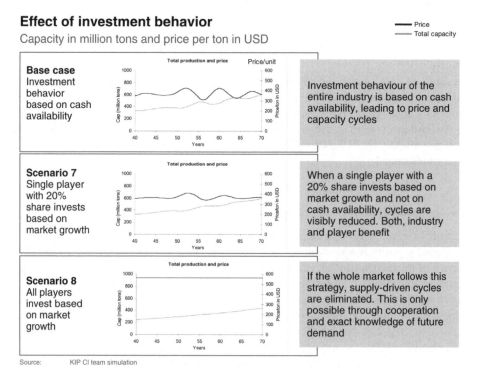

Figure 4.10   Effects of investment behavior on cyclicality

consequence, both the individual company, and the industry as a whole, benefit. In scenario 8, the whole market follows this strategy. This eliminates the supply-driven cycles.

In life, nothing is ever quite this simple, of course. Whereas in our model each company has a 20 % market share, in the real-world market, the largest ethylene company has a market share of only 4 %. Nevertheless, the model does make it clear that in certain circumstances it is possible for individual companies to change market behavior.

In summary, we have seen that even a basic feedback model is able to simulate the existence of economic cycles in an industry. In addition we have discussed how cycle amplitudes can be influenced by core parameters such as investment lead time, market growth, price sensitivity and pro- or counter-cyclical investment behavior.

4.3   DEVELOPING AN ECONOMIC MODEL OF CYCLICALITY

After having seen cyclicality at work, we now turn to look at the underlying drivers from a more fundamental point of view.

4.3.1   A fundamental law of economic cycles

In order to fully understand the basic nature of economic cycles it may be helpful to step back for a second and take a look at other scientific disciplines. Cyclicality and oscillatory behavior are a well-known, almost universal phenomenon seen in many branches of science, such as physics, biology and chemistry. Simple examples from physics include those of a swing or pendulum, the movement of a mass on a spring or a piston in a car. In biology or chemistry, cyclical behavior is observed in coupled systems such as the predator–prey cycle, as in the relationship between lynx and hares in Canada. (Figure 4.11).

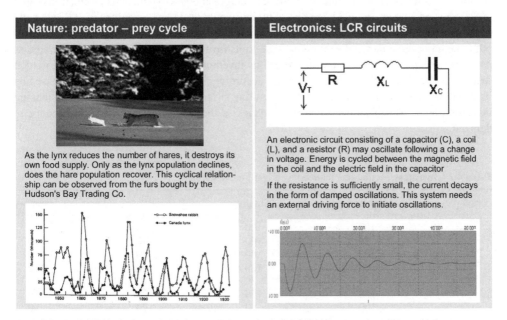

Figure 4.11 Cyclicality examples from biology and physics

Oscillatory behavior often derives from simple laws, e.g. in the case of a mechanical pendulum, oscillation occurs if its mass is accelerated by a force proportional to the displacement from its equilibrium position and is always based on a feedback loop of some kind. Can we identify a similarly simple basic law to describe the driving force behind economic cycles?

In fact we claim that the simple statement

"Companies react with a time delay to differences between supply and demand."

is sufficient to explain the basic behavior of economic cycles. Though this statement does not explain the wealth of cyclical phenomena observed in industries, it does provide a good basis for understanding the basic economic parameters that drive cyclicality.

As a start, let us look at a simple example of how companies react to differences between supply and demand. A hypothetical company, "Wheel of Fortune" (WoF), produces goods of an undefined but doubtlessly useful nature. It does not have a full view of what happens in the overall market: the company responds to what it can observe directly: its own inventory. This is a situation that many companies find themselves in, as they are separated from their customers by a number of distribution steps or intermediaries. WoF has adopted a policy to minimize its own stocks. It therefore reacts to any fluctuations in demand by correcting for these changes in a way that seeks to bring its inventory back to target in the next period. Lastly, we assume that WoF is only able to respond to changes in demand with a delay of one time period due to the lead time inherent in its production system.

In this situation, even a one-time reduction in demand triggers inventory oscillations that continue until WoF changes its inventory policy (Table 4.2). Assuming a decrease in demand from 100 to 90 units occurs in step 2. WoF observes an inventory growth from 100 to 110 units and tries to bring its inventory back to target. Without knowledge of the future demand it expects that its inventory will continue to grow if no action is taken (corresponding to an assumed continued reduced demand of 90). It therefore chooses to reduce its production output to 80 in period 3 (at an assumed demand of 90 this would lead to an inventory of 100 at the end of the period). However, the real market demand has returned to 100 units, after what turned out to be a one-time demand excursion. True to its inventory policy, WoF once again adjusts its output volume in step 4 to try and return its inventory to 100 (remember, the real market demand is not fully visible to WoF, so it acts according to what it can see happening, based on its inventory figures). In this way WoF's operating strategy, targeted at proactively managing inventory, leads to self-induced inventory cycles as the result of a one-time disturbance in demand.

Table 4.2   Inventory oscillations induced by a one-time disturbance

Period	Demand	Supply	Delta	Inventory
1	100	100	0	100
2	90	100	10	110
3	100	80	−20	90
4	100	120	20	110
5	100	80	−20	90
6	100	120	20	110
7	100	80	−20	90

4.3.2 Base parameters of simple economic oscillations

The real world is far more complicated, of course, than this simple example suggests. So let us expand on this example by examining two core parameters in greater detail:

- the reaction strength; and
- the reaction delay.

What would happen if WoF's reaction wasn't directly proportionate to the mismatch between supply and demand? So far we have assumed that WoF would try to fully compensate for the scale of a demand fluctuation and bring its inventory back to target within one period. This corresponds to a reaction strength of 2: a stock change of 10 units leads to a supply change of 20 units. At this reaction strength a stable oscillation occurs.

At all other values this is not the case, however. If WoF chooses to react with a reaction strength lower than 2, then the oscillation will dampen out over time. Conversely, if the reaction strength is higher than 2, the oscillation will increase over time, until it encounters the "system boundaries", such as, for example, the maximum production capacity of WoF's factory (see Figure 4.12). The strength of the reaction thus determines whether an economic system's degree of oscillation is dampened, stable, or increasing.

Now let us look at the second parameter, reaction delay: what would happen if the company's response time was longer than assumed so far, for instance, due to a longer production lead time? The second part of Figure 4.12 shows the oscillations resulting from reaction delays of 2, 3, and 4 periods. Two core observations can be made. Firstly, the longer the delay in reaction, the longer the period of the economic cycle. In fact, the period of the cycle increases proportionately to the length of the reaction delay. Secondly, the longer the period of delay, the weaker the strength of reaction that will lead to a stable oscillation. While for a time delay of 2 periods a reaction strength of 1 is sufficient to yield a stable oscillation, with a delay of 4 periods a reaction strength of just 0.45 will lead to the same result. In other words, the slower the economic system's response, the more vulnerable it is to being driven into cyclical behavior.

Though this simplistic model does help to illustrate some basic causes of cyclicality, it portrays business cycles as deterministic. Real-life economic cycles as seen in observed timelines remain largely unpredictable. There are several reasons for this, ranging from the surprises inherent in human behavior, to the fact that companies rarely have a clear view of all that is going on within the economic system, and regularly face unforeseen events, such as rapid changes in customers' demands and the overall economic environment. To move towards a more realistic cycle model, we need to take some of these real-life adversities into account, such as:

a) unpredictable changes to the base parameters, such as reaction strength and delay, which happen over time in response to changes in the operations, strategies, or personnel of the companies under investigation;
b) non-deterministic external disturbances (which we call "excitation", borrowing from the scientific terminology of dynamic systems);
c) differences in the characteristics of several companies (rather than one) which interact in a single market (this reflects the modeling of a system of coupled oscillators found in the study of non-trivial physical systems).

(a)

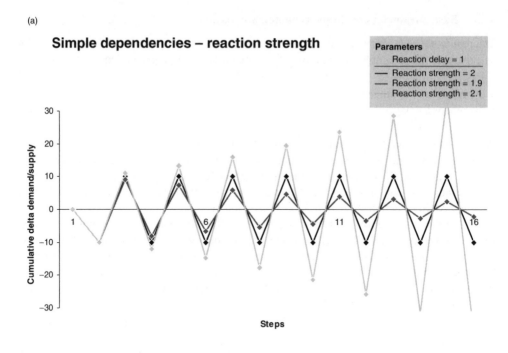

(b)

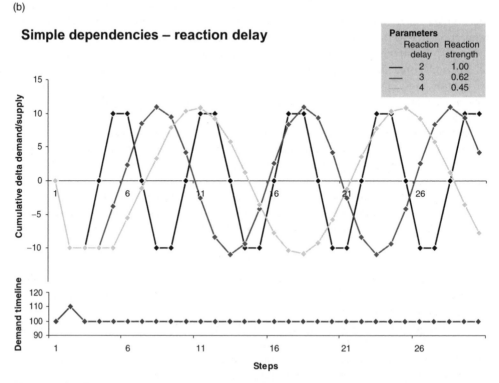

Figure 4.12   Cycle dependence on basic parameters – reaction strength and reaction delay for inventory (stock level) oscillations – in reaction to a one time external disturbance

In the following we will focus on the effects that external disturbances and the addition of further players have on cyclical behavior.

4.3.3   Reaction of cyclical systems to external "excitation"

Basic types of external excitation an economic system may be subjected to are:

- a "twang" (a one-time disturbance);
- external oscillations (continuous excitation at a single frequency);
- random (white noise) external excitation.

In the examples discussed in the last section we have already investigated reactions to a one-time disturbance and seen that even a single event can lead to prolonged economic oscillations.[5]

What happens if we couple the simple economic system as modeled above to an external oscillation? This corresponds to a company's or industry sector's link to macroeconomic business cycles. Even though these cycles are not as deterministic as the single-frequency oscillations, this simplified example might help us to uncover some of the phenomenon underlying more complex situations.

In general, when we use the simple model as outlined above and couple it to an external economic oscillation, the company's inventory fluctuates in a mix of two separate cycle periods – or, to use the more common technical term, at two different frequencies. The first frequency corresponds to the period of the external excitation and the second frequency to the period intrinsic to the system itself (this frequency is called the eigenfrequency of the system). The cycle's amplitude will grow in intensity the closer the external excitation frequency comes to the eigenfrequency of the system. If the external oscillation takes place at the actual eigenfrequency then the amplitude will continue to grow uncontrollably over time until it hits the limits of the system. Close to the eigenfrequency, the mix of the two frequencies results in a frequency pattern known in physics as a "beat" (see Figure 4.13).[6]

What does this tell us about real life? It shows that business cycles are likely to be fuelled by external excitations derived from the overall economy and that these excitations will have their greatest effect if a company's or industry's intrinsic cycle frequency coincides with that of the economy (or with other external cycles that affect it directly). If this is the case for WoF, it should be very worried indeed!

To add a little more of the uncertainties of real life to our model, we can overlay the dominant frequencies with "white noise" external excitation. Such white noise arises from the countless small effects in the business environment which influence the overall evolution of a company such as the unexpected absence of a core sales person due to sickness. In this case, even if we assume that WoF suffers from purely random excitation, its system will react most strongly to noise at frequencies that match or are close to its own resonance frequency.

Figure 4.14 provides an example of a timeline for a company's inventory which has a weak cyclical tendency (in that its reaction strength is well below the stable oscillation value) and that is subjected to random external fluctuations and a rather weak oscillatory excitation. As we see, the result starts to resemble the less deterministic patterns we observe in real life

---

[5] Introducing a one-time "twang" is particularly suited to the study of the intrinsic properties of a system since – following the initial disturbance – the system is then left undisturbed to evolve following its own properties.

[6] The frequency of the cycle amplitude modulation (the "beat") is determined by the difference between the external and intrinsic oscillation frequencies.

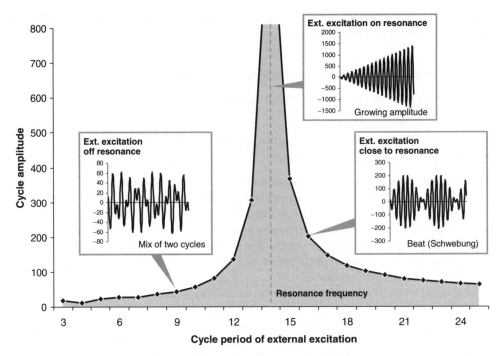

Figure 4.13 Response of a cyclic system to an oscillatory external excitation – frequency mix, resonance and beat (Schwebung)

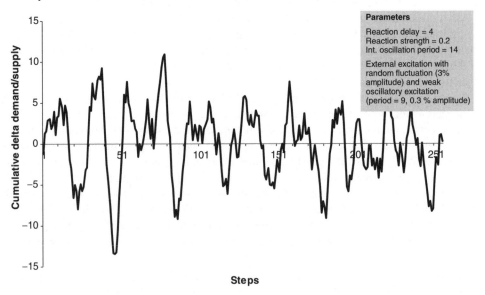

Figure 4.14 Response of a cyclic economic system to an external excitation that is a mix of random noise and a weak external cycle

systems – a seemingly erratic path over time with a cyclic component driven by the urge of the company to react to the observed differences between supply and demand.

This analysis shows the tendency to oscillate, coupled with certain unpredictable influences (which almost inevitably are present in all business situations) can lead to complex cyclical patterns that are not easy to predict. In several cases, however, the underlying parameters, such as the reaction time or the strength of the reaction, *are* under the influence of companies. If companies change these parameters they can change the market dynamics and thereby reduce the value destruction resulting from cyclicality. Simple examples of this include reducing the production or investment lead times in order to shorten the time it takes the company to react to changes in the market. We will discuss various strategies for coping with cyclicality later in this chapter.

4.3.4 Economic cycles with more than one player present

In real life, companies seldom act in isolation as they are rarely in a position to disregard their competitors. So how does the presence of more than one player affect the cyclicality model? More importantly, from a business point of view: can a company, acting on its own, reduce the impact of cyclicality on its market when there are other players present?

To analyze this further, we extend our model above by introducing a second player[7] and distinguish two basic situations:

1. Each company in the market responds solely to the level of their own inventories.
2. Each of the companies in the market responds to the overall market inventory, i.e. the cumulative difference between supply and demand.

A real-life situation is likely to be a mix of these two extremes. However, understanding the nature of both extremes will give us a feeling for the range of possible effects. In the following we assume that two companies are present in the market. This situation can easily be generalized to a greater number of companies.

Let us first take a look at the situation in which each company responds solely to the level of its own inventory. In this case, the actions of the two companies are decoupled in the modeling of this market segment. As a result, the total response will be the sum of the two individual responses. If both companies are operated and managed in a similar way then their reaction time and strength will be comparable. In this case, we can treat the two companies as a single player, sharing the same reaction period and reaction strength. This will be the case in more or less homogenous industry sectors with all participants employing a similar business model.

More commonly, however, individual companies are likely to follow somewhat different strategies in their reaction to market fluctuations. For example, one company might react more strongly than another. In addition, differences between them, in the way they manage inventory, in production lead times, or implementation times, can lead to further differences in the reaction time. In this case, each company will have its own characteristic eigenfrequency. The total response of the two individual companies will, therefore, be the product of their various eigenfrequencies and their responses to external factors.

---

[7] This is sufficient to indicate how markets with several players will behave since from any individual company's perspective all other market participants can be lumped into one aggregated hypothetical second market player.

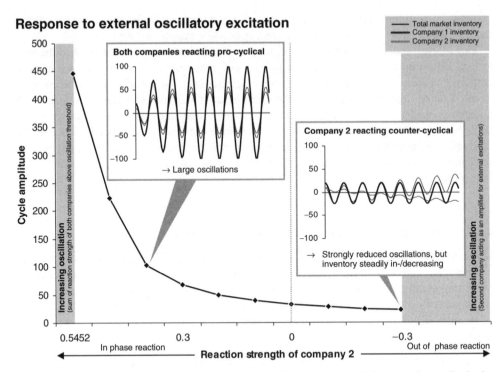

Figure 4.15 Cyclicality in a market with two players: Player 1 tries to minimize cycle amplitudes by reacting inversely to the competition (at a reaction strength of 0.3)[8]

The situation is very different in situations in which there is full market transparency and each and every company in the market responds to the overall market inventory. This is sometimes the case in situations where information on supply and demand is readily available from independent market analysts, or where companies share distribution channels or production output information. In this case, if all the companies are reacting (at least in part) to the total inventory in the segment, then any one company's reaction will be coupled to that of its competitors'.

Figure 4.15 shows an example of such a situation. This example assumes that two companies are subjected to an external excitation from a constant (deterministic) external cycle. If both companies try to reduce output at once, the total inventory will build up as their actions will reinforce each other, leading to an increase in the overall cycle amplitude (see left-hand graph in Figure 4.15).

Importantly, this situation also gives companies the opportunity to take counter-cyclical actions. A company which is fully aware of the sector's cyclical tendencies might well opt to adjust its own course of action to minimize the impact of the cycle on its business.

If one of the companies decides not to act upon changes in their inventory or acts in the opposite direction – counter-cyclical – to that of their competitors, for instance, by increasing its own inventory at a time when others in the segment are reducing theirs', the market's cycle

---

[8]The market is assumed to be driven by an external cycle of fixed frequency and amplitude.

amplitude can be reduced very significantly (as shown in the right-hand graph of Figure 4.15 – out of phase reaction).[9] Alternatively, if a company observes that the other players are acting pro-cyclically to build their capacity and inventories, the company might decide to reduce its own capacity or inventory. In this manner, the company can act to dampen the market cycles – albeit at the cost of (temporarily) losing market share. Nevertheless, this option can be of value for players with a large or dominant market share, if the benefit of reduced cyclicality is larger than the reduced profits due to a (temporarily) lower sales volume. For example, a large IC manufacturer with a dominant market share can to a large extent control the available product volume. By enforcing inventory control throughout the value chain, it could reduce cyclicality significantly. On the other hand, one reason it might not wish to do this is that smaller companies might suffer more strongly from the effects of the cycle than they do. In contrast to the situation for the smaller producers, the dominant company's higher cash buffer and greater profitability allows it to invest whenever necessary.

The impact on the cycle is greatest when one company acts to compensate for the actions of the other(s). It is important to realize that the impact of this action, in helping to minimize the amplitude of the cycle, is not solely dependent on that company's response, but also on the strength of the external excitation.

When we model the cyclicality effects produced by two players, both of which are reacting independently to the total market inventory (where each has different reaction parameters and where both are subject to random fluctuations), the resulting timeline bears a remarkable resemblance to real-life timelines (see Figure 4.16). The resonance spectrum (shown on the right-hand side of Figure 4.16 does not peak at one or the other of the player's resonance frequencies but exhibits a broadened peak, situated between the two companies' individual eigenfrequencies. This is due to the coupling of the two players in their shared market. This effect can make it very difficult for companies to understand the impact of their individual actions on the total market by looking at market data.

A specific effect present in these complex situations is that longer time cycles or fluctuations will dominate shorter time cycles. Thus, if the reaction times in an industry are shorter than the external economic cycle, the overarching economic cycle will imprint itself onto the individual industries – and the companies will follow the external cycle. In this situation, companies will also profit from shorter reaction times, as this will enable them to follow the cycle more closely and thereby incur lower losses due to mismatches between supply and demand. The fact that low-frequency, long-period changes subordinate shorter-term dynamics is also known in the theory of differential equations, where it is called "enslaving".

Observant readers might have noticed that several important parameters are missing from this analysis of economic cycles, such as price fluctuations, or the differences between long-term and short-term supply reactions (utilization versus capacity additions). While all these parameters add insight into the nature of economic cycles (and have been taken into account in the empirical based model underlying the analyses in the earlier part of this chapter), in this section we have chosen to keep matters as simple as possible to focus on the basic economic forces driving cyclicality. Nonetheless, these matters deserve a brief comment here. Price fluctuations during a cycle are a reaction to over-demand or over-supply situations, as we saw

---

[9] As can be observed, however, this can lead to an inventory imbalance between the two companies that will not be sustainable in the long run.

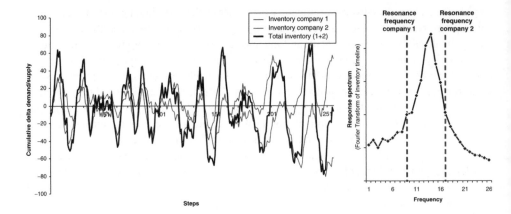

Figure 4.16 Two players with different resonance frequencies in a market driven by random fluctuations[10]

in our empiric modeling earlier in this chapter. The asymmetry between adding and releasing productive capacity explains why growing markets are less susceptible to cyclicality. While in theory capacity reductions can be executed in the same time or even less time than it takes to make a capacity addition, in practice they often take much longer to implement. This is, in part, the result of the urge companies have to see their investments pay back, as well as for other financial and contractual reasons, including those of labor obligations.

With this we close our examination of the forces that underlie economic cycles. Readers who are interested in the mathematics underlying cyclical behavior can see a more formal treatment of this matter in Appendix 4A. The appendix provides a short overview of how our statement, "companies react, following a time delay, to differences between supply and demand" may be used to derive a differential equation for economic cycles.

We now turn our attention to more practical matters – to what companies can learn from the observations and analyses we have discussed here and to the measures they have at their disposal for dealing with cyclicality in their marketplace.

4.4 MEASURES TO COPE WITH CYCLICALITY

In the preceding sections we have seen how cyclical behavior in economics can be modeled using (relatively) simple base assumptions. We have also seen how cyclicality destroys economic value and puts company survival at risk. In this section we will bring together empirical observations with modeling insights and outline some of the measures companies can take to deal with cyclicality. Clearly, certain measures, such as the formation of cartels to regulate capacity or to fix prices, are in contravention of anti-trust legislation, so are not considered here.

---

[10]To obtain the frequency spectrum as shown we have averaged the spectrums of 56 individual timelines as shown on the left of Figure 4.8.

We start with an examination of the core parameters identified above and then explore several examples of other measures companies can take.

4.4.1 Reaction delay

We have seen that the time delay between a change in supply or demand and a company's reaction to it is a core determinant of economic cycles: the longer the time delay, the longer the related cycle period. Also, the longer the time delay the more susceptible the economic system will be to fall into a cyclical pattern. In consequence, if companies or industry segments are able to reduce their reaction times, therefore, they might be able to reduce the level of cyclicality they are subjected to.

The good news is that a reduction in reaction times (i.e. investment lead times) always helps a company to reduce its dependency on economic cycles. If a company is able to reduce the time it takes to realize its investment (or its production order) this will enable it to respond to changes in external conditions more quickly than its competitors can. This will allow it to grow faster than its competitors, if there is room for growth, or to carry less buffer stock, if the market demand is dwindling.

Core measures to reduce investment lead times are:

1. **Monitor the end-customer market to enable quicker decision taking.** Many companies do not directly serve the end customer but provide intermediate products or services. These companies can tighten their link with the overall market evolution by keeping a close eye on the end-customer market. This will enable them to reduce the time it takes for this information to reach them. Carrying out market research or acting in cooperation with downstream customers are viable ways to realize this goal. An alternative is to integrate downstream segments, if the business models are compatible and the necessary means are available. Many oil and gas companies, for example, own both refineries and gas station distribution networks. This gives them a direct link to the end-customer market.

2. **Faster investment execution.** Once an investment decision has been taken, faster execution can enable a company to significantly shorten its investment lead times (in our experience, by 30 % or more). One semiconductor manufacturer, for instance, has managed to set a record by constructing a large semiconductor fab in slightly more than two years, using rigorous critical-path management. Similarly, a multinational logistics player reduced its invest- ment times (and costs) significantly by defining pre-designed modules for its distribution centers. These modules still gave it sufficient flexibility to cater to local needs while pro- viding it with optimized and reality-tested solutions to serve a wide geographic distribution network.

3. **Buffer management during the productive life of an asset.** Among the most effective means companies have at their disposal for reducing cyclicality is to monitor and manage inventory along the entire value chain. Buffers – the waiting times introduced into the value chain to even out supply–demand uncertainties – are not only costly but decouple upstream segments from downstream fluctuations. This leads to the amplification of the cycle for upstream segments. Buffers should, therefore, be reduced to a minimum. Toyota has implemented this approach in its production system by "pulling" goods – ensuring that production is based on actual customer demand – rather than pushing products into the market or onto stock. The latter can result in products being sold at high discounts to avoid obsolescence costs. Following the end-of-the-millennium bubble, the electronics and

semiconductor industry, which is challenged by product lead times of up to and beyond a year, have adopted tight inventory control mechanisms that seek to prevent excess buffers across the value chain.

The bad news for companies seeking to reduce reaction times is that there are limitations to what can be done. It is not always possible to put in place reductions that are of sufficient magnitude to ward off the adverse effects of economic cycles. Where this is the case, companies should also consider the second core cyclicality parameter – the reaction strength.

4.4.2   Reaction strength

The reaction strength is a measure of how strongly a company reacts to signals from the market. Managing reaction strength presents companies with an immediate dilemma: though they need to react quickly in order to minimize reaction delay, any overreaction will increase cycle-amplitudes and result in the self-inflicted cyclicality we observed in the case of "WoF". The question companies need to be able to answer is: how to know which signal they should react to and which they should not?

The first helpful guideline is to treat variations which have time scales that are shorter than the investment realization time differently to those that are longer than this time:

1. **Ignore market fluctuations or signals that are shorter than the investment lead time.** To avoid the overreactions that aggravate cyclicality, long-term investment decisions should be decoupled from short-term market developments ("the panic of the day"). For instance, if, in our earlier example, "WoF" had decided to ignore the market signals in any one period it would have effectively avoided getting itself into what was self-induced cyclicality. In order to stabilize their production system, a mining company we have worked with has decided to restrict the access their operations managers have to short-term information. The higher up the managers are, the less high-frequency information they are provided with. While a mining foreman gets to know the hourly changes in production volume, the shift leader only has access to volume changes over an entire shift, and senior management are only informed about weekly changes in production volume.

2. **Follow the trends which have time scales comparable to or longer than your company's reaction time.** As we have already discussed, companies can be "enslaved" by cycles that are much longer than their own reaction time. For example, a consumer goods company will have no other choice but to follow the ups and downs of the overall economy (which has cycles typically of the order of 5–10 years). Exact timing – that is, choosing the right phase of the cycle – is therefore of the utmost importance in investment. Time the investment to meet a period in the cycle in which the expected demand will support the additional volumes. This is very different to betting on a continued upward trend, the result of which is likely to see the new capacity hit the market at a phase in which the total capacity will exceed that which the market is able to absorb!

4.4.3   Two "jokers" that can help beat the cycle

If you are trapped into following a cycle there are two "jokers" that might be available to help you beat the cycle.

1. **Joker 1 – Market leadership.** If a company is a market leader (i.e. it has a market share significantly above 50 % in the relevant market), it can use its size to influence both market capacity and price (acting as a "price maker"). It can thereby reduce cycle amplitudes in two ways. Firstly, it can reduce supply in the demand troughs through temporarily "mothballing" or permanently closing assets. This will help stabilize prices and avoid buffer stocks. The same effect can be achieved in the short term by reducing the utilization of existing assets, albeit at the price of a higher fixed cost burden per unit produced. Secondly, it can bring spare capacity online during demand peaks, thus pre-empting investments by competitors. The company will only benefit from these measures if the reduction in its profit resulting from the output reduction is more than compensated for by the revenue stabilization. The more flexible the cost structure and the higher the market share of the market leader, the more likely it is to succeed.

As we have seen in the previous section even a smaller player can help reduce cyclicality through capacity additions. Since such a player will have to wager a much higher proportion of its capacity, such a move is unlikely to prove beneficial, however. The smaller player will end up carrying the full cost of the capacity reduction, while the benefits will be spread across all the market participants. Joint capacity management is a possible way out of this dilemma, as will be discussed below.

Figure 4.17 shows an example of how capacity adaptations in a commodity industry helped to end a downturn. By removing their own high-cost capacity from the market, the market leaders (producers A, B, and C) encouraged other fringe producers to reduce their own overcapacity. The initial curtailment in capacity had only a small effect on prices, due to the steep drop in demand which took place at the same time, but a second step involving the other players was effective in achieving a 30 % increase in prices.

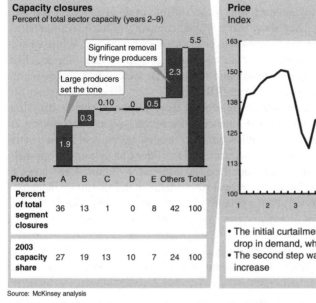

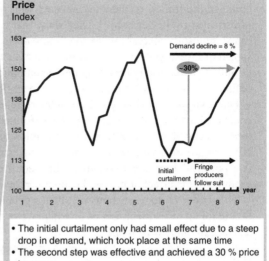

Source: McKinsey analysis

Figure 4.17   Example of effects of capacity management on cyclicality

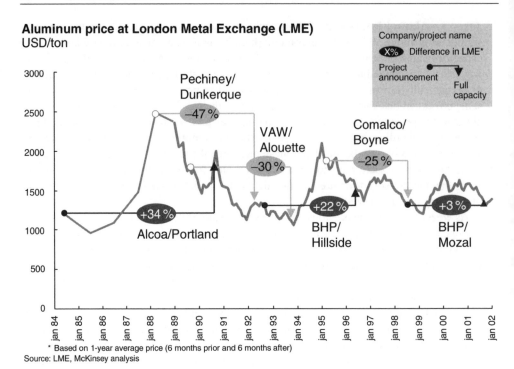

Figure 4.18 Cyclical and counter-cyclical capacity investments in the aluminum industry

2. **Joker 2 – "Deep pockets".** Companies that are not cash constrained – or have been able to build a sufficient cash buffer throughout the cycle – can use their deep pockets to optimize the timing of their investments with respect to the cycle. This effect has been investigated by Koller et al.[11] They show that a typical company's return on investments can significantly increase when the timing of its investment are optimized. While an even spread of investments over the entire business cycle yields an internal rate of return (IRR) of only 4 %, optimally timed capital expenditure results in an IRR of 9 %. Likewise, the optimal timing of asset purchases results in an IRR of 34 %.

Our own model of the ethylene industry reinforces these results. It shows that if one company invests counter-cyclically, the performance of this player is significantly increased, turning a negative NPV of minus €236 million for a pro-cyclical investment into a positive NPV of €56 million for the time-optimized investment. Thus timing an investment optimally is a powerful lever for maximizing the return on an investment. Figure 4.18 shows an example of the effect of pro- and counter-cyclical investments in the aluminum industry.

This is not to suggest, however, that a counter-cyclical timing is necessarily the best timing for an investment. Let us investigate two cases: an intrinsically driven market cycle and an externally driven one.

Intrinsically driven market cycles: A market cycle can be considered intrinsically driven if the cycle duration and amplitude is mainly the result of the behavior of the market

---

[11] Tim Koller, Marc Goedhart and David Wessels (2005). *Measuring and Managing the Value of Companies*. John Wiley & Sons Inc., p. 661.

participants themselves, rather than that of the overall economy. This is true for industries with cycles much shorter than the GDP cycles, such as the shorter 2.5-year and 5-year technology cycles of the semiconductor and electronics industries. These industries will still follow the ups and downs of the overall market but will also experience interim cycles driven by internal industry characteristics. Another case is the utilities industry which experiences short-term overhaul cycles of 3–5 years' duration overlaid with very long reinvestment cycles on the order of 20–30 years. In the case of intrinsically driven markets cycles, the cycle will be coupled to the investment lead times. All the market participants are likely to invest at approximately the same time – when cash is available – and these investments are likely to start production at more-or-less the same time, creating the preconditions for excess capacity in the market that initiates the subsequent downturn. In these circumstances, a counter-cyclical investment can be expected to earn much higher yields than a pro-cyclical one.

Externally driven market cycles: A market cycle can be considered externally driven if the cycle is imposed by external effects, e.g. the overall economic cycle. Examples of this are seen in industries such as automotive, telecom, travel & logistics, as well as – to a somewhat lesser degree – the chemicals sector. In this case, investment lead times are not necessarily matched to the cycle duration and investments should be timed to hit the right phase – typically a time when the market is hungry for more products. Optimizing the investment time in these circumstances, therefore, does not necessarily imply making a counter-cyclical investment. Since the factors driving these market cycles are external, companies might not have access to information about which phase the market is in. In these circumstances, they will have to either rely on publically available information or on their own judgment in order to decide on the optimum investment time. In either case, choosing the timing of their investment, rather than being driven by the market cycle, is likely to give them an advantage over their competitors who have less deep pockets, as these companies will have to follow the market for better or – more often – for worse.

4.4.4   Where no joker is available

Many companies have neither a dominant market position nor the necessary funds to detach themselves from cycles. Even where no joker is available to them, they can still have a couple of measures at their disposal that help them to better cope with the atrocities of a cyclical market.

1. *Diversification.* Typically, non-focused plays receive lower stock market valuations due to the fact that being present in multiple market segments carries with it the danger of insufficient management focus on any one individual segment, along with the risk of capital misallocation across the individual business units (e.g. a cash-positive unit might have to sacrifice profitable growth to sustain another weak or dwindling unit). However, diversification can be a viable measure for reducing the risks of cyclicality in much the same way that financial investors spread their investments across several instruments in order to reduce risk.[12] Companies can reduce this risk by coupling their activities in a particular cyclical market to one or several other business in other segments that are less cyclical or whose cycles are out of phase with their main business. This option should be weighed

---

[12] See e.g. Brealey, R.A. and Myers, S.C. (2000).

against other possible financial options, such as hedging or other financial investments, since these options typically demand less management attention and so do not distract from the core business.

2. ***Hedging and long-term contracts.*** If a company anticipates that the effects of price cyclicality will continue to be a problem, it can use price hedging as a source of protection. Hedging strategies include the use of (a) long-term contracts with customers and suppliers, and (b) financial instruments such as futures, forwards, etc. An example of a successful hedging strategy is that of a gold asset company in sub-Saharan Africa. In order to attract investors, it chose to hedge its revenues against price and market risks in order to reduce price volatility. It achieved this through hedging the price of gold, combined with the extensive use of contracts that would still allow it to benefit from gold price upswings. The company used a mix of contract types, such as basic forward sales, put options, spot-deferred contracts (i.e. floor-like options). As a result, it has been able to effectively stabilize its revenue and EBITDA, achieving more favorable debt leverage and stable stock prices.

Long-term contracts can also serve to reduce cyclicality risks by providing a more stable and foreseeable revenue flow. One form of long-term contract used to reduce the impact of cyclicality is the *staggered contract*. In such agreements, the contract is split into several tranches (usually three to five), each of which specifies a particular volume and price (the price is usually set at the average historical price, e.g. that of the price of steel over the last four years). Each contract tranche starts at a different point in time and is valid for a limited period (usually for two to five years). Staggered contracts have several advantages: They reduce cash flow volatility (by up to 70 % and more), are more easily enforceable due to the build in flexibility, and carry a lower risk of mispricing due to short-term price variations that do not reflect changes in the underlying basic economics.

3. **Creating capacity flexibility.** Creating capacity flexibility allows a company to adapt its output capacity to market demand, to "breathe with the cycle" without getting into an unfavorable cost position. There are several options for a company to go beyond standard asset ownership to achieve a more flexible capacity:
   (a) the use of swing assets that operate only when required;
   (b) the formation of joint ventures to share asset ownership and output;
   (c) going asset-light, using external production capacity.

Swing assets: Swing assets are assets that are utilized by a company for a defined period to bridge a capacity gap, but which are not necessarily owned by the company. This strategy can be effective in discouraging new entrants, which would otherwise seek to capture the extra demand (Figure 4.19).

Swing capacity can also be realized by building capacity flexibility into a new production site. For instance, one semiconductor manufacturer with whom we worked decided to build a 50 % safety margin into its clean-room infrastructure to allow for later expansion if the market so required. The clean-room costs accounted for only ~20 % of the total investment volume, which it considered to be a reasonable price to pay for the additional flexibility. As the upturn materialized, the fab was quickly filled to accommodate the increased production volume – and with lower investment than would otherwise have been possible.

Joint ventures: Joint ventures offer several advantages for companies that wish to make capacity additions. Firstly, for the market leaders, a joint venture between several large producers can prove very effective in discouraging fringe players from carrying out their own expansion

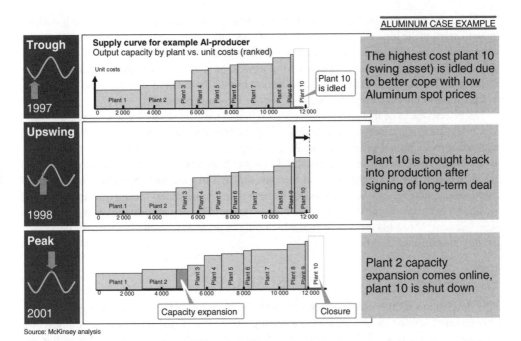

Figure 4.19   Alcoa's use of a swing asset within its asset structure

plans. Secondly, it allows the producers to cooperate in a manner that ensures that while they all benefit from a growing market they do not overbuild and add excess capacity. For such joint ventures to be successful, they need to be longer term rather than short term. One example of such a cooperation has been seen in the European steel industry. Three steel producers entered into a series of joint ventures with each other that enabled them to gradually add capacity as and when it was required. The additional capacity benefited all three companies equally. Once the last of three new steel mills had been constructed, the joint ventures were dissolved and the ownership was reshuffled, leaving each company with full ownership of a new mill. Although joint ventures often offer considerable advantages for the players involved, they are not always easy to manage, particularly as the arrangement needs to survive for a considerable number of years for it to be effective. The incentives to bind the companies into a cooperative arrangement therefore need to be strong. This goal is more easily achieved if the risks are better shared than taken alone. A clear instance of this is in sharing the risks associated with investment in a new capital-intensive technology.

Go asset light: A trend of the late 1990s, asset light production denotes the fact that part or all of a company's production is not done in-house but outsourced to an external production specialist that offers its productive capacity to several players in an industry. Such production specialists – often called foundries – are now well established in such industries as automotive and semiconductors.

   Although many companies in the semiconductor industry continue to both design and manufacture integrated circuits, they face new competition from fab-less semiconductor companies. These companies specialize in the intellectual property of chip design. Rather than producing their own chips, they farm out the actual production to merchant foundries which manufacture the design under contract. This fab-less arrangement works well for both parties as it enables them to manage the high capital expenditures of integrated circuits production more effectively, compared to the traditional Integrated Device Manufacturers (IDM). The fab-less company is able to offload to the foundry what would otherwise be a very high capital commitment. For its part, the foundry is able to keep its utilization higher than that of a traditional IDM, as it is in a position to produce chips for a global pool of fab-less companies.

The effectiveness of this arrangement is seen that in the period 1997–2004 the market share of fab-less producers increased from 7 % of total integrated circuit sales to 28 %. This is the equivalent to an annual growth rate of 21 %, compared to the average of 6 % for the industry as a whole. There is, however, a potential drawback to flexible capacity constructions that are shared between several players in the industry. All players may be betting on the same (limited) surplus capacity being available to meet their requirements during the next upturn. If the upturn materializes the flexible capacity may not be sufficient to meet the overall industry's need – leaving those players uncovered which did not manage to secure a sufficient portion of the flexible capacity in time.

4.5 SUMMARY

This description of the various strategies that can be used to beat the cycle concludes our illustration of how economic cycles are a driving force of company investments. Although we are aware that much of this is nevertheless subject to the availability of sound information and the good judgment of the management, we hope we have provided the reader with a set of instruments and distinctions to help them navigate their way through the tempests of a cyclical industry to achieve favorable returns on their investments.

We would also like to express our sincere hope that, through the improved understanding of the underlying drivers, in combination with improved transparency across the value chain, industries and industry segments will contribute to reducing cyclicality and limiting the value destruction associated with the rollercoaster ride of economic cycles.

APPENDIX 4A: A DIFFERENTIAL EQUATION FOR ECONOMIC CYCLICALITY

Basic harmonic oscillations are described by sine and cosine functions. For example, the periodic motion of a mass suspended by a string can be described by the function:

$$x(t) = x_0 \cdot \sin(\omega \cdot t) = x_0 \cdot \mathrm{Im}(e^{i\omega t})^{13}$$

where $x(t)$ is the position of the mass at time t, x_0 is the amplitude and ω is the angular frequency of the oscillation.

If the mass is given a push it will start to oscillate around its equilibrium position. The spring creates a force proportional to the distance from its starting position that always brings the mass back to its initial point of equilibrium (compare Figure 4.20).

In mathematical terms this behavior can be written as a differential equation:

$$m \cdot \ddot{x} = -k \cdot x$$

---

[13]The last part of this equation is written in terms of complex functions. Complex numbers are based on the "imaginary" unit i which is defined as $i = \sqrt{-1}$. Any complex number z can be represented as having a "real" and an "imaginary" part ($z = x + iy$). The functions $\mathrm{Re}(z)$ and $\mathrm{Im}(z)$ yield the real and imaginary part of any complex number or function.

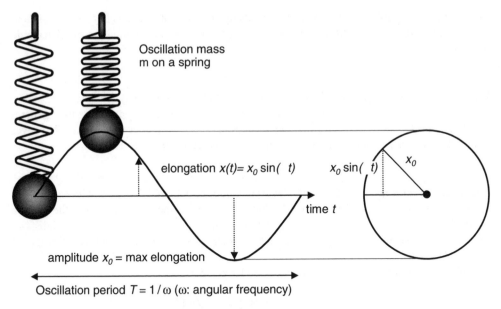

elongation $x(t) = x_0 \sin(\ t)$ $x_0 \sin(\ t)$ x_0

time t

amplitude x_0 = max elongation

Oscillation period $T = 1 / \omega$ (ω: angular frequency)

Figure 4.20   Simple harmonic oscillator – a mass on a spring

where $\ddot{x} = d^2x/dt^2$ is the acceleration (or the second derivative of the position with respect to time) and k is a constant that specifies the strength of the spring.

As economic systems show oscillatory behavior, is it possible to develop a differential equation similar to that for harmonic oscillation? Let us start from our assumption that:

"Companies react, following a time delay, to differences between supply and demand."

To rewrite this statement in more mathematical terms, we first observe that changes in inventory (or buffer stocks) of an economic good are derived from the difference between supply S and demand D:

$$\dot{I} = \frac{dI}{dt} = S - D \quad \text{or} \quad S = \dot{I} + D$$

The assumption that companies will seek to reduce their production of goods S, if they see the level of their inventory I (or the inventory in their industry) is growing, can be written as:

$$\dot{S} = \frac{dS}{dt} = -k \cdot I(t - \Delta t)$$

where k is a constant that denotes the strength of the reaction and Δt is the time delay in that reaction. Such a delay is almost unavoidable. Firstly, because a certain amount of time must pass between the moment the decision to start production is made and that when the goods are actually available. Secondly, because a certain amount of time must pass between the moment at which the inventory is counted and that at which this information becomes visible to the company. This time delay can be due to a number of reasons – for instance, because the information required is supplied by vendors further down the value chain.

Inserting the first equation into the second we obtain:

$$\ddot{I} + \dot{D} = -k \cdot I(t - \Delta t) \quad \text{or} \quad \ddot{I}(t) + k \cdot I(t - \Delta t) = \dot{D}(t)$$

In the simplest possible case, where there is no change to external demand ($\dot{D}(t) = 0$) and there is a negligible time delay ($\Delta t = 0$) we recover the basic differential equation of a harmonic oscillator:

$$\ddot{I}(t) = -k \cdot I(t)$$

Unfortunately, the presence of a time delay, which will be present in any realistic case, makes it somewhat more difficult to solve our differential equation. Producing an ansatz for a general oscillation as ($I(t) = I_0 \cdot e^{i\omega t}$) we find that a solution of this form does indeed exist. However to find the angular frequency of the oscillation ω we need to solve the equation:

$$\omega^2 \cdot e^{i\omega \Delta t} = k$$

This equation does not have a simple algebraic solution, but can be written with the help of a special function, called the Lambert W function. The Lambert W function is the inverse of the function: $x = y \cdot e^y \Rightarrow W(x) = y$. The Lambert W function is used by specialists in several fields of science and engineering, such as electronics, to solve time-delayed differential equations (*DDE*).

With this function our angular frequency can be given as:

$$\omega = -\frac{2i}{\Delta t} \cdot W\left(-\frac{2i}{\Delta t}\sqrt{k}\right)$$

where ω has both a real part, which determines the oscillation frequency, and an imaginary part, which determines whether the oscillation is damped or increasing.

REFERENCE

Brealey, R.A. and Myers, S.C. (2000) *Principles of Corporate Finance, 6th edition*. McGraw-Hill.

Right Size: Balancing Economies and Diseconomies of Scale

CHAPTER HIGHLIGHTS

This chapter focuses on how companies can define the optimum size for an investment. Finding the optimum size requires the identification of the "sweet spot" for the investment, the size of lowest unit costs at the point where diseconomies of scale begin to exceed economies of scale.

- Below the sweet spot, economies of scale lead to decreasing unit costs with increasing size. This is due to better leverage of fixed costs but also to less well-known effects such as the chunkiness of investments or technical scaling laws.
- Small is beautiful. While scale effects are generally well understood and often incorporated into the assessment of large investment projects, diseconomies of scale are almost always neglected. In consequence, companies often underestimate complexity costs, the loss of flexibility and increasing risks associated with oversized investments.
- Assessing diseconomies of scale needs to account for cost effects such as increased logistics costs, supply chain limitations, and increased management complexity, as well as risk effects such as market reaction, utilization, technology and timing risks.
- We discuss a structured approach to assess economies as well as diseconomies of scale and integrate both into a method to determine the "sweet spot" for an investment.

5.1 INTRODUCTION: THE ROLE OF SCALE IN DETERMINING PROFITABILITY

A key challenge in ensuring the success of any new capital investment project is to decide on the asset's optimum size and capacity. The choice of size can determine whether an investment will succeed or whether it is doomed to fail. A factory which is built too small to meet customer demand, for example, means the investing company can lose market share to its competitors. If, on the other hand, a factory is oversized, reduced utilization levels can wreck profitability. Once the wrong choice has been made in the decision phase it is often very difficult to remedy later, since the built-in limitations of an asset, such as the size of the building or the dimensions of critical components, can make adjustments very costly once it has been constructed.

Taking the right decision on size and capacity of an investment, however, is not an easy task because very often only incomplete information is available at the time the decision is made. Worse yet, projections of relevant decision factors such as the expected size of the market, or the specific functional and space requirements of future production technologies, can never be 100 % accurate given the intrinsic uncertainties embedded in any investment business case.

Defining the appropriate size for an investment requires finding the "sweet spot", where dis-economies of scale begin to exceed economies of scale. Notice that this necessitates analyzing economies as well as diseconomies of scale. Many companies still focus their analysis exclusively on economies of scale, omitting any quantitative assessment of diseconomies of scale. This omission may largely be due to the fact that economies of scale, such as the dilution of fixed costs, are better understood and more readily factored into investment calculations. In contrast, diseconomies of scale – especially the costs and risks associated with complexity – are more difficult to estimate and are less well-charted. In consequence, they are often omitted, although they can be of vital importance in determining the future profitability of an asset investment.

In this chapter we will examine the role of both economies as well as diseconomies of scale. We will introduce an evaluation method that enables a quick assessment of the "sweet spot" of an investment based on a structured understanding of the driving forces behind scale advantages and disadvantages.

Even though the importance of scale is widely understood, it is useful to remind ourselves of its relevance using two examples that help illustrate its role in determining the profitability of an investment.

Consider first a semiconductor manufacturer that intends to establish a new state-of-the-art 300 mm fabrication unit (a "fab"). The manufacturer faces a dilemma. A full-scale 300 mm fabrication unit (capable of producing approximately 20 000 wafers per month) costs more than $3 billion to construct. This is not a small investment, even for larger companies such as Intel, AMD, Toshiba or Samsung. Keeping the cost of the investment to a minimum is therefore a high priority. However, just downsizing the fab is not often a viable solution since the high fixed costs required to establish and equip a modern clean room facility would result in a strong cost disadvantage. For example, halving the fab output to 10 000 wafers per months would result in a unit cost increase of 10 %. A sub-scale fab, producing only 5000 wafers per month, would incur a prohibitively high cost disadvantage, adding 35–40 % in unit costs (Figure 5.1).

Utilities face a similar situation. The operating costs of running a large-scale 900 MW coal power generation unit are about 60–80 % lower than that for a small, more conventional 100–200 MW unit. In this case a physical constraint – the volume-to-surface ratio of the boiler – determines the scaling of the production costs to a large extent.

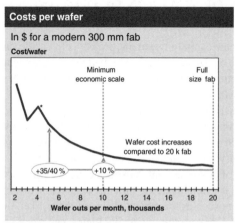

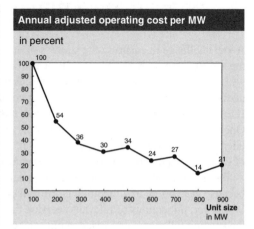

* Peak due to addition of second tool set
(needed after capacity of first complete tool set is exceeded)

Figure 5.1 Examples of scale effects in semiconductor production and power generation

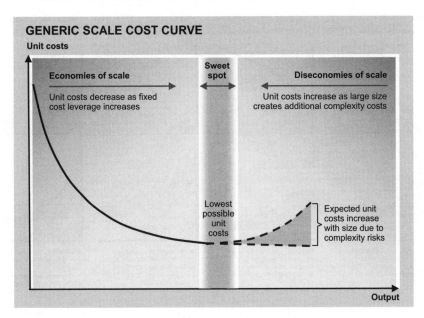

Figure 5.2 Economies and diseconomies of scale influence the unit costs of production as a function of capacity of the productive asset

It is interesting to note that in both cases the scale advantages are only partially driven by better fixed cost leverage; they include more complex scaling behavior due to technical scaling laws (in the utility case) or an improved equipment utilization in the case of the semiconductor fab. We will return to those effects in more detail below.

These positive scale effects are counteracted by diseconomies of scale (Figure 5.2) if a certain size is exceeded. The core drivers of diseconomies of scale are complexity costs and complexity risks. *Complexity costs* arise largely due to increased management, operational and logistics complexity, although other effects, such as increasing IT and control system complexity, might also contribute to increasing unit costs. *Complexity risks* are cost contributions of probabilistic nature – they may but do not have to. Examples of complexity risks are utilization, adverse market reaction, technical and timing risks.

Our experience from several scale analyses suggests that the disadvantage due to over- or undersizing an investment is typically in the range of 10 to >20 % of unit costs. Companies can therefore unleash significant value by identifying the "sweet spot" for their investments: the size that best balances the economies and diseconomies of scale.

In the following we will outline the process and logic for identifying the sweet spot of an investment. This logic has been captured in a scale-cost base model that should enable companies to complete a rough assessment of the sweet spot for their investment in minimum time.

5.2   ASSESSING ECONOMIES OF SCALE

We will first examine how to assess the four most common contributions to economies of scale. These are:

- improved fixed cost leverage (at constant variable costs per unit);
- decreased unit costs, e.g. due to technical scaling laws and increases in procurement volume;

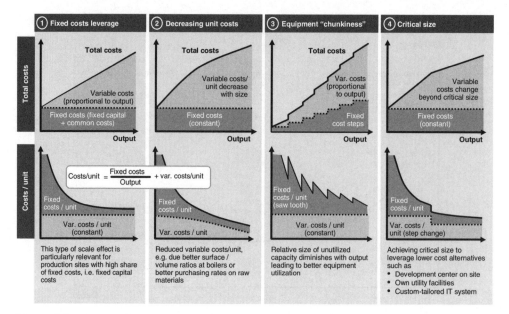

Figure 5.3   Sources of economies of scale

- improved equipment utilization, overcoming the "chunkiness" of additional capacity; and
- added features, once a critical size has been reached, that enable high-volume solutions, such as the ownership of a power plant or the creation of a development department.

Figure 5.3 summarizes the effect the four mechanisms have on total costs as well as unit costs.

5.2.1   Fixed cost leverage

In most business operations, while certain (variable) costs increase in line with output (such as the materials used or the number of labor hours spent in manufacturing an individual unit), other (fixed) costs do not scale directly with increases in production output. Typical examples of fixed costs include infrastructure costs (such as the rent or running costs of the building or production site), research and development costs, and administrative costs. Because most companies are faced with significant external demand fluctuations that arise, for example, as a result of economic cycles or product life-cycles, they usually try to keep their fixed cost burden as low as possible in order to ensure that profitability levels remain as high as possible at varying levels of output.

Unfortunately, in real life the split between variable and fixed costs is often far from clear, especially when different timescales are used in making the comparison. For instance, indirect production personnel are typically considered as a fixed cost, in contrast to the weekly fluctuations in output (i.e. people costs cannot be flexed on a short timeframe in line with demand). However, over a longer time period, say of a year or two, personnel reductions may reduce unit costs as a consequence of sustained productivity enhancement. Similarly, though development costs do not usually depend on the specific short-term changes in the sales volume of an existing product, when looking at periods of time comparable to or larger than the time it takes to develop a new product it is possible to flex the R&D costs in response to increasing or decreasing market demand.

Many companies have invented methods to turn what are apparently fixed costs into variable costs. For instance, lease contracts are employed to reduce the capital burden on production, and flexible manpower schemes (such as the "hour bank", in which overtime is accumulated in periods of high demand and reduced in periods of low demand) are employed.

5.2.2 Decreasing unit costs

In real life, of course, the (simplified) split between fixed and variable costs applies to only the most basic scale effects as actually experienced by companies. Costs do not always scale proportionately with output since variable costs per unit may decrease – or increase – as a result of the scaling-up of productive output. There can be multiple reasons for decreases in the variable costs per unit. Two causes of particular significance are those resulting from the effect of technical scaling laws and reduced purchasing costs at higher volumes.

As an example of the scale advantages arising from *technical scaling laws*, let us return to the case of a utility provider as above. Let us consider as a specific example a utility company that runs coal-fired electricity power stations. The individual power generation units are equipped with boilers of different sizes. The power output of a boiler is roughly proportional to the boiler volume, whereas investment and maintenance costs scale mainly in line with the surface area of the boiler, which in turn is proportional to the weight of the boiler body (the metal and material used to construct the hull as well as its supporting structures). The unit costs, determined as costs per output, therefore increase in proportion to the volume-to-surface ratio of the boiler. Since the volume of the boiler grows proportionally in relation to the diameter of the boiler cubed, while the surface area grows proportionally in relation to the diameter squared, the unit costs (roughly) decrease in inverse proportion to the boiler diameter or, by the same token, in line with the cubic root of the power generated (Figure 5.4).

As a result of these technical scaling properties we observe a classical nonlinear decline in unit costs, as shown in Figure 5.4.

Utilities exploit these scale advantages. While conventional boilers typically produce around 300 MW of electric power, advances in boiler technology allow for power production units as large as one GigaWatt in power output. This increase in size enabled utility providers to leverage technical scaling laws to achieve theoretical boiler operating costs which are about

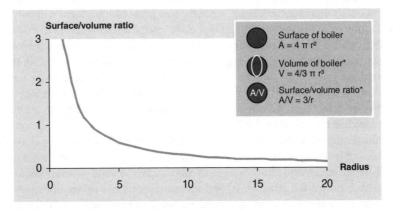

Figure 5.4 Scale effects in electric power generation – surface to volume ratio of coal boilers

a third per MW of those for conventional boilers. In reality, however, the overall unit cost reductions that utility providers have been able to realize might be significantly lower than this due to other extraneous factors, such as costs arising from engineering and overheads, which do not scale in the same manner.

To a lesser extent, the same effect may also be seen in other productive assets. Heating or air conditioning costs, for example, scale in line with the heat dissipation of the productive facility, which in turn is mostly determined by the surface area and type of surface (whether the surface is a wall, ceiling or floor) of the production facility. Scale cost advantages that arise from decreases in unit costs are not limited to those resulting from technical scaling laws but can also include reduced procurement costs as well as effects arising from higher productivity (in terms of direct labor hours per unit). These advantages might, for instance, be the result of employing machinery capable of a higher throughput in a larger scale facility, or the better utilization of maintenance experts.

5.2.3   Equipment utilization/chunkiness of capacity

Another major contribution to economies of scale arises from the fact that often capacity cannot be added incrementally but only in "chunks" of a given size (e.g. a new piece of manufacturing equipment). Each new chunk leads to a step change in unit costs for the first output that requires this new investment. The larger the size of the facility, however, the smaller the relative contribution of the chunk to the total unit costs. Larger-scale facilities have more flexibility than smaller ones in being able to distribute the impact of investment chunks, thereby achieving a higher average utilization. In consequence, increasing the overall size of an asset reduces the impact of investment chunks on unit costs.

To illustrate this point, let us consider the simple example of a laminate producer. Laminates form the base plates of printed circuit boards (PCBs). The base plates are typically single or multiple layers of epoxy resin coated with copper or other conductive materials. Pressing the layers together is a critical and capital-intensive step in the production process. In this process, heavy pressing machines bond the metal sheets to the epoxy layer by applying high mechanical pressure at a controlled temperature. The utilization level of the press is a significant factor in the overall production costs.

Let us assume a laminate producer is already employing two presses and has to respond to an increase in demand by installing an additional machine. Due to the additional cost of the extra press, the producer's unit costs will jump, since the new piece of equipment will only be utilized to a small fraction of its capacity: an effect that often leads decision-makers to first consider all other possible options (such as operational enhancements or new manning schemes) to cover their capacity constraints before deciding to add any new equipment. Assuming that the cost contribution of one press to the total unit cost of a laminate is 8 %, then adding a third press (at low utilization) to the plant will increase overall unit costs by 4 %. If the facility were twice the size, however (and therefore already employed four presses), adding an additional press would only increase the unit costs by 2 %.

Semiconductor manufacturers are a prime example of an industry that faces challenges from the chunkiness of its equipment assets. The semiconductor manufacturing process requires a number of different equipment families, such as lithography (to write structures onto the wafer), chemical etching (to fix the structures), and measurement tools (to monitor the structuring results). Figure 5.5 exemplifies the effects of equipment chunkiness on the investment cost curve (for simplicity we assume three classes of equipment only).

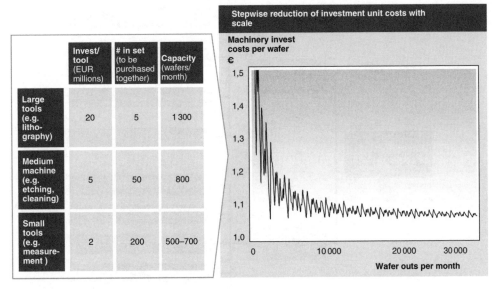

	Invest/ tool (EUR millions)	# in set (to be purchased together)	Capacity (wafers/ month)
Large tools (e.g. litho- graphy)	20	5	1 300
Medium machine (e.g. etching, cleaning)	5	50	800
Small tools (e.g. measure- ment)	2	200	500–700

Figure 5.5   Effects of chunky investments and equipment utilization on scale cost curve

The unit step cost associated with each new group of equipment tools is visible in the graph on the right-hand side of Figure 5.5. It is clear that the range between ineffective (low) and effective (high) equipment utilization in terms of investment costs per wafer narrows in line with the increase in the size of the plant (dropping from >20 % for productive capacities of below 5000 wafers per month to <3 % for capacities above 20 000 wafers per month). Since unit demand can only be predicted with limited accuracy, a semiconductor company, in effect, sees an effective unit cost averaged out over a range of capacity utilizations. Increasing the size of the fabrication unit thus increases the expected average utilization of the plant's equipment. Even though this is a simplified example (many more than three equipment classes exist in a real semiconductor fab), it captures the basic scaling behavior arising from the very chunky nature of the capacity additions in this industry.

5.2.4   Critical size

We only briefly mention the fourth scale effect contribution – the addition of new, dedicated features to an existing asset. Such additions can reduce unit costs but typically only become economically viable above a certain critical size. Examples of such capital additions include the construction of a captive power plant (with the purpose of potentially reducing energy costs and decreasing the risk of breaks in power supply), the installation of sophisticated factory automation systems, or the introduction of R&D and support units dedicated to a specific asset.

5.3   DETERMINING DISECONOMIES OF SCALE

While most effects of economies of scale are incorporated into the assessment of large invest-ment projects, their counterpart – diseconomies of scale – are often excluded from economic assessments. This can lead to a bias towards oversized assets.

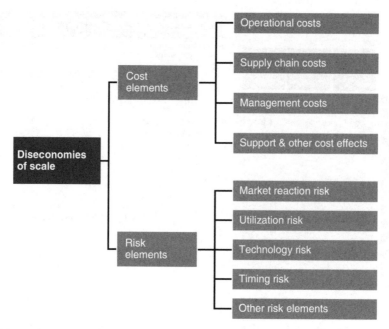

Figure 5.6 Main drivers of diseconomies of scale

In the following discussion we will discuss core contributions to diseconomies of scale. We differentiate between deterministic elements (those arising from increased unit costs) and non-deterministic elements (those arisring from increased risk), as shown in Figure 5.6.

There are four major cost elements driving diseconomies of scale:

- operational costs;
- supply chain costs;
- management costs; and
- support and other costs.

While in most cases the impact of scale diseconomies can be readily predicted, this is not the case for risk effects. Risk effects are inherently probabilistic in nature, so although a foreseen risk might well occur, it does not do so inevitably. This makes risk effects more difficult to assess than cost diseconomies of scale. Currently, few companies factor complexity risks into their investment decision-making process.

Despite these difficulties, certain risk effects are readily measurable. For instance, the effects of increasing the span of control in relation to increasing size can be assessed without difficulty, once the basic organizational structure and the targets for the spans of control have been determined. Other aspects are more difficult to measure, however. For instance, assessing the potential likelihood of a technology failure, such as a control-board breakdown, requires a detailed understanding and statistical failure analysis of all the critical components of the board.

We have identified four main risk types that give rise to diseconomies of scale:

- utilization risk;
- market reaction risk;

- technology risk; and
- timing risk.

In the following we will investigate the individual cost and risk elements in a little more detail.

5.3.1 Cost elements

In order to gain a better understanding of diseconomies of scale we start with a closer look at the cost diseconomies of scale.

Operational costs

Typically, as discussed in the section on scale advantages, operational costs are decreasing with size – mainly due to better fixed cost leverage. However, there also are a number of effects that lead to increasing costs with scale. For example, if the production materials have to travel a longer distance from the docks to the plant, the increased transportation costs will give rise to increased handling costs per unit. As a result, increased scale can in some circumstances lead to additional unit costs for large-scale operations. Some of the most relevant effects are:

- **Downtime.** Typically, larger-scale production facilities experience longer setup and changeover times than smaller ones. This can be due, for example, to the use of larger and more complicated machines in the bigger plants, as well as the additional time it takes to maintain and repair such machines.
- **Transport.** Transportation costs (for both automated and non-automated means of transportation) tend to rise faster than is proportional to the increase in scale for a number of reasons. For instance, additional costs can result from the increased average distance that each unit needs to be transported from the plant, or to the increasing investment in transportation (e.g. because forklift trucks are no longer practical, a conveyer belt has to be installed).
- **Other operational waste.** Operational waste has a tendency to grow disproportionately with increased size, if not managed carefully. Operational waste includes:
  - the growth of intermediate inventories, due to increasing batch sizes in production. This often leads to longer waiting times of materials and increases the total lead time of products to the customer;
  - overcapacity and overproduction at the various value steps, due to the improper leveling of capacity;
  - overproduction, due to the greater difficulty of matching production output to demand;
  - increased defect rates, due to a reduced focus on the individual production units, a greater separation between the fault generation step and the next quality check point, and the increased difficulty in detecting the root causes of the problems.

Keeping operational unit costs under control at increased scale requires fighting all kinds of operational waste. The strategies to achieve this goal have been described extensively in books on Lean manufacturing.[1]

---

[1] Compare e.g. John Drew, Blair McCallum and Stefan Roggenhofer (2004). *Journey to Lean: Making Operational Change Stick*. Palgrave Macmillan.

Supply chain costs

Local supply constraints can lead to increased component or materials costs. As an example, consider the case of coal power generation plants. Optimally, these should be located as near to the source of coal as possible, that is, as close as possible to the coal deposit or the docks. However, if the demand of a single power plant or the size of the local cluster exceeds that of the local mining or shipping capacity, adding additional power generation capacity might be uneconomic due to the extra costs of transporting the additional coal from further afield.

Main reasons for increased supply costs per unit of output are:

• Suppliers might be operating at a point beyond their own optimum scale, causing increased complexity costs for the supplier, which are reflected in higher prices.
• The major suppliers (with low prices) might reach their own capacity limits and, therefore, need to rely on additional suppliers (with higher prices).
• Additional suppliers might be located further away from the investment, once again leading to higher transportation costs (e.g. as in the supply of coal for utilities).

At larger production volumes these effects can reduce or reverse volume bundling effects (higher discounts at larger purchased volumes).

Another effect that is more difficult to quantify is the increased complexity of the supply chain. Larger operations might require a more complex supply chain, for instance if several suppliers have to be used rather than one. As a result, management costs per unit will increase and – what is often more relevant – it might become more difficult to manage and maintain the quality and on-time delivery of parts supplied.

Management costs

Management costs often increase at a rate faster than the increase in unit output due to the increased management complexity that larger size engenders. Typically, with any increase in the number of people involved, the number of possible interpersonal interfaces increases quadratically.[2] Companies try to counteract this effect by establishing hierarchical reporting lines, but a certain amount of networking across organizational boundaries is usually necessary to manage cross-functional issues. In matrix organizations this effect is strongly aggravated, since every person has more than one reporting line and both matrix dimensions need to grow with increasing size.

As a result, the number of organizational layers required to keep the span of control at an acceptable level also increases and, in consequence, the management cost per unit rises. In addition, there is further hidden cost in that each new organizational layer typically increases the time it takes management to react to and resolve problems (Figure 5.7).

Measures companies can use to help mitigate the increasing costs and complexity that result from expanding their organization include the following:

• Keep the number of organizational layers to a minimum.
• Replace matrix structures with single reporting lines wherever possible.
• Minimize administrative and other overhead functions.

---

[2] A simple analogy can help illustrate this effect. If n people meet at a party and everyone wants to shake hands with everybody else (i.e. with $n - 1$ people), the total number of handshakes is $n * (n - 1)/2$. Taking the number of handshakes as an indicator of the required communication lines in an organization, we see that communication costs and management complexity can be expected to grow proportionally to the square of the size.

Increasing scale makes additional management levels necessary

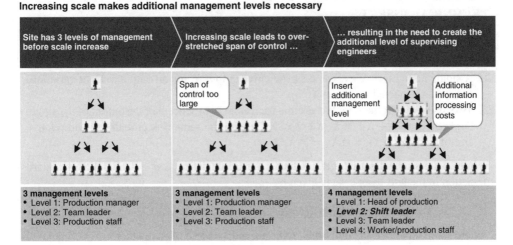

Figure 5.7   Increasing organizational complexity with scale

Designing the organization to reflect the company's most important business needs will help to avoid complex, matrix-type organizations and minimize the required interfaces between the different departments.

Support and other costs

Overheads, such as IT, office and other facility costs, also tend to increase at a faster rate than proportional to the increase in production. A typical example of this kind of diseconomy results from the extra costs of the sophisticated IT necessary to facilitate the increasingly complex information flows between employees and management. Another example would be increasing measure and control complexity leading to a higher disturbance rate requiring more and higher skilled personnel.

Establishing firm overhead targets and stringent IT governance can help mitigate these problems and keep costs under control, even with increased size.

5.4   RISK ELEMENTS

Before we look at the analysis of the individual risk elements in more detail, let us first consider why there is reason to believe that increased scale can lead to increased risk – or to put it the other way around, why splitting a larger asset into smaller units might help reduce risk.

The main effect of increased risk arises from the fact that an incident, such as the failure of a main component or the effects of a fire, can shut down an entire large-scale facility, whereas it is very unlikely that similar events will occur simultaneously in a number of smaller units. This is similar to the rationale that capital market investors use when they spread their total investment across several investment opportunities to "diversify risk" (the mathematical foundation of this point is discussed in the technical insert below).

TECHNICAL INSERT

Distributing operational risk

Consider two basic scenarios:
1. A single large asset: We assume a productive output X and an output risk (or variation) to have an expected impact ΔX.
2. Two assets of half the size: We assume each asset to produce half the output of the single larger asset ($X1 + X2 = X$, $X1/2 = X/2$) with the same risk probability and relative size of risk, i.e. $\Delta X_1 = \Delta X_2 = \Delta X/2$.

While in the single asset case the output standard deviation is $\sigma = \sqrt{\Delta X^2}$, the standard deviation in the two-asset case is given by

$$\sigma_{1/2} = \sqrt{\Delta X_1^2 + \Delta X_2^2} = \sqrt{(\Delta X/2)^2 + (\Delta X/2)^2} = \sqrt{\Delta X^2}/\sqrt{2} = \sigma/\sqrt{2}$$

where we assume that the individual risks are independent of each other.

Thus, for the two smaller assets the risk factor is $1/\sqrt{2} = 71\,\%$, i.e. 29 % smaller than that for the single large asset.

It is important to realize, however, that this simple argument only holds true if the risks are independent of scale (the output deviations are thus proportional to the scale of the output, i.e. $\Delta X_1 = \Delta X_2 = \Delta X/2$). This is a reasonable assumption in a number of cases. For instance, in the case of power generation units, one can assume that downtime risks are largely independent of scale. Consider, for example, a 300 MW power generation unit which has a risk of 2.0 % unplanned downtime. If two 150 MW units are used instead of the single unit and these two units each have the same downtime risk, the above argument holds true and the two plants have a reduced combined output risk of 1.4 % (Figure 5.8).

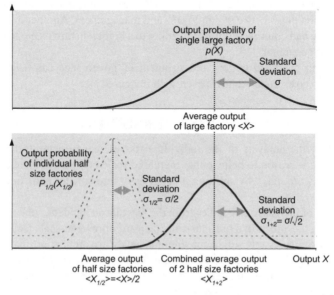

Figure 5.8   The reduced output risk of two smaller production units compared to one large unit

In the following we will take a more detailed look at utilization risks in order to illustrate the methodology applicable in assessing contribution to diseconomies of scale. The same methodology can and has been applied to the other risk types but will not be discussed in detail here.

5.4.1   Utilization risks

Though a single incident, such as the failure of a mechanical part, is no more critical for a large plant than it is for a small one, the larger the size of the plant the greater the potential loss of production. Similarly, it can also prove to be more difficult to manage sales demand where production is concentrated in one large fabrication unit. Risks such as these may lead to an increasing risk of non-utilization for larger facilities.

We use a five-step process to assess the contribution of a risk to diseconomies of scale:

1. Generate an option tree to separate the relevant options for managing risk from each other and to link these to their respective economic impact.
2. Select the relevant branch of the tree for a given investment.
3. Define the probability distribution of the underlying risk driver.
4. Calculate the resulting unit cost function for selected confidence levels.
5. Integrate the risk component into the overall scale-cost curve at the defined confidence level.

We exemplify this process for utilization risks.

Step 1: We first need to identify all relevant branches of the risk tree for utilization risks. This requires thinking through the various options available to a company when managing utilization (compare also Figure 5.9). In the best case, if there is sufficient demand to fully utilize the installed capacity, no additional non-utilization costs will be incurred. If this is not the case, however, the company is likely to react in one of two ways. Firstly, if the production is readily scaleable it might opt to reduce its output and accept a higher fixed cost burden on each unit of production. Secondly, if the company is unable or unwilling to reduce production output it will need to somehow fill its capacity. It could do this either by continuing to produce the same product or by utilizing the spare capacity to produce other products. Producing more of a product than the market demands will either increase the company's buffer stocks (thus incurring related storage and/or obsolescence costs) or it will force it to make the products available at a discounted price. The production of additional products is likely to result in a margin differential between the original product (which can be assumed to have the highest margin, as this was the first choice) and the additional product.

Step 2: The next step is to select the relevant branch for a given investment. In the example depicted in Figure 5.9, the company opts for the easy way out and decides to produce extra stock. While this keeps production operations undisturbed, the company incurs storage costs and runs the risk of having to scrap some of its production if it cannot sell this at a later date.

In principle it is, of course, possible to select a combination of options to handle utilization risks, or to switch between options over time. While it is possible to model such cases,[3] in order to keep this discussion simple, we assume that the company has chosen only one branch of the risk tree.

---

[3] In the case of multiple options being used, the individual assessments can be added using probability weights for the different options. If a switching occurs over time, one assessment needs to be used until the switching point and a different one after the switching point.

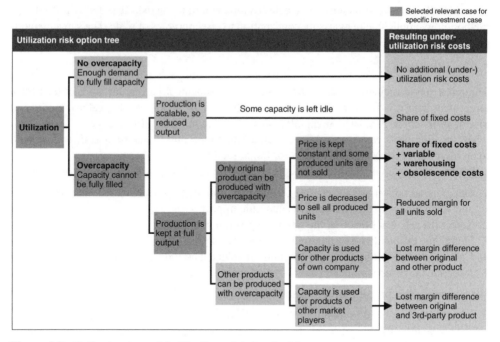

Figure 5.9   Option tree to model utilization-related scale risks

Step 3: The main driver underlying utilization risks is the uncertainty about future demand (including demand volatility). While it is often impossible to predict future demand accurately, it may well be possible to make an assumption about the possible demand range based, for example, on historic demand volatility and insights about expected market developments. In the simplest case, this can be achieved through estimates of high, medium, and low demand. To obtain a continuous distribution, we assume a normal, Gaussian demand distribution characterized by an estimate of the average and the standard deviation of demand. If more information is available (e.g. that upward fluctuations in market demand are more likely than downward fluctuations), this knowledge can be built into the distribution curve.

Step 4: Based on the assumed distribution curve, we can calculate the economic risk resulting from underutilization as a function of the scale of the investment (Figure 5.10). For outputs significantly smaller than the expected sales demand, the utilization risk is negligible; at output capacities above the expected demand level, higher and higher levels of utilization risk are incurred. In real life, a certain amount of overcapacity is often unavoidable, even when the demand level is well understood. The extra capacity is necessary to buffer volatilities in supply and production.

Step 5: Once the basic risk model has been established, it can be integrated into the overall scale cost-curve. First, the appropriate "confidence level" needs to be chosen. This level can be that of the expected average value (50 % confidence), a one-standard-deviation tolerance (67 % confidence), or any other level that is deemed appropriate, depending on how critical additional unit costs are from a business perspective.

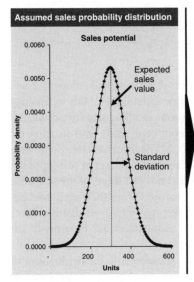 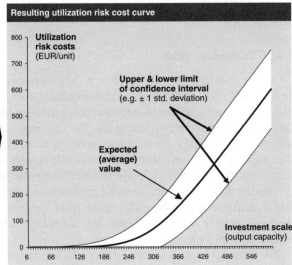

Figure 5.10   Deriving utilization risks

5.4.2   Market reaction risks

Another source of risk is that competitors can, and often do, react to capacity additions. The larger the chunks of capacity that are added, the higher the risk of adverse price reactions in the market. In such cases, competitor reaction can put product prices or market share at risk, depending on the size of the capacity that is added.

Typically, a market reaction is only seen if a market reaction threshold is exceeded. As an example, a telecommunication company that we know found that price changes or network coverage extensions only led to a measurable change in customer behavior if they exceeded 10–15 %. Once this threshold is crossed, competitors have a number of choices. They may decide to either keep their own capacity constant – and to reduce their price – or to change their capacity as a reaction to the initial added capacity. If competitors keep their capacity constant, the company making the original investment might have to lower its price in response and thus, in effect, enter into a price war; or it can maintain its own price at the previous level, running the risk that it might lose market share (as compared to its original business case assumptions). A competitor might also opt to reduce its production capacity in order to keep the market prices stable. Lastly, competitors might opt to add additional capacity in order not to lose market share. This will put both the price of the products and the market share of both companies at risk.

Successfully predicting and pre-empting competitor reactions can, therefore, have a significant effect on outcomes. A big market player might, for instance, announce significant new capacity additions well in advance of the actual investment, in order to deter competitors from making their own investments. This pattern is seen in the semiconductor market, for example, albeit not always played with success. If competitors are not deterred by such announcements, then excess capacity is built up in the industry, which can prepare the ground for a future price war that will put every company's margin at risk.

Based on the notion of a reaction threshold, we assume a reaction s-curve typically used to describe threshold phenomena also in other fields of science. This reaction strength increases drastically around the reaction threshold. Away from the threshold the reaction slope is much more shallow.

5.4.3 Technology risks

No matter what the size of an investment, the diseconomies resulting from technology risk will be increased if a company makes a commitment to a single new technology. If this technology proves not to be feasible or fails to meet the desired specifications and productivity targets, this can severely impact overall unit costs. The challenges telecom companies have faced in the introduction of the new generation of mobile networks (3G/UMTS) illustrates this point well. The telecom companies had to decide whether they should enter the market at full (optimal) scale, providing network coverage to serve all their areas and not just those of dense traffic, or whether they should take a staged approach, extending outward from their core markets. Almost universally they have chosen the latter approach. Their reasoning was that it reduces their risk, both in terms of whether the technology works as intended and in terms of the market demand for the new technology.

The main driver of technology risks is the uncertainties associated with the deployment of a new product or process technology (for more details on process technology risk effects see Chapter 3, Right Technology). Suffice to say, several scaling behaviors are possible, ranging from scale independence (as when there are fundamental problems with the new technology) to step-change behavior (as when critical parameters cannot be met above a certain size). We assume a "softened" step function in our analysis: this step function can be adapted to both these cases, if the parameters are chosen appropriately. The resulting unit cost curve is also depicted in Figure 5.11. Note that the level of uncertainty is typically highest in the "switching" range, the point at which any variation in the parameters has the strongest effect on the outcome.

5.4.4 Timing risks

The last type of risk we consider is the risk of delay in the realization of an investment. It is often the greatest fear of a project manager that the investment project will not be completed

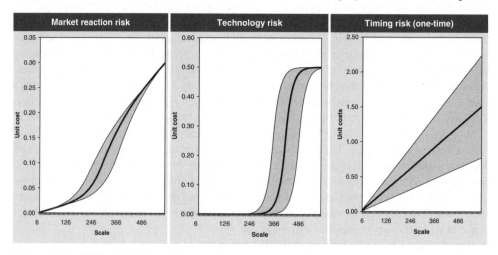

Figure 5.11 Utilization risk modeling – unit risk curves for different risk types

by the date originally targeted. There are 1001 things that can – and often do – go wrong during a large-scale project, so such fears are not unreasonable. Delays in realization typically reduce the investment return, since the production volumes that have been targeted cannot be fully realized, or are realized at a later date. If time-to-market is critical for a product, these effects can be drastic. For microprocessor companies, the company that is first-to-market often realizes a value 30–40 % higher than those that follow in its wake.

There are several branches to the risk tree for assessing timing risks. If the new capacity replaces an existing production line, or if alternative production capacity is available, the only material risk is in the productivity difference between the new and old technologies. If the productivity gain is not sufficiently large, the cost of the investment could lead to a reduction in the margin. If no replacement capacity is available, however, a delay in implementation can either contribute to short-term losses in sales and margins during the period of delay, or lead to a long-term reduction in volumes or margins.

5.5   AN APPROACH FOR FINDING THE "SWEET SPOT"

Having discussed the three main components that contribute to the scale cost curve – decreasing unit costs due to economies of scale, increasing unit costs, and risks – we can now bring these elements together. To provide an overview, we will briefly introduce a scale effect model we employed to assess the overall scale cost curve and then discuss the results of scale-cost assessments based on two case examples: an automotive company and a chemicals production plant.

5.5.1   Scale effect model

All economy and diseconomy of scale effects we have discussed have been incorporated into a mathematical model that can provide a quick assessment of scale effects. We have tried to balance the requirements for completeness and accuracy with the desire that it should be simple to understand and easy to use. In order to achieve this goal we have focused on a number of core input parameters that drive the assessment logic.[4]

The model inputs are structured in three areas: general parameters (such as fixed or variable costs, stepped or fixed investments), the expected ramp-up and operation time, and the relevant output range. These parameters are used as the basis for the assessment of economies of scale. A second set of parameters is used to determine the complexity costs following the structure outlined earlier in this chapter. These are based on a combination of the driver parameters (e.g. internal transportation costs) and their scale elasticity (e.g. the percentage change in transportation costs for a given increase in capacity). The complexity risk parameters follow the logic outlined earlier in this chapter: you first select the relevant branch of the option tree, then specify the probability profile of the main risk driver, and compile the economic impact figures.

The model then uses these inputs to calculate a scale unit cost-curve: the output includes all the economies and diseconomies of scale. From this output curve the scale cost-dependence and the sweet spot can be determined (Figure 5.12).

---

[4] In this model approximately 20 base parameters are used to characterize the investment and its relevant scale range and approximately 10 parameters are used for the assessment of the individual scale risk elements.

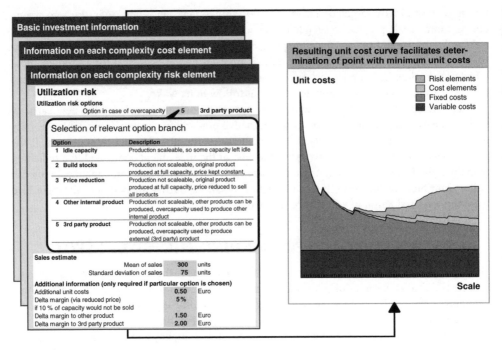

Figure 5.12   Scale model inputs and outputs

5.6   REAL-LIFE EXAMPLES

We will now look at a two (fictitious) application examples of scale cost-analysis:

5.6.1   Automotive industry case example

After inserting values typical for a compact car production line in the relevant economy and diseconomy of scale categories, we obtain the scale cost-curve for an automotive plant as shown in Figure 5.13.

The graph shows that there are significant diseconomies of scale at output sizes in excess of 80 000 cars a year. Prior to taking into account diseconomies of scale, the actual capacity – based on an example from an East European car production plant – was set to 125 000 cars a year. The inclusion of diseconomies of scale reveals that, in fact, the scale sweet spot is 16 % less than this at 105 000 cars per year.

In this case the plant size is only slightly in excess of the ideal scale, and so its excess capacity can be managed satisfactorily (with a calculated cost effect of <1 %). In many other cases, however, car makers have discovered that their plants are far too large and are moving more and more towards a "small is beautiful" approach. As a result, several companies have recently taken decisions that favor a smaller plant size than was the norm in the past. General Motors/Opel, for example, has chosen to construct its Eisenach and Gliwice plants with an output of 70 000 cars per year, less than a quarter the size of its plant in Bochum, which has a capacity of 300 000 cars per year.

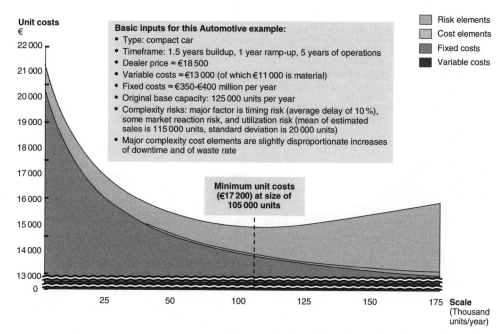

Figure 5.13   Scale cost curve example – automotive, compact car

Returning to our present example, if the management had chosen to establish a production facility with an output of 175 000 or above, in the belief that "bigger is always better", the scale risks might well have led to unit costs well above the cars' actual sale price!

In this example, the risk-related scale effects dominate the outcome, while the contributions of scale cost disadvantages are relatively minor. This is because the operational, supply chain and organizational cost effects can be controlled relatively easily, e.g. by employing lean production techniques. In contrast, the diseconomies of scale, which are driven largely by timing and utilization risks, are much more difficult to overcome. Being late in the ramp-up, for example, could seriously compromise the company's ability to introduce a new model into the market at a price that is competitive and in sufficient quantities to justify the investment. This would sabotage the economics of its expansion strategy. Developing a factory of too large a size could easily lead to poor utilization of the productive asset, burdening it with high and unsustainable overheads and putting the potential profits at risk.

5.6.2   Base chemicals case example

As another example, let us look at the case of manufacturers of base chemicals such as polyethylene or petrochemicals. After inserting estimates for the scale cost and risk elements, we obtain a scale sweet spot of around 400 000 tons per year (see Figure 5.14). The actual size of such plants as observed in the field is approximately 20 % larger than the calculated optimum size (but again at an only slight (~1 %) cost disadvantage).

It is, of course, dangerous to generalize about the scale considerations in chemicals plants based on this one example from a company focused in commodity chemicals, as chemicals plants vary quite significantly depending on their specific segment of activity.

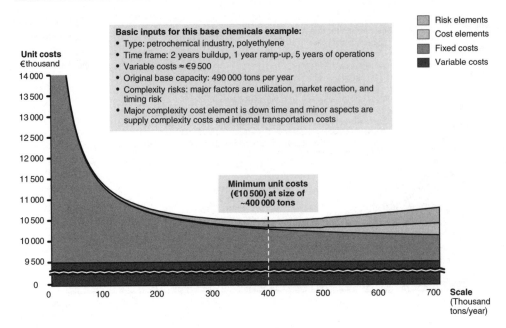

Figure 5.14 Scale cost curve – base chemicals example

Most commodity chemicals are by definition needed in large quantities, so commodity producers have, over time, sought to create large sites that integrate a number of production lines. Colocating plants allows the companies to benefit from substantial economies of scale and low internal logistics costs (because all the production steps are in close proximity to each other). Colocation also provides them with the ability to use production byproducts as the base inputs for other chemical processes. The flip side of these advantages is that these players face an increased operational risk: disruptions to one process can severely affect the whole production site.

Certain industries face more complex scale scenarios. Consider, for example, investments in modern telecom networks, such as 3G mobile phone networks. For a company in a medium-sized country, such as France or Germany, the investment necessary to establish a large-scale 3G mobile network infrastructure is of the order of €1–4 billion (this excludes the sometimes tremendous cost of obtaining the 3G license itself: in Europe such license fees are themselves in the multi-billion Euro range). Determining the optimum size for the network (including the rollout of the network from the urban to rural areas) typically requires an in-depth analysis that compares the costs for establishing the additional coverage to that of the potential additional revenues. Since this goes well beyond the scope of unit-cost assessments, this analysis requires an in-depth assessment of scale effects that maps benefits and costs along several different market scenarios. This task is obviously of much greater complexity than for some of the industries described earlier, and will require a dedicated analysis to incorporate specifics of the network topology.

5.7   SUMMARY

We hope these examples have served to illustrate the importance of considering diseconomies of scale, not just economies of scale, when determining the viability of an investment. It should have become clear that the impact of diseconomies in counterbalancing economies of scale varies significantly between industries and between segments. We also hope that the examples have shown that a basic model as discussed above offers a practical approach to help managers identify the scale sweet spots for their investments and optimize return on investment.

REFERENCE

Drew, J., McCallum, B. and Roggenhofer, S. (2004). *Journey to Lean: Making Operational Change Stick*. Palgrave.

Right Location: Getting the Most from Government Incentives

CHAPTER HIGHLIGHTS

Government incentives can have a significant impact on the longer term returns of an investment and are often a major consideration when deciding on an investment's location. However, there is often little transparency about the range of incentives available and the conditions attached to them. In this chapter we shed some light on the various categories and types of incentives that are available. The chapter provides:

- a general framework, designed to help classify and assess the various investment instruments that are available;
- a worldwide screening of incentives, providing an overview of the available incentive instruments as well as numerous examples;
- an analysis of the impact incentives have on a business investment case in reducing upfront investment, enhancing the value creation in the ramp-up and early production phase, and by improving long-term cash flow.

Location is of vital importance in determining the success or failure of an investment, yet deciding on the right location is a far from simple task. Decision makers need to take into account a wide range of factors that can have a significant impact on the final outcome. This decision-making process is made more complicated because these factors can change over time.

Fortunately, certain specific factors tend to be of much greater importance than others in determining the viability of location. A survey by Abele et al. (2008), for instance, shows that the two factors consistently the most important in determining the attractiveness of a production location are labor costs and market proximity. This survey also indicates that government incentives, such as taxes and subsidies, are highly relevant when choosing between different countries or regions when siting a production plant. Interestingly, incentives prove especially important for "leaders" (i.e. companies which have extensive experience in setting up new plants – see Figure 6.1).[1]

In this chapter we will focus on just one location criteria: government incentives. We have chosen to look at this factor in detail because many companies struggle to model the impact of incentives on their business plans, as well as how they should manage the incentives within the overall project. Also, we feel that valuable advice on other factors, such as material, labor, and logistics costs, is readily available or is highly dependent on the specifics of an investment such as the availability of skilled labor or local know-how and clusters.

There are several perfectly valid reasons why incentives are difficult to manage: there is often limited transparency about which instruments are available, what the application process is, and

---

[1] Please see Abele et al. (2008) for a detailed discussion on selecting the right investment location.

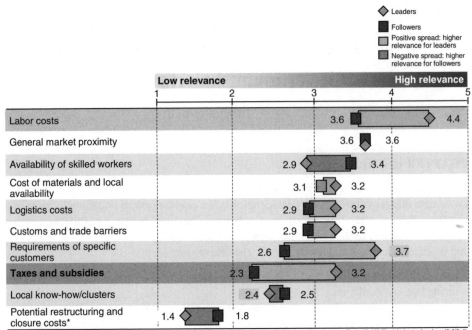

Figure 6.1   Relevance of location criteria at the country level[2]

under what conditions a company becomes eligible for incentives. As a result, companies often have to spend significant time, resources and energy in clarifying these issues, particularly with regard to the structure, size and conditions of the incentives package that might be available to them. To help companies through this process, we will provide an overview of the various incentive instruments that are available internationally and discuss how they can affect an investment business case. The chapter focuses on answering three core questions:

- What are the different types of government incentives?
- What is the likely economic impact of the various incentives on a business plan?
- What is there to learn from the experience of companies that have made use of them?

6.1   GOVERNMENT INCENTIVES: AN OVERVIEW

In 2007 the EU spent about €190 billion on incentives,[3] the equivalent to approximately 8 % of all total private investment in the EU (Figure 6.2). The EU is not unique in its level of government support. Similar levels of incentives are seen elsewhere in the world – albeit often with much less transparency regarding the actual levels of expenditure involved.

The impact of government incentives on business is substantial. In some cases, incentives can account for as much as 25 % of the total investment. So although incentives might not be a dominant factor in investment decisions, they can certainly tilt the balance in the final

---

[2] Abele et al. (2008), p. 39.

[3] This number includes non-investment related incentives.

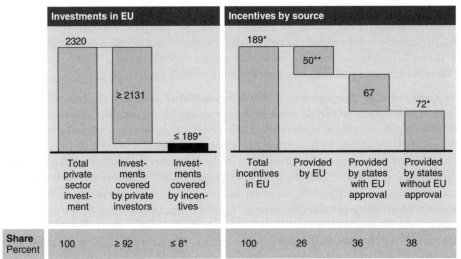

* Contains non-investment-related incentives or subsidies
** Regional aid by EU for 2007-13: EUR 347 billions
Source: McKinsey analysis, Eurostat, DG Competition

Figure 6.2   Government incentives in the EU by source (EUR billions, 2007)

choice between several different investment options, especially with regard to the location of that investment.

Leveraging government incentives is an art rather than a science. The ability to secure incentives often depends on the company having access to the relevant information, to government institutions, and to other decision makers.

Here we provide investors with a brief overview of what to expect worldwide. Due to the nature of the subject, the information in this section can neither be fully comprehensive nor conclusive. Nonetheless, we hope it will shed some light on what is a largely uncharted area and that the information provided here will help decision makers judge the applicability and relevance of the various incentive instruments open to them.

Let's start by defining what we mean by government incentives: any financial aid and concession that has a monetary value and that can be granted in favor of certain industries, institutions, or groups of persons.

It is well understood that state aid leads, in the long run, to a higher tax burden and to market distortions. As a result, in general, such incentives are provided only where a government thinks there is good reason to justify them, for example, that they will lead to a reduction in unemployment, or to an increase in regional development, or will help to protect the environment. Such government incentives have several different objectives and can have a wide range of beneficiaries. For the purpose of this book we focus solely on government incentives that are targeted at company investments.

6.1.1   Creating public-private, win-win situations

Investment resources are not unlimited, neither at the company level nor at the state or government level. This leads to competition for resources: there is competition between companies to obtain the incentive resources and competition between the different government authorities in attracting businesses to their region. Though there is competition, there is also the opportunity for alignment between the interests of business and government.

The basic objective of government incentives is to serve the public interest by creating a win-win situation for the region, the country's economy and the company. Although we are interested mostly in the company perspective on incentives, let us take a quick look at the core reasons for believing that such win-win situations are indeed possible.

There are four main reasons why **governments** provide incentives:

- **Support regional development and the formation of industry clusters.** Governments support investments in certain areas to strengthen the local economy, to prevent imminent decline in public welfare, or to compensate for economic or structural imbalances. These incentives have proven to be particularly effective if they help create or foster economic clusters, that is, by creating a network of interrelated economic activities in close geographic proximity to each other. Such clusters can leverage regional synergies and create the critical mass necessary to attract talent, suppliers and other resources to the area.[4]
- **Reduce unemployment.** Governments try to create jobs by attracting capital investment to regions of high unemployment.
- **Protect the environment.** They provide incentives that help fulfill the government's obligation to protect the environment.
- **Support technological progress.** They also provide incentives to encourage companies to develop and use innovative technology, with the aim of strengthening the future prospects of local or regional industries.

Typically, there are four economic reasons why **companies** might apply for incentives:

- **Secure investment funding.** Government incentives can make a significant contribution to funding capital investments, e.g. through the provision of grants, equity stakes, or infrastructure.
- **Enhance profitability.** Tax relief and other cost-focused incentives, such as labor grants, can enhance the profitability of investments.
- **Improve financing conditions.** Governmental guarantees or loans can improve the financing conditions for an investment, thereby reducing the overall level of interest on the debt.
- **Safeguarding investments.** Governmental support is stronger when there is a financial link with the company. Such a link might also help to minimize approval difficulties or risks.

Government incentives can create economic value for a region when they are provided for investments that have a fair chance of economic success and where there is sufficient focus on a particular industry. They are likely to fail when they are spread thinly across many industries, where they tend to quickly wither away without creating any lasting, sustainable, structural impact. To create the right focus, the government needs to carry out a proper assessment of the potential investors and the likely impact that the prospective investments will have on the regional economic network (in the ideal case, in developing an economic cluster).

An example of the positive effects government incentives can have has already been mentioned briefly in Chapter 2 – those provided by the Free State of Saxony. The incentives helped stimulate the development of a regional semiconductor cluster that has become known as "Silicon Saxony". These incentives were a good investment from the state's perspective: By providing incentives of $\sim$ €900 million the state has, to date, been able to generate more than €2 billion of economic value. Figure 6.3 shows that the direct effect of additional tax income alone has more than compensated the state's cash expenditures, the breakeven point being reached at the end of the fourth year from the start of the investments. If indirect benefits, such

---

[4] See e.g. Porter (1998).

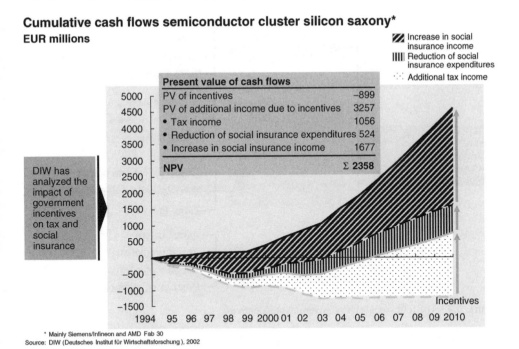

Figure 6.3   Impact of government incentives on Saxony's economy

as the reduction in social insurance expenditure and the increase in social insurance income are also included in this assessment, then the State of Saxony's incentives started to pay back from the very first year.

Not all incentives follow the Silicon Saxony pattern. Sometimes incentives are paid out over the longer term in order to sustain industries that would otherwise succumb to competition, or to alleviate the short-term impact of a structural transformation of the economy. These types of incentives are properly termed "maintenance subsidies" and should be considered quite separately to investment subsidies as discussed here. Rather than supporting new investments, long-term incentives are mostly consumptive in nature and have only limited impact on future value creation. We have therefore excluded them from this investigation.

6.2   COMMON TYPES OF INCENTIVE INSTRUMENTS

So far we have looked at what motivates governments to provide incentives and companies to seek them out. Until now we have talked of incentives as if there is only one type. In reality, of course, there are many different types of incentives, all of which have a very different impact. We will now look at the range of incentives offered, who provides them, and under what circumstances.

We distinguish three major categories of government incentive instruments: subsidies, financial support, and tax relief; along with one further category of miscellaneous, though nonetheless important, incentives, which we describe for the sake of completeness as "other" (Figure 6.4).

In an effort to create some transparency in what is otherwise a rather opaque topic we have screened the publicly-available data from 17 countries around the globe, all of which are

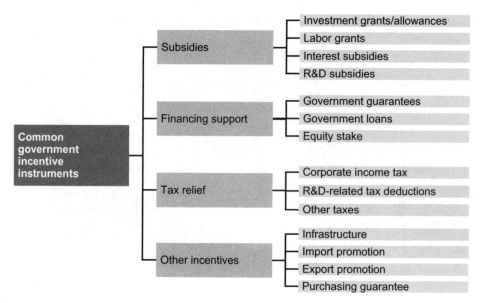

Figure 6.4 The four categories of government incentives

prominent destinations for investments. Figure 6.5 provides an overview of the information collected. We are aware that, despite our best efforts, these data reflect only a small subset of the total number of existing incentive instruments and that this landscape changes all the time. Nevertheless, we hope it will give managers a head start in screening the incentives available to them.

ESTIMATES BASED ON LIMITED DATA

– No data found   ○ Descriptive data available   ◑ Medium impact   ◐ Low impact   ● High impact

	Subsidies			Financing support			Tax relief			Others		
	Investment grants	Labor grants	Interest subsidies	Guarantees	Govt loans	Equity stake	Corporate income tax	R&D-related	Other taxes	Infrastructure	Import promotion	Export promotion
Bahrain	–	◑		–	○	–	●	–	○	●	●	○
Belgium	◑	◑	○	–	◑	–	◑	◑	○	–	◑	○
Brazil	–	–	–	–	○	–	●	–	○	●	○	○
Canada	–	◑	–	○	○	○	◐	◑	○	–	◐	○
China	–	–	–	–	◑	–	●	◑	●	–	●	●
Czech Republic	○	◑	–	–	○	–	●	–	–	◑	◑	○
France	◑	–	–	–	◑	–	◐	–	○	–	–	○
Germany	●	●	–	○	○	○	–	○	–	–	–	◐
India	○	–	–	–	○	–	●	●	○	○	○	●
Italy	◑	●	○	–	○	○	◑	●	○	◑	–	○
Japan	◑	–	–	○	○	–	◐	○	–	–	○	○
Mexico	–	–	–	○	○	○	◐	–	○	–	–	○
Russia	–	–	–	–	–	–	◑	●	○	–	○	–
Singapore	◑	○	–	–	○	◑	●	●	–	–	–	○
Spain	○	●	–	○	○	–	◑	◑	○	○	○	○
UK	◑	○	–	–	○	–	◑	●	○	–	○	◑
US	–	○	–	–	○	◑	○	●	○	–	–	○

Figure 6.5 Overview of incentive instruments

TECHNICAL INSERT

Overview of common types of government incentives

Table 6.1 summarizes the major types of investment incentives together with specific examples of where they can be found. The countries mentioned here are merely examples, incentives of the same type often being found in several other countries as well.

Table 6.1   Overview of common categories of government incentives

Class	Type	Description	Examples	Country
Subsidies	Investment grants	Upfront subsidies, limited to a certain amount or provided as a percentage of the investment within its first year.	Grants of up to 65 % of total investment in overseas territories, 10–20 % in other areas.	France
	Interest subsidies	Reimbursement of interest expenses up to a certain amount or percentage.	Full compensation of interest.	Belgium
	R&D subsidies	Money given to cover/reduce R&D expenses, provided as fixed amount or as percentage of R&D costs.	Several types, with a wide range of conditions. Typically awarded to individual institutions or beneficiaries based on specific research proposals that are screened by expert committees.	Several EU countries
	Labor grants	Grants for reducing the cost of labor, e.g. as a fixed amount per year per worker employed, or as a reduction of non-wage labor costs for every person formerly unemployed.	Subsidy of $11 925 per year for the first 3 years for each Bahraini employed. Assistance for training redundant workers.	Bahrain UK
Financing support	Equity stakes	Mostly government-mediated/facilitated with private equity partners; however, sometimes government itself will take an equity stake.	Federal program "Technology Partnerships Canada" provides Canadian companies with venture capital for private research.	Canada
	Government loans	Usually loans made with a preferential interest rate (in comparison to the market).	Interest-free loans of up to 50 % of a project's total costs.	Belgium

(*Continued*)

Table 6.1 (*Continued*)

Class	Type	Description	Examples	Country
	Government guarantees	Enables a company to obtain credit at reduced interest rates and close to the risk-free rate.	Credit guarantee programme.	Mexico
Tax relief	Corporate income tax	There are many different ways in which governments can reduce the tax burden, e.g. by reducing the corporate income tax rate, by reducing the taxable amount (i.e. through tax deductions), or by releasing companies from the duty to pay taxes, initially and up to a certain amount (tax credits).	No tax payable until the investment generates profit, then 50 % for the first five profitable years thereafter. In special economic zones (SEZs), reduced corporate tax rate of 15 %.	China
	R&D related tax deductions	Usually a tax deduction; sometimes credits as percentage of R&D costs.	R&D expenditure fully depreciated within two years. Tax deduction for R&D expenditure. R&D tax credits.	Russia Brazil Canada
	Other taxes	Other taxes can also be used as a lever, e.g. VAT reduction in special economic zones.	VAT tax rebate within SEZ. Reduction of industrial property tax.	China US
Other incentives	Infrastructure	Government provides the infrastructure required by the company, e.g. free land, new roads.	Free land for plant sites. Subsidized utilities. State construction of utility facilities and roads.	Brazil Bahrain India
	Import promotion	Reduction of customs duty on goods such as materials or machinery.	Duty-free import of materials and machinery.	Russia
	Export promotion	Usually provides export financing or insurance for the export process.	Export financing. Export guarantees.	Germany

We will now investigate each of the four incentive categories in a little more detail.

6.2.1 Subsidies

Subsidies are probably the most typical and direct form of government incentives in which the government provides cash for an investment, given that certain criteria are met. These criteria are linked typically to a government objective (e.g. that a certain number of jobs should be created, or specific know-how should be built up within the region), or have been established to prevent the potential misuse of incentives (e.g. to ensure that the investment does not result in a company obtaining a dominant or monopolistic market position). The latter objective can be pursued, for instance, by setting a market share threshold that defines the maximum share that is acceptable for entitlement for subsidies.

Subsidies, in the form of investment grants or allowances, are usually beneficial to a company, especially during the first period of an investment during which the asset is being set up. This makes subsidies the first choice for investors that are facing financial constraints in the investment and ramp-up phase.

The actual mechanism for how such subsidies work varies considerably. Governments employ a variety of approaches in timing the payout of such incentives. In some, the subsidies are provided upfront. More often, however, they are given only after the investments have been made by the company. As a result, in some cases the company concerned only receives the subsidies following a substantial delay of up to a year or more. While it is understandable that governments should want to see proof that the planned investments are actually being made and that they are in compliance with the specified requirements, such a long delay in making the payment can undermine its basic purpose of seeking to alleviate the company's financing constraints. While in most cases such subsidies are no doubt nevertheless welcome, this arrangement requires the company to produce interim financing to bridge the gap between the time when the expenditure is made and that when the company finally receives the subsidy. If a government wanted to speed up this process without endangering the efficacy of the subsidy process, it should seek to keep the implementation of the subsidy regulation as simple as possible. A single inspection visit to the investment site can prove a far better check on the quality of an investment than any amount of form filling.

Table 6.2 shows examples from our incentive instruments screening.

6.2.2 Financing support

Financing support is targeted specifically at alleviating the financing burden of the proposed investments. Government loans and loan guarantees are typical forms of this category of incentive. A government loan requires the government to act in effect as a credit bank and to hand out its own cash. In the case of a guarantee, the government acts as a guarantor for a loan or credit. This does not require the government to provide cash upfront but allows companies to achieve more favorable credit terms. Whichever approach is used, the government has to make an assessment of the economic risk associated with the investment. Clearly, the danger for the government is in backing an overly risky investment.

Of late we have also seen a growing willingness for governments to take an equity stake in new investments. Either they can carry this entrepreneurial risk directly, or they can place it with an institutional intermediary such as a government-owned enterprise. A government stake may enable the company to achieve lower debt-equity leverage than would otherwise be possible. It can, therefore, make a crucial investment contribution, making an investment possible that otherwise might not have been feasible.

Table 6.2   Examples of investment subsidies and labor grants

Instrument	Selected examples with significant impact		
Investment subsidies	Germany	France	Japan
	EU legislation allows subsidies for regions of Eastern Germany to continue until 2013, to a maximum of 30 % of the investment. For example, high-tech fab in Silicon Saxony: investment subsidies of $500 million in 2003 out of a total investment volume of $2.4 billion.	Subsidies to PAT areas (priority development areas) of up to 65 % of total investment in overseas territories, and 10–20 % in other PAT areas (through investment subsidies and interest subsidies).	About 40 local authorities grant subsidies to investments in local production capacity. The limit of subsidies for new plants depends on the region. The upper range, in Hokkaido for example, is 10 % of the investment volume.
Labor grants	Italy	Spain	Belgium
	Grants equal to 80 % of the wages for all formerly unemployed workers for up to 12 months; subsidies for new employees for 4 years. For instance, in Sicily this is equivalent to about €500 per person/month.	Subsidies provided for job creation for people who have previously been unemployed for >6 months. For example, companies receive a 20 % reduction in the person's payroll for first year; 25 % if that person is female and given a full-time contract; if that person was employed for >1 year, then >50 % during first year and 45 % during the second year.	Employment plan includes a reduction in social security contributions (75 % in the first year, 50 % in the second) for all employees unemployed for the previous year. This provides a reduction in the total annual payroll costs of 19 % in the first year and 13 % in the second.

Though there is undoubted risk on the government's part in taking an equity stake, there is the advantage that it can gain access to information on aspects of the investment, such as job creation or compliance with legal and environmental standards, which it might otherwise not have full access to. When a government takes an equity stake it is entitled to expect a reasonable return on its investment, reflecting the level of its economic risk, just as in the case of any other investor. Sometimes, however, government institutions also seek to secure guaranteed cash back-flow and back-up securities, disregarding the fact that investments bear an intrinsic risk of failure and success cannot be guaranteed for a shareholder. As this can lead to excessively lengthy negotiations, or even to their failure, government institutions would be well advised to involve intermediaries in such negotiations, as they require a good understanding of the commercial terms typical of such an arrangement.

Examples from our incentive instruments screening are shown in Table 6.3.

Table 6.3 Examples of financial incentive instruments

Instrument	Selected examples with significant impact		
Financing support/ equity stake	Singapore	Germany	US
	The Economic Development Board, through its investment arm (EDBI), takes stakes in selected projects. EDBI manages a fund of more than $6 billion dispersed between >280 projects in Singapore and elsewhere	For example, $320 million in manufacturing plant made by the "Free State of Saxony investor consortium" (out of a total investment volume $2.4 billion)	Investments by Maryland Department of Business and Economic Development and North Carolina Technological Development Authority in emerging technology companies. North Carolina's investments >$0.5 million
Government loans	China	Belgium	France
	The Bank of China offers fixed-asset loans, working-capital loans, and accounts-receivable financing. It gives priority to export-directed and advanced technology enterprises.	The European Investment Bank (EIB) in Luxembourg is a competitive source of borrowing for financing capital expenditure in Belgium. Certain loans are offered interest-free. Loans can cover up to 50 % of a project's total costs.	Project location and scope determine investment assistance. In PAT (priority development areas) assistance covers 11.5−23 % of the amount invested in land, plant and equipment by large corporations.

6.2.3 Tax relief

Tax relief is a popular incentive tool made use of by governments in many parts of the world, including the US and China. Its popularity probably arises from the fact that it does not require the government to dedicate any of its own cash in the arrangement, nor does it require it to take on any risk related to the investment. From the company's point of view, tax relief usually does not provide any help in the financing phase, but it does allow for enhanced profitability later on.

Tax relief can prove very attractive for companies that intend to establish a presence in a new location, especially in locations which offer potentially strong growth and the possibility of securing attractive profits during the period of tax relief. Governments no doubt hope that the companies they attract will stay well beyond the period of tax relief, so that the country can benefit in the longer term from increased employment and the additional purchasing power of the company's employees.

Typically, tax relief is provided for a specific period, ranging from three to ten years, though there are exceptions that provide relief for periods well in excess of this. Much

Table 6.4   Corporate income tax relief and R&D-related tax deductions

Instrument	Selected examples with significant impact		
Corporate income tax relief	Bahrain	Brazil	China
	Bahrain is essentially tax-free (only a few items are subject to tax). There is no taxation on personal or corporate income and no withholding or VAT tax.	Up to 75 % reduction in corporate income tax in special regions (the Amazonas and North East regions).	Tax benefits in the special economic zones (SEZs) include corporate tax reduction to 15 % (from the normal rate of 33 %); reduced further to 10 % for exporting enterprises. The "2 + 3 year" policy provides exemption from tax for the first 2 years and tax at 7.5 % for the following 3 years.
R&D-related tax deductions	Singapore	Italy	India
	Incentives include a double deduction for R&D expenditure: one or more years at "pioneer status" which offers exemption from company tax for 5–15 years.	For tax purposes, research expenditure can be deducted from taxable incomes either all in one go, entirely in the year of the outlay, or at an annual rate of 20 % in the year the expenditure was made and the following 4 years.	R&D expenses, including capital outlays (though not for land purchases), are fully tax-deductible in the year incurred. Tax holidays are available to companies engaged exclusively in scientific R&D with commercial applications.

more rarely, tax relief can apply for an indefinite period. Many of the companies which established a presence in China in the pioneering years were able to make use of tax agreements. Bahrain – which, in essence, is tax free – is trying to use its tax-free status to attract new industries.

Table 6.4 outlines some examples of the various forms of tax relief and R&D tax deductions provided by countries selected from our incentive instruments screening.

6.2.4   Other types of government incentives

In addition to the three major categories of incentives, there is a wide range of other instruments open for use by the government in supporting investments – albeit many of these are somewhat less transparent than those mentioned so far.

Such incentives take many forms, for example to further infrastructure developments such as improving roads, creating better railway connections, putting in place a dedicated and reliable source of electricity, or providing clean water. By providing such incentives, governments can reduce the operating costs of a productive asset. These incentives are particularly relevant in regions where the required infrastructure is not yet present or where it is highly inadequate and where it will be costly to install or upgrade.

While in many rural areas of Europe companies are expected to cater for their own needs, in other regions of the world, as in some countries in the Arabian Gulf, governments consider infrastructure development as their core task, and try to manage economic growth through its provision. Bahrain, for example, provides government-subsidized access to utilities for foreign investors, as well as a 100 % rebate of property rentals in government industrial areas for the first five years after the company has set up there.

Another special form of government incentive is that for the promotion of imports and exports. Examples of such incentives include free trade zones in China, reduced tariffs on industrial goods in the EU and, more generally, the selective reduction of customs tariffs.

While infrastructure support is often necessary in order to attract new business, international bodies are putting import and export promotions (as well as purchasing guarantees) under increasing scrutiny, as these incentives are believed to distort trade.

Table 6.5 lists examples of infrastructure support and import-export promotion selected from our incentive instruments screening.

Table 6.5   Infrastructure and import-export promotion

Instrument	Selected examples with significant impact		
Infrastructure	Brazil	Bahrain	Czech Republic
	State and municipal governments sometimes offer low-cost or even free land for company production sites. The local government may also provide the infrastructure (such as roads and sewerage systems).	All industries in Bahrain, including foreign-owned firms, benefit from government subsidies for utilities. 100 % rebate on rental fees in government industrial areas for the first 5 years, for all industries.	Depending on the size of the investment, the Czech Republic offers certain infrastructural benefits, e.g. provision of roads to connect the plant to the highway. In other cases, the municipality industry parks come equipped with the necessary infrastructure.
Import-export promotion	China	Belgium	Bahrain
	Free trade zones (FTZs, also known as bonded zones) offer attractive tax and customs incentives to foreign investors. These zones allow tax-free imports; there is no VAT on traded goods or processing activities within their boundaries.	No tariffs on industrial goods traded with countries of the European Economic Area (EEA) or with Switzerland.	In January 2002 Bahrain reduced customs tariffs to 5 % for all imported goods (except alcohol and tobacco), and entirely exempted 417 food and medical items from all customs duties.

6.3   THE FINANCIAL IMPACT OF INCENTIVES: A MODELING APPROACH

So far we have surveyed the various types of government investment incentives that are available to investors. We now turn to look at their impact on the economics of an investment case. From the company's point of view, we will answer the question about how to decide, in cases where there are a choice of instruments, which is the right one to choose.

To help provide the grounds for answering this question, we have established a basic business case model that allows us to calculate the specific impact of the most commonly-used incentive instruments.

We employ three basic parameters to assess the economic impact of the various incentive instruments (Figure 6.6):

- **Financing contribution.** This quantifies the effects of the various incentive instruments in reducing the upfront financing burden of an investment, typically, in the first two years following the decision to invest.
- **Value creation within the first 10 years of an investment.** This parameter measures an incentive instrument's overall contribution to value creation in relation to the economic value of the investment. We use the change in net present value (NPV) over the first 10 years

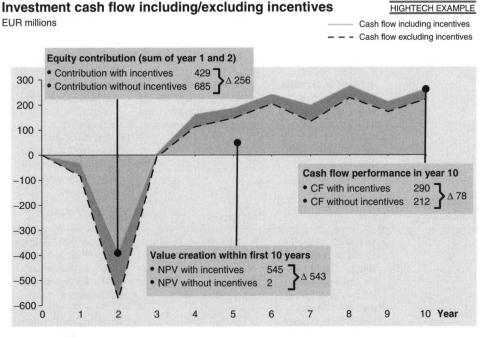

Figure 6.6   The three parameters used to measure the economic impact of incentive instruments[5]

---

[5]The numbers in Figure 6.6 reflect an example investment from the high-tech industry with an assumed total investment volume of €1 billion.

as the measure of its value creation.[6] Since this parameter integrates the impact of both the financing and profit aspects in one number, we consider it to be the most significant of the three parameters. In case of doubt, therefore, we recommend decision makers use this parameter as the leading one.

- **Cash flow performance in year 10.** This parameter measures the actual delta (in cash) received by a company as the result of a given incentive instrument for a particular investment. This parameter should provide a good indication of yearly economic impact after all major transitory effects have disappeared. It is of particular relevance for those companies, such as utilities or infrastructure companies, that are interested in achieving the highest long-term return on invested capital (ROIC). We have chosen cash flow rather than net income in order to strip away any bookkeeping and accounting effects that could otherwise cloud a decision-maker's judgment.

These parameters provide a solid base for making a comparison of the various types of incentives that are available, although companies should adapt them to their specific needs when assessing their individual investment case. Using these parameters, it is possible to establish how the different government incentive instruments would affect an investment.

In order to make these effects more tangible, we will refer to industry examples throughout this section to illustrate the various effects. In particular, we will use the example of an investment case from the high-tech industry: an LCD screen production facility with a total investment of €1 billion, and a cash flow profile that shows an investment period of two-to-three years followed by a ramp-up period of approximately two years and an operating life extending beyond the 10-year horizon. This example forms the quantitative backdrop for the numbers presented here. Figure 6.7 shows the impact of several incentives on the cash flow curve of this investment.

6.3.1 General impact of subsidies

As mentioned above, subsidies are focused on the first period of an investment. They would be particularly relevant in our LCD example as the investor is planning to enter the LCD market for the first time. Normally this would mean that they would incur high start-up costs without any initial cash returns from their operations. Of all the possible incentive alternatives, subsidies therefore provide the highest contribution to value over the 10-year period for the LCD company. It should be borne in mind, however, that this outcome is dependent on the specific choice of parameters used in the model and the outcome can look quite different in other industry segments. For instance, industries with more long-lived investments, such as utilities, face a very different challenge. The investment payback for a new power plant or water system, which might have a lifespan of several decades, can be fairly long term. If long-term tax relief is available, therefore, it might prove more advantageous to the company than a one-time subsidy.

---

[6] We limit ourselves to a 10-year period to avoid the pitfalls that reside in the calculation of the terminal value which is often highly sensitive to even minor changes in technical parameters. Companies, in any case, tend to be most interested in understanding an investment's value creation during its first 10 years, as the number of variables beyond this period lead to a high degree of uncertainty (and inaccuracy).

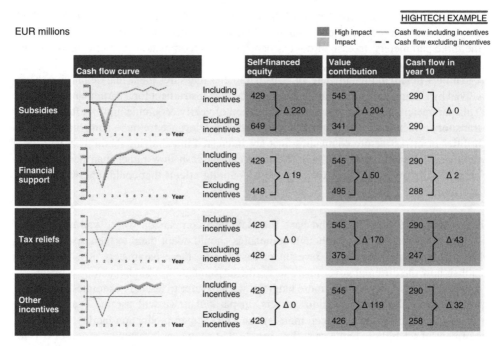

Figure 6.7   Impact of size and timing of various incentive instruments

6.3.2   General impact of financing support

The impact and timing of financing incentives, such as government loans or guarantees, is typically neither particularly short term nor particularly long term, but affects the investment case for as long as external financing continues to be necessary and has not yet been paid back. As repayment periods typically extend over a period of 3–10 years, this is the time during which companies can benefit from financing support. It is particularly helpful for companies that require high debt leverage and which face difficulty raising the necessary external funds. Figure 6.7 shows that, in our LCD example, financing support has a somewhat limited economic impact when compared to other incentives instruments (again, this depends on the specific situation – there are many exceptions).

The timing and impact of equity stakes depend largely on the specific form of the instrument that is used. Since government institutions often try to protect themselves against any economic risk, companies might consider ensuring that any equity stake has the provision of a call option, so as to provide a structured route for either party to exit the equity link before the originally targeted end-date is reached.

In the case of our LCD example, financing support can help the company to bridge the limitations in its finance during the difficult ramp-up phase.

6.3.3   General impact of tax relief

The various forms of tax relief, such as reduction in income tax or deduction of R&D and other expenses, are typically of limited duration, though relief for periods as long as 20 years or more is not uncommon. This makes tax relief the incentive instrument that has the longest-lasting effect. It is a particularly important incentive for long-lived investments. In our comparative case analysis of the LCD investment, tax cuts, together with subsidies, have the highest impact of all the government incentives (Figure 6.7).

Other incentives can also provide significant, often long term, contributions, making an investment viable which would otherwise not be. For example, in our LCD example, if the government provides infrastructure, in the form of a good road connection to the airport or separate utility plants that reduces the risk of power or water outages, this may provide a value contribution to the project that is able to tip the scale when making a decision about location. Since infrastructure investments are durable, their largest impact is in terms of the overall 10-year value creation and (as well as the continuing impact on the cash flow after this period).

6.3.4   Specific impact of incentives on different industries

How do the specific investment profiles typical of different industries affect the attractiveness of the various incentives? Figure 6.8 summarizes the effects of incentive instruments on two different industries: semiconductor fabricators and chemical plants. In both cases the industries show very different profiles.

Semiconductor industry: The high demand for upfront cash investments in the semiconductor industry puts a strain on even the most potent players in the market, making subsidies and grants particularly attractive to the industry. Today, a state-of-the-art 300 nm semiconductor unit costs \$3.0–3.5 billion. These are substantial sums even for the largest companies in the industry, such as Intel, NEC or Samsung.

Chemicals producer: In this case, the long research cycles and complex process developments required prior to the initial investment mean that there is often a long delay before an investment starts to pay back. Before cumulated positive cash flows can be realized the production plant has frequently been in operation for several years. This investment-asset profile, together with

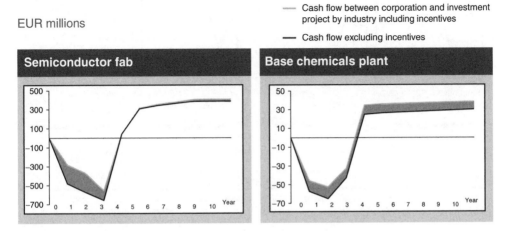

Figure 6.8   Comparison of attractiveness of incentive instruments in two industries

the tight margins of the industry, puts special emphasis on long-term performance and makes tax incentives – or, potentially, other long-term incentives such as favorable import-export arrangements – particularly significant for the industry.

6.4   GEOGRAPHICAL DIFFERENCES IN INCENTIVE STRUCTURES

In a globalizing economy, companies are often willing to consider a range of different locations for their fixed capital investments. So how do the geographical differences in incentive structures affect the economics of an investment? We have used our model to compare the typical incentive structures in four locations, using the example of an automotive production site as a sample investment. The four locations are the EU, the US, China, and Bahrain. Figure 6.9 summarizes the results of this comparison.

The EU: The total picture of EU incentive packages includes R&D grants (depending on the nature of the intended technological development) and financing support. Of late, EU government authorities have become more reluctant to provide loans but credit guarantees are still not uncommon.

The overall attractiveness of the incentives structure provided within the EU is greatly reinforced by the reliability of the system by which a company's eligibility for the incentives is assessed. If the company can prove that they meet the incentive's criteria, they are then legally entitled to receive those incentives. This provides planning security to the company planning the investment, meeting its need to control the overall risk. As a result of this security, €200 millions in incentives in the EU might well be considered to be more attractive than a 50/50 bet on €300 million in incentives elsewhere.

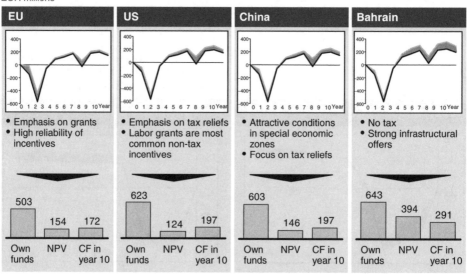

Figure 6.9   Comparison of the impact of incentive packages on different countries

The US: Tax relief is the most common form of government incentive in the US. This relief can take several different forms, such as tax relief on wages or sales, or corporate tax or property tax relief. Which particular varieties of tax relief are available varies from state to state. Examples include the five-year wage tax credit for each newly hired employee offered in New York, a property tax cap at $100 million in Oregon, or the provision of access to tax-exempt, county-owned land in Arizona and New Mexico. Other incentives include state-issued development bonds and equity financing, which are provided by the economic development boards of Maryland and North Carolina, and government support for technology development and employee training.

China: China focuses its incentives on special economic zones (SEZs), such as those of Hong Kong and Shanghai. As in the US, the focus is on providing tax relief. In the SEZs, ETDZs (economic and technological development zones), and "open cities", any foreign investment in manufacturing enterprise is entitled to a five-year tax holiday, consisting of full exemption in the first two years and a halving of tax for the following three years, beginning from the first year the investment is in profit. The tax benefits in the SEZs include a reduced corporate tax rate of 15 % (compared to 33 % elsewhere in China) which may be further reduced to 10 % for enterprises exporting goods from China to other countries. In terms of financial aid, the Bank of China offers loans against fixed assets, working capital loans, and financing for accounts receivable. The state governments also provide financing for up to 15 % of investment costs. Last but not least, imports into the free trade zones are tax free and VAT is not imposed on any trade and processing activities carried out within their boundaries.

Bahrain: Bahrain is in many ways representative of the rapidly developing economies of the Middle East and elsewhere. However, it has gone one step further than most in making itself a tax-free location. There is no taxation on personal or corporate income and no withholding or VAT tax. In addition, the Economic Development Board (EDB) offers an investor facilitation service to first-time investors that are interested in investing in Bahrain. This service includes acting as the first point of contact, understanding the objectives of investors, providing them with information regarding the relevant procedures for setting up a business, and helping them form a network of contacts within the kingdom.

Of course, we do not suggest that the automotive plant should be built for example in Bahrain, as several other aspects (proximity to suppliers and sales markets, availability of qualified employees, etc.) are also relevant and more important than government incentives. However, we advocate thoroughly quantifying and modeling the potential impact different incentive structures have on the economics of an investment and consider this in the choice of the right location.

6.5 MANAGING GOVERNMENT INCENTIVES

Companies that wish to make use of government incentives need to make sure that they not only make a proper assessment of the economic impact that the available incentives will have on their investment but that they approach the application process in the right way. Based on our own experience, we summarize a few guidelines on the right approach for dealing with government incentives:

- **Give the process due importance.** Managing incentives needs to be an integral part of investment management, due to the huge impact it can have on the success of an investment.

- **Select only the most appropriate incentives.** Pursuing too wide a range of incentives, or ones that are inappropriate to the needs of the investment, can easily dissipate resources. The right focus is to select the incentives that best meet the investment's needs:
  - Cash: in investments where there are financing constraints focus on cash incentives.
  - Tax relief: if financing is not problematic, then tax relief is often the most attractive instrument.
  - Dependability: the reliability and dependability of the government's incentive structures is often more important than the size of the incentives package being offered. A thorough assessment of the incentives process requires a full understanding of the legal situation as well as the application procedures: it almost goes without saying that this varies significantly between countries.
- **Start early and commit the necessary resources.** Because the incentives environment is complex, the process of application and negotiation often takes considerably more time and resources than first envisaged.
  - Timing: It is always important to start the process as early as possible. If the location for the investment is not yet settled, then it is sensible to start negotiations with more than one government, choosing the location that looks most propitious in terms of the overall package. In this respect it is important to define early on the potential win-win situation for the company as well as the region and to convince key stakeholders on a national, regional and local level.
  - Regulatory requirements: The application will require careful drafting and a good understanding of the government's decision-making process. Investing the time and resources in getting this right the first time around can significantly accelerate the approval process.

6.6 SUMMARY

We have argued that the "art of obtaining" governmental support can and should be structured in the same professional manner as the other aspects of a capital investment. Companies can create a lot of value by being better informed about the opportunities and pitfalls of government incentives. We hope to have provided some helpful information to this end.

REFERENCES

Abele, E., Meyer, T., Näher, U., Strube, G. and Sykes, R. (2008) *Global Production: A Handbook for Strategy and Implementation.* Springer.
Porter, M. E. (1998) *The Competitive Advantage of Nations.* Free Press.

7

Right Design: How to Make Investments Lean and Flexible

CHAPTER HIGHLIGHTS

In this chapter we show how Lean thinking and principles can be extended from operations to investment design. We illustrate how this can enable investors to carry out the execution of investment projects in a time- and resource-efficient manner, overcoming many of the limitations typically found in existing production plants, and creating a flexible design capable of responding to changing conditions. The chapter will describe how to:

- design a standardized "investment system" to enable a company to bring new capacity to the market more quickly and at lower cost while at the same time increasing the asset's flexibility. This outline will include a look at the set of technical tools and practices, the required management infrastructure, and required mindsets and behaviors;
- integrate the investment system with the main elements of the Lean production system in terms of the project objectives, design principles, and project targets;
- optimize the design process at the macro-, midi- and micro-levels, according to the Lean principles established in the design phase.

While the rest of this book provides advice on how to make the right basic design choices this chapter is focused on design execution – how to build an investment system and core tools to make it run.

7.1 LEAN DESIGN AS A COMPETITIVE ADVANTAGE

Companies that are able to bring capacity of the right quality onto the market at lower cost and at a faster pace than the competition are likely to capture a solid share of new market opportunities. Developing a *system* that enables them to do this systematically will ensure these companies will gain a significant advantage in terms of their long-term cost position. This distinct competitive advantage will, in turn, help fund future investments.

Developing additional *flexibility* is also likely to be very important, as growth is not likely to follow a straight line (historically, it has never done so). This need for flexibility is reinforced by the changes in demand patterns: the emerging demands of the world's markets reflect an increasing diversity of new and quickly changing tastes and needs, resulting in ever-shorter product lifecycles.

7.1.1 The Lean way: moving from capital investment projects to a Lean design system

In the current investment environment effectively carrying out investments has risen higher on the agenda of many CEOs and CFOs. A company's skill in investment management has become a core capability to build and maintain industry leadership. To achieve excellence in investment execution "just" running projects may not be good enough for a company any more since the success of an investment project often depends on the quality of the manager heading the project and knowledge is not systematically carried over from one project to the next.

To be able to consistently deliver excellent investment results, companies may have to establish an investment system – just as modern manufacturing is based on a production system. But what precisely is the difference between running a series of investment projects and building an investment system? A system integrates learnings and best practices from individual investment projects into a consistent way of working, a "standard", that specifies targets, roles and responsibilities, processes and tools, as well as mindsets and behaviors. By leveraging the experience from each project to enhance the standard, companies can significantly reduce the dependency on the experience of individuals as well as the risk of project mismanagement.

The starting point – developing a "production system perspective"

It is now well understood that a superior production system gives a manufacturing company a distinct edge over its competitors. Toyota is the classic example of the impact this can have: its path to becoming the number one car manufacturer has been reliant on the development of a particularly robust system. This "Toyota Production System" has enabled the company to significantly increase the pace of its improvement while removing waste from its operating plants and achieving rapid growth – all without ever losing its grip on performance.

What Toyota has demonstrated in the automotive industry has been achieved in other industries too, as described in detail in books such as *The Machine that Changed the World,* and *Lean Thinking.*[1] Lean or "Lean-6sigma philosophy", whether or not coupled with Total Productive Maintenance (TPM) tools – as is mostly the case in process industries – has become the strategy by which companies are progressively eliminating waste, variability and inflexibility – not only in their facilities, but also in the supply chain with which they operate.

In order to capture the full growth potential of an investment, it is necessary to use the frame of such a production system. New investments are no longer viewed as isolated, standalone technical projects but become part of a fully consistent set of assets, operated within a well-defined production system (Figure 7.1). Companies that fail to adopt such concepts will be beaten twice: firstly, in terms of industrial performance, as their operations will be less effective; and secondly, in terms of the time it takes them to build up capacity, as for each new investment they will have to reinvent the wheel rather than follow well-established standards and procedures.

A system is more than a set of tools

In many cases, companies which have decided to develop and implement a Lean production system have merely copied Toyota. Many have failed, at least in part and often by a fair margin,

---

[1] Womack et al. (1990). This is the seminal book on Toyota's Production System and is largely responsible for stimulating interest in the company's Lean operations in the West. For more recent thinking by the same authors on how the concepts of Lean operations can be applied more widely see, Womack, J. P. and Jones, D. T. (2003).

Examples of companies with established production systems

Company	Core elements/principles	Quotes*
TOYOTA	• Toyota Production System (TPS) • « Toyota way »	"The 'Toyota spirit of making things' is referred to as the "Toyota Way." It has been adopted, not only by companies inside Japan and within the automotive industry, but in production activities worldwide"
ALCOA	• 5 defining strategies • Alcoa Business System (ABS)	"Keeping the focus: ABS shapes our business to meet the needs of our customers"
Danaher	• « Voice of the customer »	"We base our strategic plan on the Voice-of-the-Customer. Robust, repeatable processes yield superior Quality, Delivery, and Cost that satisfy our customers beyond their expectations."
Valeo	• 4 directions, 5 core axes • Roadmaps • Valeo Production System (VPS)	"At the heart of the 5 Axes methodology (Involvement of Personnel; VPS; Supplier Integration; Constant Innovation and Total Quality) is the Valeo Production System (VPS)."
GE	• Vision of future as deployed through 1–3 prioritized cross-business themes • 6 sigma philosophy	"Across the Company, GE associates embrace Six Sigma's customer-focused, data-driven philosophy and apply it to everything we do."

* From companies' websites
Source: Websites, literature

Figure 7.1   Examples of Lean and 6-sigma production systems

to reach the same level of excellence. They have done so because they have copied the exposed part of the iceberg, rather than looking at the system as a whole. This has led them to focus on implementing a set of tools, such as kanban, 5S, SMED, or value stream mapping. What they have failed to do is to emulate the integrated nature of the three dimensions of a full system (Figure 7.2):

1. **Technical operating system.** The set of specific tools (e.g. 5S) and practices (e.g. operating standards) that are needed to sustain and improve performance.
2. **Management infrastructure.** The (organizational) structures, processes and (IT) systems necessary for managing your system. In particular, the way in which performance is managed at all levels of the organization through a set of cascaded indicators and reviews. These indicators aim to identify and eliminate gaps with standards practices as fast as possible, and as close to the shop-floor as possible.
3. **Mindsets and behaviors.** All the "softer" aspects that ensure the other two dimensions form an integrated system. This is the element that ensures that each employee lives the system of his or her company.

At Toyota the system is based on two building blocks: TPS (Toyota Production System) and the "Toyota Way". Both these building blocks reinforce each other and ensure that all plants, whether they are brownfield or greenfield, and whatever country they might be located in, live and operate with the same practices and culture.

3 dimensions of a production system also apply to an investment system

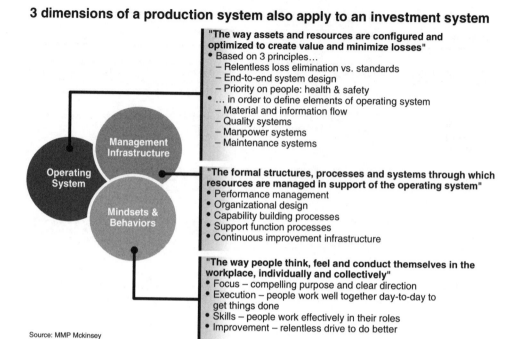

"The way assets and resources are configured and optimized to create value and minimize losses"
• Based on 3 principles...
 – Relentless loss elimination vs. standards
 – End-to-end system design
 – Priority on people: health & safety
• ... in order to define elements of operating system
 – Material and information flow
 – Quality systems
 – Manpower systems
 – Maintenance systems

"The formal structures, processes and systems through which resources are managed in support of the operating system"
• Performance management
• Organizational design
• Capability building processes
• Support function processes
• Continuous improvement infrastructure

"The way people think, feel and conduct themselves in the workplace, individually and collectively"
• Focus – compelling purpose and clear direction
• Execution – people work well together day-to-day to get things done
• Skills – people work effectively in their roles
• Improvement – relentless drive to do better

Source: MMP Mckinsey

Figure 7.2   The three dimensions of a production or investment system

7.2   THE THREE DIMENSIONS OF A LEAN CAPITAL INVESTMENT SYSTEM

A Lean capital investment system is in effect a machine to scope, design, construct, and ramp-up projects in the optimal economic conditions and with the shortest lead-time. Conceptually, the investment system delivers projects that are fully compatible with the production system. Like the production system, the investment system should be Lean (no waste, no variability and flexible); however, its output is not products or services but assets.

It can be structured along the same three core dimensions as an operating system:

1. **Technical system.** The "operating" system to carry out an investment project, eliminating waste as far as possible. The focus of this dimension is on getting the technical design of a new asset right.
2. **Management infrastructure.** Like operations, investment projects benefit from clear structures, processes and systems as well as from a stringent performance management applied to investments projects.
3. **Mindset and behavior.** Successful execution of an investment project requires a close link between business objectives and the behavior of individuals trying to achieve these objectives. As with any operating system, the softer aspects – how humans are linked with the system – are a core ingredient to getting things right that need to receive proper management attention.

In the following sections we will explain how each of the three dimensions of the Lean capital investment system ought to be developed, how the system should be adapted to local market conditions and, depending on the level of the company's "maturity", how you can get started in putting these things in place.

The first and largest segment of this chapter is devoted to exploring the constituents of the technical system with a section at the end dedicated to the two other core dimensions.

7.3   DIMENSION 1: THE TECHNICAL SYSTEM

For the sake of practicality, this next section presents the tools and practices required as part of the Lean capital investment system in the sequence in which they are normally used in a project. The objective is not to produce an exhaustive list but to highlight the key elements of the system. These elements also apply to companies which invest sporadically.

7.3.1   Start with project objectives, design princisples, and target setting

As surprising as it may sound, many projects do not have formal and well-documented objectives and targets. As a result, the link between what is required of the investment in terms of its business objectives, the industrial objectives and its technical performance is often left unclear. This significantly blurs the focus of the design team and limits the management's ability to make the right decisions and tradeoffs. Moreover, the design principles that should arise from the production system requirements, and which the project team needs to follow, are frequently missing or unclear.

To give some indication of the type of objectives that are required, we include here a **project objectives charter** from the automotive sector (see Figure 7.3). Each charter requires a precise definition (or at least a good understanding) of the specific objectives as well as boundary conditions applying to the investment at hand. It is our firm conviction that a project charter should be written down at the start of a project to provide a written agreement on the purpose and direction of the project. The charter should be as concise and precise (quantitative) as possible to provide guidance and focus to the project team.

Since the challenge to establish proper quantitative and qualitative investment targets is substantially more complex than developing the project objectives charter we will look at this aspect in more detail.

Often companies set targets based on benchmarks of capital expenditure derived from their experience in past projects in combination with top-down NPV/IRR targets. The danger is that this type of target can skew the output of the project team as it tries blindly to meet the target without having adapted the targets to the project's objectives. In the worst case, this approach can lead to the project's failure, as the team takes risks in order to reach targets that have not been properly assessed beforehand. Though management may readily recognize the shortcomings of its targets, it frequently fails to provide the project team with any alternative. The reason why it fails to do so is that it does not have an appropriate model for target setting, one that is sufficiently challenging whilst taking full account of the embedded risks.

In the best case, operational project targets are linked to business objectives in a **value driver tree** that breaks down the overall project impact to operational and project KPIs that are meaningful to the project members and can be allocated to project work streams such as production yield, number of people employed (FTE) or the ramp-up time to full capacity. The

Project		Date	Dept	Team

Industrial objectives	Changes
• Build a steel plant in geographical area X producing X Mt per year at X Euro/t leading to an NPV of EUR X million • Launch production before 200X • Integrate new plant with down stream processes using a pull system at weekly frequency	

Key value creation dimensions (productivity, volume, margin)	Key industrial success factor	Function performance
• Cost reduction to improve productivity (X) • Improvement of service level (X) • Volume increase (X)	• Low investment and optimized operating costs • Outsourcing of non core business activities	• Produce X Mt/y of steel with an optimized OEE • Achieve lowest production cost for finished goods • Ensure optimized loading of assets

Upstream supply chain		Downstream supply chain	
Impact	**Resources to involve**	**Impact**	**Resources to involve**
Close plant A	• Supply chain manager • Plant manager • Program director	Start new ordering and transportation system for cold phase (pull)	• Program director • Supply chain manager • Plant managers

Source: Disguised client example

Figure 7.3 Example of a project charter sheet (simplified)

overall project impact needs to be specified by a value measure such as NPV, EVA[2] or NROI[3] in order to integrate investment as well as operating cash flows.

There are two tools that can make a true difference in this area: business simulations and a Lean technical performance map.

The use of high-level business simulations (such as Monte Carlo-type simulations) can help to quantify the risk inherent to an investment and establish its maximum investment level. The approach is used to calculate the probability of meeting a predetermined financial target (see Figure 7.4). Much of the value added by this simulation approach resides in forcing the project team to carefully examine the selection and quantification of their parameters, such as demand, raw materials costs, capacity utilization, all of which impact significantly on the investment value and its modeling. As a result of such analyses, particularly in uncertain market environments, management will often decide upon a maximum investment level much lower than that originally suggested by the project team. One reason why this happens is that the simulation overcomes the natural tendency to overestimate demand and to underestimate its variability (in terms of the demand level and mix).

The use of scenario tools such as a Monte Carlo simulation is not the end of the task. Though they can set the bar for the maximum level of the investment, such tools do not give a true indication of the optimal outcome, nor of the level of operational risk embedded in the project. It is here that the Lean technical performance map comes into the picture.

Developing a Lean **technical performance map** helps management gain a deeper understanding of the investment. It can also help focus project resources on the critical elements

---

[2] EVA (economic value add) = NOPLAT (net operating profit less adjusted tax) − WACC* IC (invested capital).

[3] NROI (Net Return on Invest) = NPV of operating cash flows/total project NPV (incl. investment cash flow).

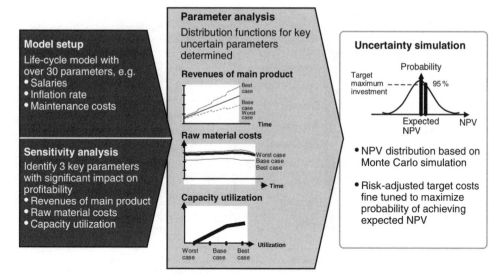

Figure 7.4   Monte Carlo simulation – analysis over life cycle

during the basic design phase. From a technical standpoint, developing a technical performance map requires: identifying the key technical parameters at the right level of granularity (e.g. the OEE of key equipment, energy consumption, material yields), as estimated in the first project draft plan; benchmarking these with past projects (both internal and external ones); and assessing the Lean limits (this should be a standard skill of the project teams). See Figure 7.5 for an example of a list of operational parameters.

There should be two outputs from the map: (1) a list of the main opportunities for performance improvement, and (2) a list of the main areas of risk. In projects where the target is far from the Lean limits, bridging this gap should become the priority for improvement. In projects in which the target is very close to the Lean limits (or far ahead of other benchmarks), the potential risks of the investment need to be analyzed carefully in order to make sure that there are no unsupported assumptions inherent in the plan.

7.3.2   Value engineering and Lean tools

Value engineering tools have become standard in many companies, although they are not always implemented with sufficient rigor. Their impact can be complemented by the addition of specific Lean tools. While value engineering tools help in the structuring, Lean tools make clear what excellence means. When used to enhance the basic design of an investment, these Lean tools contribute to faster project development times and ensure a deeper level of optimization. We have tested their use in a wide range of sectors, including automotive and assembly, semiconductors, furniture, metals and mining, and petroleum and energy. We recommend that they should be used in the following sequence.

1. The first step is to conduct a detailed **functional analysis** of the investment project. Each of the functions[4] is identified and labeled and then detailed at the subfunction level. The target

---

[4] We use the term "function" to denote a certain well defined step in the production sequence that typically serves a specific purpose such as e.g. body painting.

Key operational parameters*

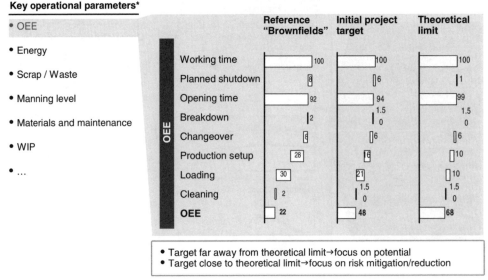

* Non exhaustive, depending on cost base structure
Source: Disguised client example

Figure 7.5   Targets for key operational parameters

performance for each of the functions is then set, based on readily measurable objectives (e.g. OEE, speed, units per hour, energy consumption, or reliability). The preliminary technical solution should then be described (e.g. two cranes of a defined type and specification), and the associated capital expenditure and operational expenditure requirements listed. In addition, each function is either categorized as value-creating, incidental (e.g. necessary, but not adding value, such as cooling storage between two equipment phases), or waste (e.g. storage that is not essential to the process). The objective of this step is to increase the value from the value-creating functions, while reducing the other functions to a minimum, eliminating them wherever possible.

2. The second step is to **select technology or process alternatives** for each of the functions, focusing firstly on the most important functions (Figure 7.6). Our experience shows that it is very important to conduct cross-functional brainstorming sessions to produce these alternatives and, whenever possible, to involve suppliers in the sessions.

3. The third step is to **optimize the technical solution** for each function, segregating what is fundamental and essential from what is optional. This exercise identifies the minimum technical solution (MTS) and is critical to eliminating "gold plating". Each of the optional items (those that are not on the MTS) then need to be evaluated separately, the evaluation being carried out following the calculation of the individual option's NPV (Figure 7.7). This ensures that the inclusion of any optional items in the project is the result of a rational management decision based on the assessment of whether or not the value they create is sufficiently high to justify the additional investment.

The three value engineering steps are a fairly robust way to progressively strip a project of all that is unnecessary for its success. In many cases, this process will not only reduce the costs of the investment but will also increase the reliability of the asset, as the approach also reduces

Generation and analysis of functional alternatives

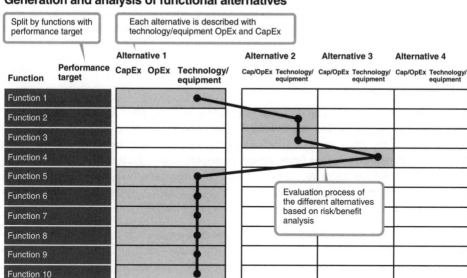

Figure 7.6 Functional alternatives and analysis

Eliminate gold plating while being innovative on value creation

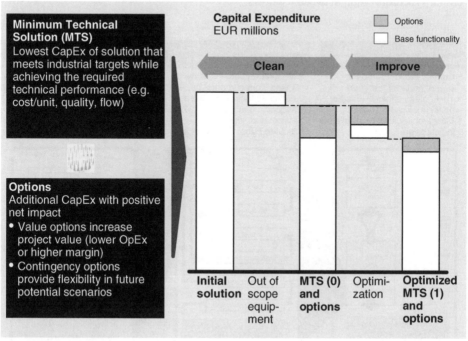

Figure 7.7 Minimum technical solution (MTS) and options

complexity. However, completing these steps is in no way a guarantee that the project is the best possible project. It will only free it of unnecessary extras and increase consistency. More robust tools are necessary to achieve a fully Lean project, one that will allow the company to extract as much value as possible.

7.3.3   Design optimization

The next stage of the investment design is to optimize the investment by carefully analyzing all sources of waste, variability and inflexibility inherent in the basic design on three levels: the macro, midi, and micro level (Figure 7.8). Companies that have already developed a Lean production system and formalized their design principles are at a great advantage here, as they will possess a solid first draft of the design, and so at this point will be able to focus their energies on fine-tuning. Those that have not yet developed such a production system will need to work harder at each of the following three levels of the design:

- **Macro design.** At this level the project team needs to ensure that the overall factor layout works smoothly and is waste-free. The focus is to "right-size" the overall investment and to optimize the macro-layout and flows. Coming back to our discussion on target setting, it is at this level of the design that the project team should challenge the performance targets wherever the initial proposal is far from the Lean limits, and propose new solutions. In terms of flows and layout, the project team needs to work on eliminating all unnecessary space, and ensure that the products flow naturally. Whenever possible, flows dedicated to one value stream or product line should be favored, and equipment capacity and speed adjusted to ensure synchronization between the flows.

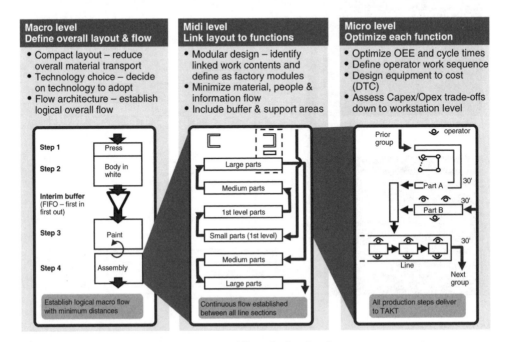

Figure 7.8   Design optimization at macro-, midi-, and micro-level

- **Midi design.** The focus at this level is to optimize the "value loops". A value loop is a stream of operations that work together, rather than individually, to add value to the product. Often value loops are separated from each other by storage (e.g. for cooling or testing purposes). Within each value loop, the flows need to be optimized further and the shop-floor organization and staffing need to be defined. It is at this level that the team should ensure that the design of the equipment takes into account what has been learnt from past experience (e.g. in terms of failure modes, maintenance space requirements, and so on), so that the performance can be optimized.
- **Micro design.** At this level, the equipment design needs to be analyzed in greater detail, all the unnecessary subfunctions removed (unless they bring a specific value), and the human–machine interfaces optimized through the simulation of key operations. It is at this level that Design-to-Cost (DTC) workshops should be organized in conjunction with suppliers in order to further improve the performance and costs of critical equipment.

The three principles for obtaining an optimal design using this process are: 1) use all the tools described here within the design process; 2) ensure they are all used in an iterative manner, each taking account of the other; and 3) that the people using them have been properly trained in their use.

Good project design requires adequate time and resources. Time and again, this is where we see the value of putting in place a formalized production system, as it provides guidance in the principles of design, as well as comprehensive data on failure modes, OEE, and waste.

7.3.4 From the basic design to start of production

Though this is not a handbook on project management, it is nevertheless important to stress a few key points that are fundamental to producing a successful project outcome. It is not our intention to list all the tools and concepts that are necessary for ensuring a project follows all the best practices but to outline core principles.

- **Standardization of design.** Whenever possible, an optimized modular design should be used as the standard for a particular process. The production system provides the design principles. These are then translated into an optimized basic design per work package or module. This basic design becomes the de facto standard for that given project type. The overall standard is the combination of standard modules (including a limited number of defined variants). These modules become the reference building blocks for all future projects – the "Lego" blocks of a factory design. Whenever a similar project is initiated, therefore, the project team should start from the standard modules and assess whether there is any need for, or benefit from, customization. This assessment needs to be based on an analysis of the value that will be created in comparison to the additional costs incurred (e.g. in terms of additional engineering, loss of volume-based rebates with suppliers, increased lead time). This way of working not only saves a significant amount of planning time and resources but also makes sure that prior learnings are incorporated into all future designs.
- **Smart contracting.** It is very important to determine the best possible sourcing strategy, especially in terms of whether to make or buy an item, managing the supply market dynamics, and matching the availability of internal and partners' skills. In some cases, the optimal solution is to outsource certain project modules to the supplier, thereby focusing internal resources on the most critical areas. Indeed, suppliers are often able to add significant value to a project. It is frequently the case that a supplier has a broader and deeper experience of a

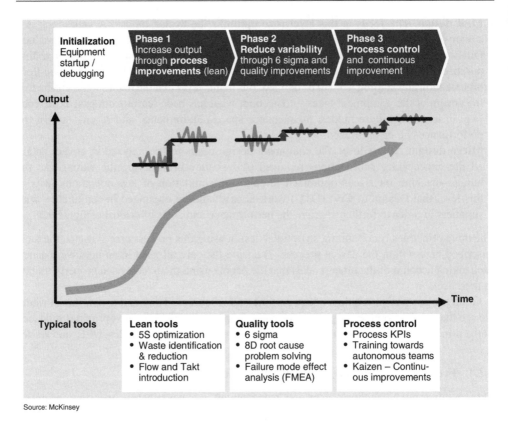

Source: McKinsey

Figure 7.9   Lean construction in the various ramp-up phases

particular task than does the company (as they supply many different customers). Similarly, the value of redesigning versus buying off-the-shelf is often very limited or even negative.

These decisions are analogous to those faced in the question of standardization: when does the company have an interest in customizing versus standardizing, taking into account the requirements of the company's production system and its business objectives? This question needs to be followed by a second: when should this be done in-house and when should it be subcontracted? Whatever the decision for each module, we strongly recommend that project teams should involve suppliers upfront in the design phase, as their experience will allow the company to reach a better solution than they could on their own – and to reach it faster. Protecting the outcome of such collaboration is, of course, key, but as the priority is to eliminate waste and variability in the design, wherever humanly possible this aspect should not be allowed to hamper the project team in reaching an early decision about cross-functional optimization.

- **Lean construction.** Lean tools and practices can also be useful in the construction phase. Their use can significantly reduce the lead time and level of risk in the project. Two important elements should be considered here. Firstly, the design should take into account the construction and ramp-up costs and the project's timing. Here again, it is important to be forward looking and to rely on cross-functional teams to establish the costs and timing, as this allows the project leaders to understand the implications of early design decisions. Secondly, Lean construction should be seen as a manufacturing activity. It is vital that

Lean production principles are formalized within the production system at this stage. Our experience shows that the rigorous application of critical-path management (leveraging Lean tools such an SMED and pre-testing/assembling at suppliers) can save 25–50 % in terms of construction time.

- **Lean ramp-up.** During the ramp-up phase, two organizations need to co-exist: the plant/line organization and the project team. The plant/line organization will own the asset and be responsible for it in day-to-day operation. Best-practice companies also add a separate ramp-up project team. This is responsible for addressing the specific issues faced during the ramp-up phase up until the point where production reaches 100 % of what has been projected. The ramp-up team applies specific process control and Lean tools that allow it to progressively raise the average production volumes while reducing day-to-day variability. These ramp-up tools should be fully integrated into the Lean investment system (Figure 7.9).

7.3.5   Anchoring tools and practices in formal standards

Project organizations often lack the formal standards that need to be deployed in each and every project. To put this right, the Lean capital investment system needs to formalize all the tools and practices described above, as well as others such as stage gates, a risk register, and critical path management. These standards should describe what the practice is and how to put it into practice, illustrating this with real-life examples of its application. Each of these standards needs to have a clearly identified owner and should be reviewed regularly, based on knowledge gleaned from recent projects.

7.4   DIMENSIONS 2 & 3: MANAGEMENT INFRASTRUCTURE, MINDSET AND BEHAVIOR

The technical system with its set of tools is the most visible element of the Lean capital-investment system – but the tools in themselves will have little impact without the right organization, performance management, and people and knowledge processes. Again, rather than listing every aspect, we will focus on the important elements that are often disregarded or not managed carefully enough.

7.4.1   Project organization and performance management

Developing the right organization to manage projects necessitates developing the right frame of reference for the company project teams and carefully monitoring their performance.

- **Project organization.** In terms of organization, two key decisions should be made. Firstly, what is the right form of coordination and/or integration between the engineering, production, and purchasing functions? Secondly, under which umbrella should the project managers and technical teams be located? There is no one-size-fits-all answer to these questions. However, two features will always be necessary whichever design is chosen. Firstly, deploying an investment system always necessitates having good control over key resources. Secondly, the design needs to ensure that the group has critical mass. In particular, senior project managers and senior technical experts should not be fragmented across the organization or too many projects at the same time. This sometimes requires the company to develop a central pool of such resources.

- **Performance management** is a key component of a Lean capital investment system. All the projects should be audited to ensure that the standard practices and tools are implemented according to the established guidelines. This audit should be carried out alongside the traditional project reviews and close-file review processes. If any gaps with the standard practices are identified, the causes should be addressed immediately (e.g. through remedial training). Compliance with these standards should be a significant dimension in the evaluation of project teams. Finally, performance management should also seek to identify areas where standards need to be improved. The project teams should be given the responsibility for proposing and implementing improvements (e.g. by introducing simplified methods for small projects). Performance management should also be rigorously enforced for suppliers through the use of standard score cards.

7.4.2   Institutionalization and learning

Institutionalization and learning are two aspects of the same coin: what the organization as a whole learns from a project's management, and what the individual learns.

For the organization as a whole, the integration of what has been learnt during a project, in terms of how problems have been identified and resolved and how standards have been improved, is essential to ensure continuous improvement of the Lean capital investment system.

At the level of the individual, the company needs to put in place a people development system. This should evaluate each member of the project team using a competence grid to map out a clear development path for each person. It should show both the desired growth trajectory and their current competence gaps. Training should be made available to all the team members wherever appropriate in order to help them bridge any gaps that have been identified. Each of the training modules required to achieve this should be formalized and standardized to ensure that everyone in the team is brought up to the same standard of competence and shares the same level of knowledge and capabilities.

7.4.3   Adapting the system to local specifics: project design cannot be "one size fits all"

The project's design needs to be adapted to the local conditions in which the investment is to operate to ensure that it has the optimal configuration. This means that the design needs to be adapted to local factors costs, quality requirements, and local characteristics such as the skill levels of operators, environmental regulations, management style, local turnover, and logistics constraints. This does not mean that our strong preference for standardization (based on optimized design and aligned with the production system principles) need not apply. On the contrary, formalizing the production system and standardizing asset design allow the designer to focus on only those areas that need to be different, whereas companies with few standards very often have difficulty even in identifying what needs to be different. Unfortunately, all too often we see designs that have not only not been optimized (they are too complex, with poor flows) but which are also not adapted to the local conditions either. In such circumstances, it is not surprising that the company concerned finds it hard to achieve steady-state performance and so struggles with a long and slow ramp-up, the correction of which consumes a great deal of high-level resources.

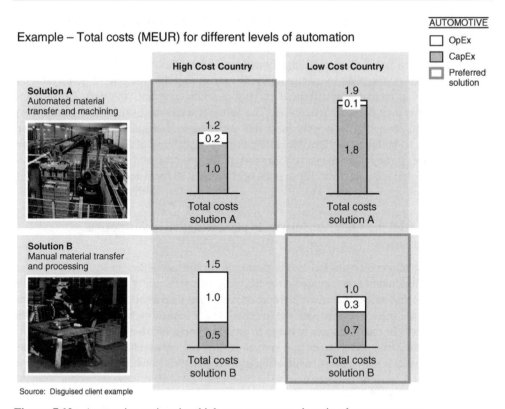

Figure 7.10 Automation options in a high cost country vs. those in a low cost country

These local differences need to be identified at the outset in the design of any new process or product. For example, when developing the Minimum Technical Solution and the design principles, a company should ask itself what these would mean in a high-cost vs. a low-cost country. If the company does this at the outset, the list of options and variants for the key design choices can be outlined upfront, taking into account their likely context. This will enable the company to fully standardize around a "mid-stream" solution or, alternatively, to implement a core platform that can, depending on the location of the plant, accommodate slight variations in the design as regards the level of automation used, for example (Figure 7.10).

7.4.4 Getting started

It should be clear by now that for companies which have already developed a Lean production system it is a fairly easy step to move to the next level and, using the same principles, build the three dimensions of their Lean capital investment system. For the majority of companies that have yet to achieve a best-in-class production system or a Lean capital investment system, the priority is to develop both as quickly as possible. The good news for companies that have yet to start on this path is that they need not wait for the whole company to move to the new production system and then develop the Lean capital investment system afterwards: they can put both in place simultaneously in their next green-field investment (or even in a significant brown-field one). Once they have done this, they will have the experience to roll out the production system to their other sites.

7.5   FLEXIBILITY: JUST WHAT CUSTOMERS AND THE COMPANY NEED AND NO MORE

In the introduction to this chapter, we highlighted the need for flexibility. Flexibility is essential because demand is uncertain by nature and will vary during the lifecycle of an investment. Capital plans that cannot adapt to these varying requirements faces the risk of destroying significant value over the asset's lifecycle. The value of a new investment is therefore very much related to its ability to exactly meet this variation in demand. This means that new capacity needs to be inherently flexible. Designing the right level of flexibility into the new capacity to meet these requirements is a core task of the project team.

Excellent design requires flexibility in plant operations at all three design levels: the macro-, midi-, and micro-level (Figure 7.11).

7.5.1   Macro-level flexibility: modularity in plant design to ensure flexible, cost-efficient assets

A common trap that companies fall into in their hunt for the most efficient scale is to be lured into capacity investments that are based on overly optimistic forecasts of demand growth. While it is clearly true that bigger plants can be more cost efficient than smaller ones, it is just as true that the larger the plant or equipment, the tougher the consequences when that investment is not fully utilized. In many cases it is better to sacrifice some of what appears potentially to be "optimal" industrial performance but what, in reality, can only realize the projected higher overall NPV under a very narrow range of industry and market conditions. Also, as we have seen in Chapter 5, scale advantages need to be balanced with scale disadvantages due to rising complexity costs and increased risk.

This is not to suggest that overcapacity is always a bad thing. For example, sizing a factory's building size and infrastructure to leave room for later growth may significantly increase the ability to scale capacity with demand at low additional cost. Also it sometimes makes sense to exceed short-term demand requirements and build temporary overcapacity upfront as a deterrent to competitors.

Flexibility at all 3 design levels

Design level	Description
Macro level flexibility	• Modular design • Minimize efficient economic scale • Include continuous improvement rate in design considerations
Midi level flexibility	• Base design on value streams, not on machine type clusters • Adapt layout and equipment to module specifics and cater for product diversity • Balance performance with flexibility
Micro level flexibility	• Design work cells to work productively at different production levels • Optimize man-machine interface for flexibility (e.g. rapid change in manning, operating procedures and sometimes tool arrangement)

Source: McKinsey

Figure 7.11   Building in flexibility at all three design levels

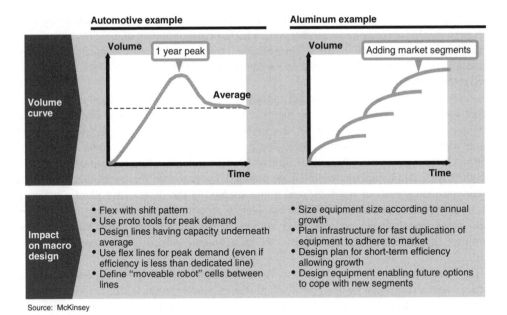

Figure 7.12 Automotive and basic materials industry examples of adding capacity blocks

In general, however, overcapacity is something to be avoided since any unused capacity will add to the fix cost burden to be carried by each unit of output. Though there is obviously no magic bullet here, increasing the modularity of the investment most often leads to greater value. **Modular design** makes sense because it not only enables investors to add blocks of capacity as demand levels increase, but helps manage the risk exposure due to demand fluctuations. Modular design is inherently flexible because it allows investors to take account of resource constraints and grow in line with demand in a larger variety of markets rather than betting critical resources on a fixed projection of the future that may or may not turn out to be correct.

Once a company has developed its production and Lean capital investment systems and packages of "standard, optimized modules", this opens the way for greater flexibility. Standard packages are faster to implement, reducing both the time-to-market and the risk exposure. They are also cheaper. This is important, for this can help reduce the gap between the economics of the smaller plant compared to the larger one.

There is no single correct size for a modular design. The size of the capacity blocks depends on the minimum efficient economic scale of an investment, which differs from industry to industry (Figure 7.12). The nature of the industry may also determine the overall impact of modularized and standardized designs in reducing costs and improving the time-to-market.

When establishing the ideal target capacity level, the project team will also need to understand and take account of the rate of continuous improvement that can be achieved in the initial years, as this can serve to reduce the overall capacity that will be necessary longer term.

7.5.2 Midi-level flexibility in plant design: cater for product portfolio diversity

In order to increase the degree of flexibility in plant design at the midi-level, the layout and equipment requirements will need to be adapted to the specific requirements of variability in the product portfolio. Demand is not monolithic: the demand for each individual product has a set of specific characteristics, such as different engines, accessories or outer appearance for cars personalized according to customer demands. The most important of these characteristics, which need to be taken into account when adapting the design to facilitate greater flexibility, is the maximum product volume and its variability, and the number of product variants that need to be considered.

One way to significantly improve flexibility is to base the plant organization and layout on **value streams** (e.g. one that looks at the production process from start to end) rather than machine type clusters (e.g. moulding, assembly, etc.). The latter approach leads to design teams trying to optimize machine utilization rather than process effectiveness. In this way utilization takes precedence over cycle time and overall output leading to misincentivation of the work force and hampering overall asset productivity. However, there are other challenges when optimizing each of the individual value streams in the design of a plant. Often not all of the various **value streams** can be completely separated from each other. In reality, in many cases, certain heavy and expensive equipment has to be shared across value streams. However, this should be the consequence of an economic calculation and not the starting point.

The value streams will have a range of characteristics. Depending on the demand profile, certain value streams can be designed for high-run products (products that are high-volume, low-variability). In these cases, achieving maximum performance will be the most important factor and the need for flexibility will be of less importance. In contrast, in other cases, peak performance can be sacrificed to ensure better flexibility. This will allow the asset and the surrounding organization to better react to changes in demand or to the introduction of new product variants. Designers should calculate or simulate effective production capacity throughout the value chain in the design phase to identify and right-size bottlenecks before the start of operations. The plant designers also need to adapt the layout in the interests of increasing flexibility and leverage opportunities to develop more flexible equipment. Potentially, they could also share small-size assets across value streams in order to absorb peaks in production, while calibrating the streams themselves for average demand.

These decisions depend on a thorough economic assessment that balances the costs and benefits of flexibility in order to find the right equilibrium for each product or group of products (see Figure 7.13). As we saw in the previous section on macro-level modularity, it is important to start with standardized production and Lean capital investment systems in place, as this will drive the design and help avoid reinventing the wheel each time a new investment is made.

Once the midi-level design has been completed, the project team will have developed a perspective on the correct organization of the value streams, adapted the process design to accommodate the product specifics, accommodating the associated flexibility that is necessary, and established the right sequence for each of the modular capacity additions. The next step is to focus on the more tactical flexibility needs which will address day-to-day or week-to-week changes in demand.

7.5.3   Micro-level flexibility in plant design: design for iso-productivity

A major problem almost all plants and production lines are faced with is in having the right capacity to absorb the daily, weekly and monthly fluctuations in demand. This is not to suggest that the roots of this problem are the same in all cases. The way this problem arises in assembly is obviously different to the way it happens in "continuous" processes in which, though the

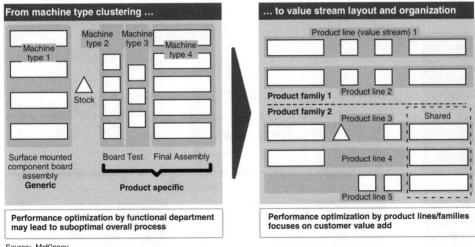

From machine type clustering ...

Machine type 1
Machine type 2
Machine type 3
Machine type 4

Stock

Surface mounted component board assembly

Generic

Board Test   Final Assembly

Product specific

... to value stream layout and organization

Product line (value stream) 1

Product family 1   Product line 2

Product family 2   Product line 3   Shared

Product line 4

Product line 5

Performance optimization by functional department may lead to suboptimal overall process

Performance optimization by product lines/families focuses on customer value add

Source: McKinsey

Figure 7.13   High-tech example of midi-design flexibility

overall demand may not vary much in volume, the changes in the production mix produce a different and distinct set of challenges for shop-floor teams. There are many different ways to address this problem, of course (e.g. in terms of workforce organization), but we have found that asset design has an important role to play here. Flexible designs can allow the lines to work at different production levels while maintaining overall productivity, thereby allowing the plant to absorb short-term peaks and troughs in demand (Figure 7.14).

Developing this level of flexibility in the design requires incorporating this aspect as a key parameter in the micro-design phase. At this level, it is necessary to draw the layout of the optimal man-machine interface. When this is done well, it becomes possible to run a line at different levels of output without any significant drop in productivity, through rapid changes in manning and operating procedures and, sometimes, of layout. This is true, in particular, for the automotive and assembly industries, as well as for heavy industries that make use of discrete tools that require a significant amount of labor. For continuous processes, the objective is slightly different: that of being able to adapt the operating team routines and standards to any change in the complexity of the mix, or to peaks and troughs in demand. This obviously has less impact on the design.

For design teams with limited experience, working at the midi-level and micro-levels can be a real challenge. Nonetheless, working at these levels is a good use of design resources, as the flexibility gained from de-bottlenecking assets can have a significant impact on the overall project value. Best results are achieved on the midi-level if shop floor operators are involved already during the design phase.

Currently, few companies carry the design process systematically through each of the three levels. However, this level of sophistication is becoming more and more important for companies that want to get the most out of every euro or dollar spent. The increased flexibility this process offers allows them to be more responsive to customer needs and this, in turn, enables them to actively differentiate themselves from their competitors and thereby reduce their market risks.

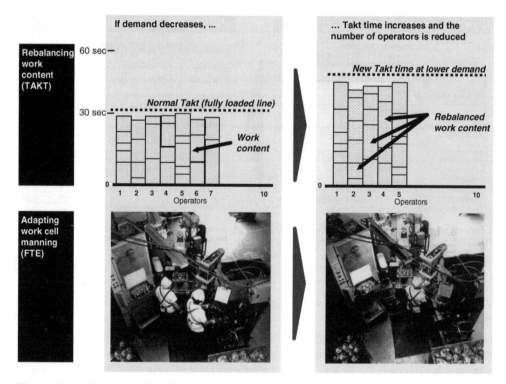

Figure 7.14   Micro-level flexibility in plant design

7.6   HOW TO AVOID CREATING A FRONT-PAGE DISASTER: ANTICIPATING WHAT CAN GO WRONG

All too often a project fails to deliver upon its predicted economic returns or industrial performance (Figure 7.15). Analysis shows that such failures result mostly from one or more of three causes:

- misunderstanding about the true nature of customer needs and the demand profile, leading to unused capacity or significant missed opportunities;
- limited knowledge about or absence of production principles, leading to gold-plated investment and/or lengthy ramp-up;
- weak project management basics: in particular, insufficient performance management and poor decision-making processes, weak risk and project management tools and processes, and insufficient cross-functional cooperation.

These problems can be addressed through better performance management and decision making, the use of the right tools, and better cross-functional co-ordination. We will examine each of these aspects.

Main reasons for investment failures

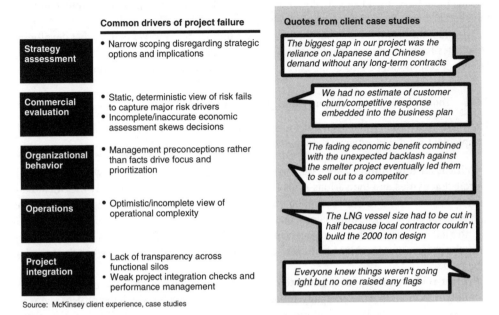

	Common drivers of project failure	Quotes from client case studies
Strategy assessment	• Narrow scoping disregarding strategic options and implications	*The biggest gap in our project was the reliance on Japanese and Chinese demand without any long-term contracts*
Commercial evaluation	• Static, deterministic view of risk fails to capture major risk drivers • Incomplete/inaccurate economic assessment skews decisions	*We had no estimate of customer churn/competitive response embedded into the business plan*
Organizational behavior	• Management preconceptions rather than facts drive focus and prioritization	*The fading economic benefit combined with the unexpected backlash against the smelter project eventually led them to sell out to a competitor*
Operations	• Optimistic/incomplete view of operational complexity	*The LNG vessel size had to be cut in half because local contractor couldn't build the 2000 ton design*
Project integration	• Lack of transparency across functional silos • Weak project integration checks and performance management	*Everyone knew things weren't going right but no one raised any flags*

Source: McKinsey client experience, case studies

Figure 7.15 Failures are typically driven by a range of issues, many nontechnical

7.6.1 Performance management and decision making

The need to develop a Lean capital investment system is underlined by the frequency of project failures. Many projects do not deliver their expected return because the processes used to manage their performance are weak, the decision mechanisms unclear, and the supporting project management tools not formalized or standardized.

It is essential that all the processes in the organization should be aligned to *make the investment risks transparent*, and to identify these risks as soon as is it humanly possible to do so. Earlier in this chapter, we outlined the need to identify risks at a relatively detailed level early on in the target-setting stage. During the design phase and in later project phases, the risk analysis needs to be updated frequently and action taken to mitigate these risks. Unfortunately, because the discipline this requires is largely dependent upon cultural reinforcement within the organization, communicated through the performance management system and training, it is frequently not given sufficient emphasis. As a result, project teams tend to overlook the importance of risk analysis and are often poor at evaluating the degree of risk, either underestimating it or overestimating it, slow at evaluating the likely impact of the risks, and even slower in taking action to mitigate them.

In mega-projects two failings tend to make these problems significantly worse. Firstly, where the *leadership is weak* in its project management and/or is fragmented, or lacking in sufficient control, this reduces the ability of the company to react in a timely manner to new risks as they arise. At the higher levels of mangement this can result in a situation in which nobody within the organization is likely to have a full understanding of (or responsibility for) the problem. Lower down the organization, it can lead to the staff feeling that they do not have the authority to speak up about the potential dangers. Secondly, because teams and even management have a tendency to shy away from problems, as most people are reluctant to be the bearer of bad news, the potential problems are not addressed squarely.

Together, these two failings have led to many a project disaster. We believe that developing clear rules for managing and auditing risks, in combination with regular reviews of leadership effectiveness, should be two of the core elements of any Lean capital investment system.

7.6.2   Tools which every company and project team need to master

There are four project management tools which are essential in any company. These tools complement solid performance management principles and sound leadership.

- **Critical path planning.** This tool provides the company with a clear view of the different project activities and the various steps involved in each project (Figure 7.16). Critical path analysis is essential in identifying the various tasks, the drivers that influence them in terms of cost, quality and time dimensions, and the linkages between these tasks. The use of critical path analysis ensures that a project's milestones are defined clearly. This provides clarity for the project managers by identifying each of the critical decisions and when they need to be made.
- **Project reviews and quality gates to ensure convergence towards the gates.** It is particularly important that the company should develop a process by which the project teams all converge towards the key project milestones or "gates". This process will help make certain that most of the issues are resolved prior to the gate being reached, thus ensuring that the

Define

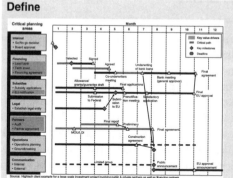

5 steps towards an optimized critical path
- Generate a plan including all relevant steps. Minimize level of detail by focusing on measurable end products
- Identify interconnections/ interdependencies between the tasks
- Parallelize task to a maximum, cut out waiting times
- Identify and minimize the critical path items
- Remove/mitigate risks on critical path and for near-critical path items

Track and Manage

4 "golden rules" of critical plan execution
- Conduct weekly review of progress vs. the critical path plan with all major parties present
- Define and track progress, result and impact KPIs to create and maintain focus
- Pro-actively identify and resolve obstacles to ensure plan adherence
- Define and review relevant milestones with decision takers to ensure mgmt. involvement

Source: McKinsey

Figure 7.16   Critical path – Key success factors

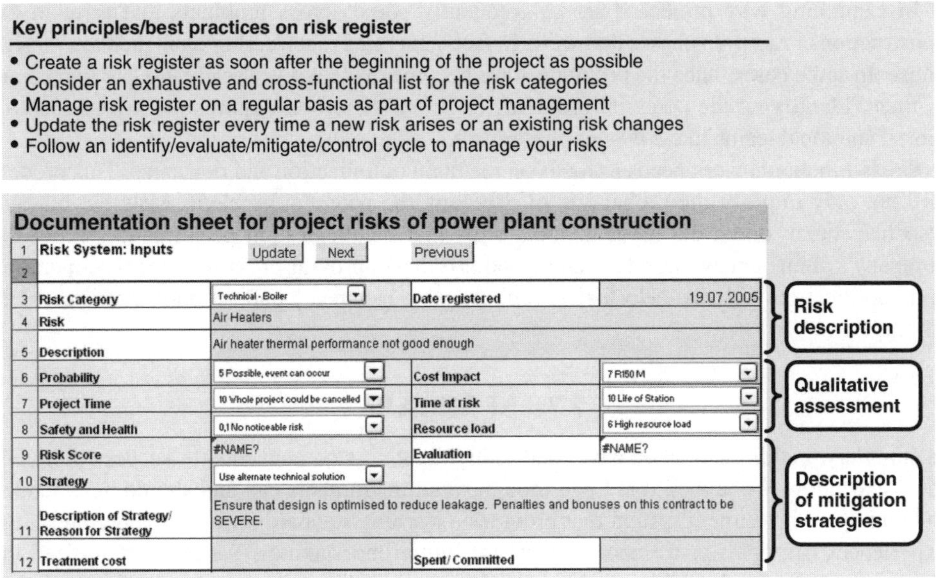

Key principles/best practices on risk register

- Create a risk register as soon after the beginning of the project as possible
- Consider an exhaustive and cross-functional list for the risk categories
- Manage risk register on a regular basis as part of project management
- Update the risk register every time a new risk arises or an existing risk changes
- Follow an identify/evaluate/mitigate/control cycle to manage your risks

Documentation sheet for project risks of power plant construction

1	Risk System: Inputs	Update Next Previous				
2						
3	Risk Category	Technical - Boiler ▼	Date registered		19.07.2005	Risk description
4	Risk	Air Heaters				
5	Description	Air heater thermal performance not good enough				
6	Probability	5 Possible, event can occur ▼	Cost Impact	7 R150 M ▼		Qualitative assessment
7	Project Time	10 Whole project could be cancelled ▼	Time at risk	10 Life of Station ▼		
8	Safety and Health	0,1 No noticeable risk ▼	Resource load	6 High resource load ▼		
9	Risk Score	#NAME?	Evaluation	#NAME?		
10	Strategy	Use alternate technical solution ▼				Description of mitigation strategies
11	Description of Strategy/ Reason for Strategy	Ensure that design is optimised to reduce leakage. Penalties and bonuses on this contract to be SEVERE.				
12	Treatment cost		Spent/ Committed			

Source: McKinsey

Figure 7.17   Risk register: database example

gate becomes much less of an administrative progress-review and more of a problem-solving and validation session that focuses on the key risks and opportunities. It is critical to put such gates in place at all the major decision points (or crossroads): the failure to address important issues at these points has the potential to lead the project into the unstable ground created by "soft agreements" within the organization. The gates help ensure that the project does not pass these decision points without all the issues being addressed.

- **Risk register.** This is a dynamic list of all the project's risks and the associated plans to mitigate them. An example of a risk register is shown in Figure 7.17.
- **Standardized work packages.** As such, this is not primarily a method to control risks. However, the more formalized and standardized the reference design of a technical module is, the less room there is for uncontrolled risks. In fact, standardization makes it easier to focus risk management on any new areas of risk; it is much harder to avoid unforeseen problems when each new project starts from a blank sheet of paper.

7.6.3   Cross-functional coordination

We have already seen that many improvement opportunities require cross-functional coordination. This is also true in risk identification and mitigation. The more complex the project, the more likely it is to generate grey areas in which no single department or expert group has a good understanding of the full picture. This situation gives rise to risks which are particularly difficult to anticipate.

As we discussed in Chapter 2, the ultimate goal for a company is to adopt a comprehensive view of the risks across all the phases of the project and its technical functions and to produce an integrated approach to managing them.

In examining why projects fail, we frequently come across problems that arise in the construction or ramp-up phases that were, in fact, generated much earlier on in the basic design phase. In some cases, once the problems have become evident it is already too late to respond to them. Identifying the potential problems early on, therefore, requires the involvement of cross-functional teams in the design phase itself.

Cross-functional work needs to focus on the main optimization and risk areas. This process will not only improve the probability of detecting the potential problems early on, but will also help break down the organizational silos that handicap high performance. From the company's point of view, an added benefit of this is that improving cross-functional cooperation and coordination will also help foster a culture of transparency and action-oriented problem solving.

7.7   SUMMARY

In summary, in this chapter we have tried to highlight core components for successful investment execution. We argued that Lean thoughts and instruments can and should be extended to build up an investment system that provides a learning standard for a company to leverage experiences from past investment projects for future undertakings. We also emphasized the necessity to cater for flexibility needs across the macro-, midi- and micro-levels of asset design to mitigate the risk of plan uncertainties or unforeseen changes in demand as well as other external factors.

We have given an overview of selected tools that we have found to be helpful in exercising projects across a broad range of industries. We hope that these thoughts and tools will allow investment managers to avoid common pitfalls such as misreading true market needs, gold plating investments, insufficient project management skills or lack of cross-functional cooperation.

REFERENCES

Womack, J. P., Jones, D. T. and Roos, D. (1990) *The Machine that Changed the World: The Story of Lean Productivity*. Macmillan.

Womack, J. P. and Jones, D. T. (2003) *Lean Thinking: Banish Waste and Create Wealth in Your Corporation*. Macmillan.

8

Right Financing: Shaping the Optimal
Finance Portfolio

CHAPTER HIGHLIGHTS

The composition of the financing portfolio is often critical to the longer-term success of an investment project. In this chapter we discuss how the project's financing can be made cost-effective while maintaining the liquidity throughout the early stages of the project. The chapter illustrates:

- why banks are at an advantage in negotiating finance;
- how to develop a thorough analysis of the project's likely cash flow curve over its lifetime. This will produce a good understanding of the project's assumptions and interdependencies;
- how to assess all the project's risks and to quantify their potential impact, identifying which risks can be mitigated and which can not;
- an outline of the ideal composition of a project's financing portfolio.

8.1 WHY FINANCING MATTERS

Investment decisions always have an impact on financing: each euro, dollar or yen a company invests has to be raised somehow. Therefore decisions on capital investments and decisions on finance cannot be wholly separated.

Large capital investments are usually financed using a portfolio of financing instruments that balance the necessary trade-offs. The most significant of these trade-offs is that between debt − which forces a company into a rigid repayment schedule − and equity − which has no repayment schedule but which produces a higher cost of capital.

One of the major obstacles companies struggle with when composing the right financing portfolio is that there are a wide range of finance instruments available in myriad possible combinations (see Figure 8.1 for a select overview).

If the future cash flows of an investment were certain and managers did not have to worry about market volatility, financing investments might be easy for companies to plan and to manage. However, future cash flows are uncertain and most financing instruments require a definite amount of cash at a particular point of time. The key question for management, therefore, is how to combine the available finance instruments in such a way so as to avoid over-financing the investment and secure liquidity at all times.

Each financing solution is investment-specific: the chosen approach has to reflect the individual business risk and the level of confidence the management has in the cash flows that will be generated. All too often, however, the financing for the investment is not tailored to

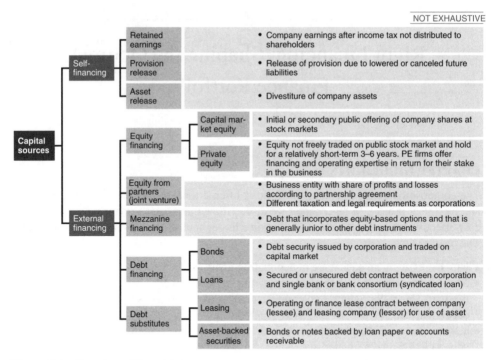

NOT EXHAUSTIVE

Figure 8.1 Overview of financing instruments

the appropriate risk exposure or tuned to the predicted cash flows but follows some general pattern that might be wholly inappropriate to the particular needs of that investment project.

As an example of how projects can be financed effectively, let's look at what banks do, as they have more experience than most investors in this area. First of all, it is interesting to note, project finance is one of the most profitable business segments in bank financing (Figure 8.2). The pretax ROE after risk costs was between 45 % and 50 % before the financial crisis in October 2008. This high level of profitability is due to the fact that banks have a very sophisticated and quantitative understanding of the risks of large projects; they apply a rich portfolio of instruments to mitigate these and so adjust their pricing to take account of them. Banks carefully quantify the expected credit loss, which is calculated as equal to the product of the probability of default and the potential loss when that default occurs. The risk-adjusted return, which is defined in relation to the risk capital, is then calculated as the sum of the income from the interest margin plus fee, minus the operating costs and the expected credit losses. The risk capital buffers the bank against unexpectedly high credit losses. The ratio of risk-adjusted return to risk capital has to be above the bank' hurdle rate, which is typically 15–25 %.

Banks use some well-proven quantitative instruments in order to minimize credit losses. These include levers for risk mitigation, pricing, and covenants:

- The levers for risk mitigation include:
  - hedging risk drivers, e.g. hedging gas prices or currency rates;
  - grid pricing, i.e. linking the cost of financing to, for example, earnings in the form of EBITDA;

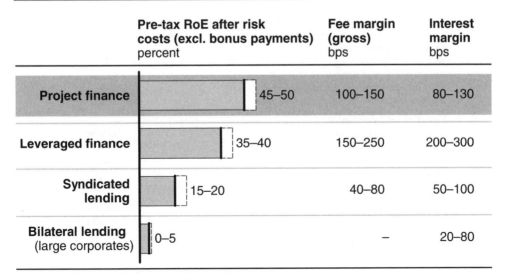

	Pre-tax RoE after risk costs (excl. bonus payments) percent	Fee margin (gross) bps	Interest margin bps
Project finance	45–50	100–150	80–130
Leveraged finance	35–40	150–250	200–300
Syndicated lending	15–20	40–80	50–100
Bilateral lending (large corporates)	0–5	–	20–80

Figure 8.2   Project finance from a bank's perspective

- guarantees from the project construction companies, e.g. EPC guarantees; a major part of the timing risks and technical risks can be mitigated in this manner;
- export credit agency guarantees, which can eliminate a major part of the political risks;
- collateralization.
- Where the risk exposure can be quantified satisfactorily, pricing can take account of inherent risks. The selection of deals can also be made risk-dependent in that, if the risk exposure of a deal is above a certain threshold level, the financier will not make an offer. Similarly, margins can be adjusted to reflect the inherent risk of an investment.
- Finally, the financier can ask to participate in the upside of an investment through covenants, profit-linked mezzanines, and direct equity stakes.

In this manner the bank, as the financier of a large project, can extract good value from the project, carefully quantifying and then managing the risks. The bank is at an advantage, as it is able to understand and quantify the risks involved while still being paid to carry the risks that they have managed away.

Our objective in this chapter is to describe a three-step approach to help management determine a bespoke financing portfolio that will provide the right level of finance appropriate to the degree of the investment's risk exposure.[1]

Step 1 evaluates the investment's cash flow parameter. Step 2 assesses the risks associated with the investment. Step 3 uses the results of the first two steps to compose the financing portfolio.

---

[1] It is not the objective of this chapter to go into every aspect of financing an investment (for example, we do not address the question of assessing on- or off-balance sheet financing) or to examine every detail of the theory of financing and valuation. Brealey and Myers, *Principles of Corporate Finance* and Koller et al., *Valuation* are among the standard texts on the subject.

Table 8.1   Details of CCGT case example

Project information	
Start year of project	2008
Length of CAPEX period	2 years
Start-up year of power generation	2009
Ramp-up phase to reach production peak	2 years
Power plant information	
Maximum output power	400 MW
Fuel	Natural gas
Efficiency	56 percent
CO_2 emission	388 kg/MWhe
Financial information	
Construction costs	€200 million
Fixed O&M costs	€10 200/MW
Employees	40
Total labor costs/employee	€70 000
WACC	8 percent

This approach can be illustrated using the hypothetical example of a €200 million investment in a 400 MW combined-cycle gas turbine (CCGT) power plant. Table 8.1 shows the details of the CCGT plant that will be used in this example.[2]

8.2   THREE-STEP FINANCING APPROACH

Let's now look at each of the three steps in financing the CCGT investment in some detail.

8.2.1   Step 1: Evaluating the investment's cash flow parameters

The key to determining the right financing portfolio is to develop a detailed understanding of the expected cash flows of the investment. The first step, therefore, is to produce a forecast of the cash-flow curve of the investment project. The best approach is to develop a financial model of the project that includes all the relevant variables, such as market price in liquid time horizon and estimated market price in illiquid time horizon, market share, unit variable costs, and fixed costs – as well as the interdependencies of these variables and how they develop over time. We are aware that some managers believe that building models (or detailed business plans) is a waste of time. However, in our experience building such a model forces the company to think more deeply about all the variables involved in executing the project and enables them to identify and question the assumptions that are being made about its likely success. This process greatly reduces the risk of failure. As Brealey and Myers say in *Principles of Corporate Finance*: "Model building is like spinach: You may not like the taste, but it is good for you."[3]

---

[2] Some assumptions have been altered to better illustrate our key points (e.g. construction costs are higher in reality, and ramp-up phase to reach production peak is usually shorter).

[3] Brealey and Myers (2000), p. 270.

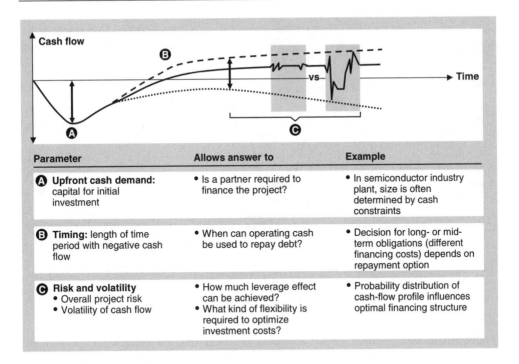

Figure 8.3 Cash flow curve

The predicted cash flow curve of the project is a synthesis of all the relevant parameters necessary for developing the finance portfolio (Figure 8.3). First of all, it shows the upfront cash demand (A).

The predicted cash flow curve shows the length of time in which the investment will generate a negative cash flow (B). This allows the investor to assess when cash from operations is likely to be available to start repaying debt and opportunity costs. How long it is before the investment starts generating cash can significantly affect the financing costs, and this information will shape the decision as to the finance portfolio in terms of the combination of short-term, long-term, or mid-term repayment options.

The cash-flow curve also shows the risk and volatility of the potential investment (C). It indicates whether the same profit can be expected annually or whether the cyclicality of the industry is likely to allow reasonable profits only during the peak period of the cycle (as has been the case in several industries such as petrochemicals and steel). If the cash-flow curve is predicted to be smooth during the investment's operation, this will allow a greater degree of leverage in financing as there is less risk of illiquidity, i.e. periods of cash shortage are unlikely.

Figure 8.4 shows the cash-flow curve for the power plant investment of our case example. Point A indicates that the investment will incur an annual net cash outflow of approximately €100 million during the two-year construction phase (resulting in an upfront cash demand of ~ €200 millions). The repayment of interest and principal using cash from its operation becomes feasible from year three onwards, the point when the cash flow becomes positive following the completion of construction. At this point the plant is still being ramped up to full

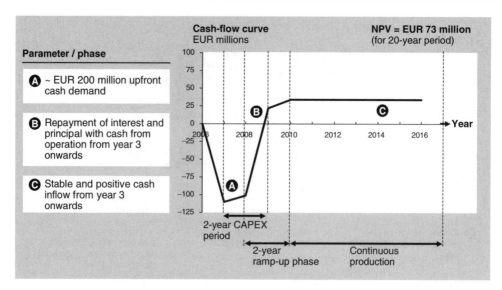

Figure 8.4   CCGT investment cash flow curve

production, though revenues are already being generated (B). The cash flow is positive and stable from year four onwards, as the power plant enters its continuous production mode (C). By using the given cash flow data, a calculation of the NPV over the first 20 years following the start of construction results in a positive value of €73 millions.

8.2.2   Step 2: Assessing investment risks

The cash flow curve modeled in Step 1 reflects only one possible cash flow scenario – the one management in charge believe to be most likely. In Step 2, management need to make sure that they fully understand the risks inherent in the project. To do so, they need to assess what could go wrong (e.g. in terms of delays to the plant's construction) or what might benefit them unexpectedly (e.g. in terms of the potential increase in demand for their product). The impact of these risks should then be mapped into the cash-flow curve.

This risk assessment has three main benefits:

1. It helps to identify and quantify the impact of all risks, as well as the probability of their occurrence. This allows management to establish the levels of confidence they can have in the various financial parameters, based on the cash-flow-at-risk concept or alternatively NPV@risk. In the light of this, the investor might wish to take the opportunity to revise or optimize the business plan so as to reduce the impact of any uncertainties or potential weaknesses.
2. The risk assessment also supports the distinction between risks that can be mitigated and those that cannot. It is therefore the starting point for developing a strategy to minimize risk exposure, both during the project planning as well as in the operation of the business. This classification of the various risks ranks each risk according to its potential negative impact. This makes it obvious to management which of the risks it should give high priority to mitigating and which it needs to continue to observe to reduce their potential occurrence.

3. The risk assessment helps management gain a deeper understanding of the investment's overall risk exposure. Besides highlighting the risk to cash inflows, it also enables the calculation of a project-specific WACC. This can be used by management to reduce the overall financing costs. In particular, the risk assessment is helpful when negotiating any premiums that might be requested by outside investors to compensate for the project's risks.

A risk assessment provides managers with invaluable knowledge. Even if the project's risks turn out to be wholly diversifiable, managers still need to understand what could potentially cause the venture to fail. Once they know this, they can decide whether it is worth trying to resolve these uncertainties. In our example, further investigation of future electricity demand and the price of gas could provide the decision-makers with the foundation for establishing the optimum size for the power plant. Further talks with potential suppliers might possibly help them to achieve a better estimate of the expected ramp-up time and construction costs. Similarly, further scenario analysis could lead to a better understanding of future CO_2 emission costs.

A thorough risk assessment has a more general benefit too. The sooner the plant's managers can identify any potential circumstance that might produce a negative NPV, the better. Even if they do decide to go ahead based solely on the present information, they will nevertheless need to be aware of the danger signals, as well as be in a position to plan the action they will take if things do go wrong.

The risk assessment is carried out in three steps: (1) risk identification, (2) risk simulation and quantification, and (3) risk classification.

Risk identification

The objective of this step is to compile an overview of all the risks that are relevant to the investment, to estimate the potential impact they could have, and the probability that they might occur. This is typically done using a "risk heat map" that plots the likelihood of downside occurrence for each risk against its expected (financial) magnitude.

The six potential categories of risk include business and market risk, technology risk, implementation risk, financial risk, political and legal risk, and operational risk.[4] Expert knowledge is useful in establishing the probability of whether a particular risk will occur or not. For example, a survey of investors showed that they believed that there is a 5 % probability that tax liabilities will increase by 50 % due to the cancellation of tax subsidies. Interpreting this slightly differently means, on the other hand, that they believe there is 95 % probability that the tax subsidies will continue and that liabilities will not increase by as much as 50 %.

In the case of the CCGT power plant, we first need to model the investment project and describe the types of risks that apply to this type of project and to this project in particular. The next step is to establish the nature of the impact of the potential risk on the project's financial performance, e.g. whether it impacts its predicted cash inflow or estimated tax liabilities.

We then define the probability distribution functions and assign each risk with a probability of occurrence. For example, the project's investors expect natural gas (fuel) prices to be €50 per MWh. This assumption is built into the basic business plan and the investors have not allowed for any variation from this price over the full 20-year period of the project. In other

---

[4] These risks are described in detail in Chapter 3.

words, the plan presently has an error tolerance of zero in regards to the forecast (average) fuel price.

On the other hand, the plan recognizes that fuel prices are volatile and has given a range of possible estimates for energy trading. Prices are forecast to fall as low as €40 per MWh and to rise as high as €60 per MWh.

Combining these two numbers we see that the business plan has a forecast of gas prices with an error tolerance of 0 but with a price range of plus or minus 20 %. If the energy trading department has in fact given the plan the lowest and highest possible outcomes, actual fuel prices should fall somewhere within this range with near certainty (i.e. 99 % of the time). If the forecast errors are normally distributed, this degree of certainty requires a range of plus or minus three standard deviations.

Other distributions could, of course, be used. For example, the project management department might allow for delays in the construction of the CCGT power plant of, for instance, up to two years in duration; the legal department might expect tax subsidies to be cut during the lifetime of the project and has assigned this a probability for this happening of 30 % for the year after next. Both these risks require a probability distribution function with discrete steps. Similar inputs must be made for all the risks identified in Step 1.

For the purpose of demonstrating the risk assessment process, we have chosen four risks that the CCGT power plant project faces (Figure 8.5). This is not intended to be an exhaustive list of all the possible risks inherent in a real-life situation.

Risk 1: Delays during the construction phase. Delays to construction will postpone the start of the cash inflow from its operation (that is, prevent the company from selling power to its customers). At the same time, however, the financing and fixed costs occur as before (i.e. we assume there is no increase in financing costs or penalty payments due to this delay).

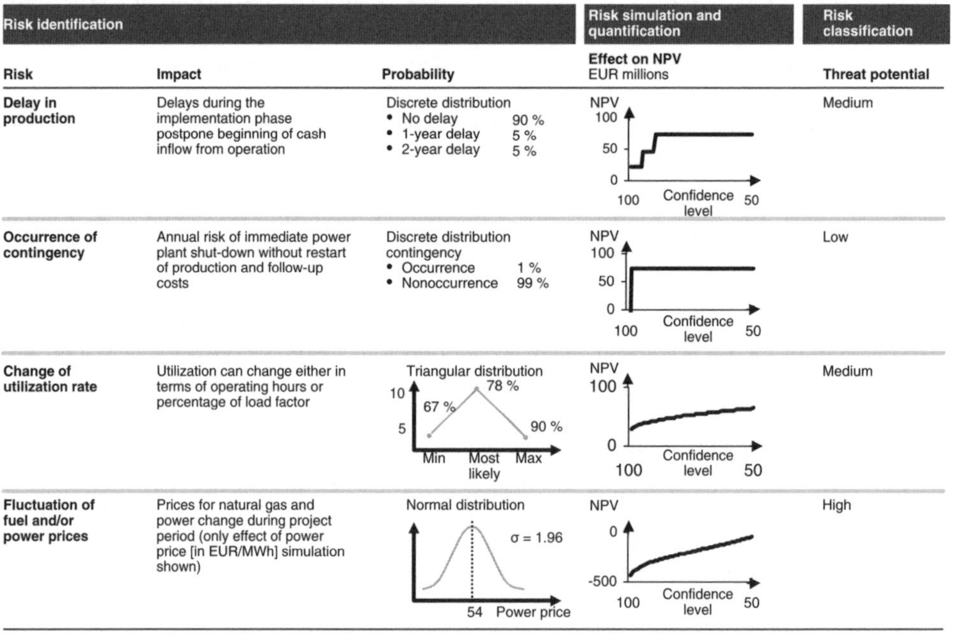

Figure 8.5 Result of risk assessment for our CCGT power plant

Figure 8.5 shows that, based on their past experience, the investors believe, with a probability of 90 %, that there will be no delay in production and that the NPV will result as planned. However, they also believe that there is a 5 % probability that there could be a 1- or 2-year delay that might significantly reduce the expected NPV.

Risk 2: Occurrence of contingencies. Contingencies that would have a severe impact on the profitability of the project include a fire that destroys the production facility, and security concerns or environmental regulations that require the complete shutdown of the plant. The probability distribution functions and the resulting NPV curves for these contingency risks are discrete. For example, an insurance coverage could compensate for the negative effect on NPV in the case of a fire. In our example, the investors see an annual probability of 1 % that an immediate power plant shutdown might occur. In other words, there could never be 100 % confidence that the expected financials of the project will be realized.

Risk 3: Changing utilization rates. The utilization levels of the CCGT plant could fluctuate depending, for example, on the energy demand, maintenance cycles, the average power output, and the overall number of operating hours (expressed as full-load hours of production). A triangular input function produces the probability distribution of the plant's utilization levels (the percentage of possible full-load hours (x-axis) versus the probability of that utilization (y-axis) under regular operating conditions. The complete shutdown of the plant due to contingencies are not reflected here in order to avoid double-counting risks. The shape and type of this function will normally be based on industry averages or expertise within the company. Under the current assumptions, the project NPV will be lower than in the first business plan scenario, but even taking into account the risk of fluctuating utilization, the plant's NPV always remains positive.

Risk 4: Fluctuations in fuel prices. Fluctuations in the price of raw materials are the most difficult risks to estimate accurately. Even sophisticated predictions of natural gas prices often turn out to be wrong and the complex correlations between fuel costs and power prices are very difficult to model with any degree of certainty.

In our model we have used a probability distribution function to model the risk of gas prices using historic data and based on common assumptions about the likely future development of gas prices. The result is a normal price distribution with a peak in the expected future price of natural gas. Historical gas price fluctuations determine the standard deviation of this function. The impact of these price fluctuations on the project's NPV is enormous and negative NPVs can be expected with a high degree of confidence.

Risk simulation and quantification

In this step, investors can use a Monte Carlo simulation to model all the risks identified in Step 1 and to determine the most likely impact of a single risk, or a combination of risks, on the key financial parameters. A Monte Carlo simulation enables managers to inspect the entire distribution of project outcomes.

Monte Carlo simulations have been developed for just such a task – and are designed to take account of all the possible combinations of variables. The Monte Carlo computer simulation samples the probability risk distributions and calculates as well as records the resulting cash flows for each period. After many iterations (in the case of this example, 10 000 iterations),

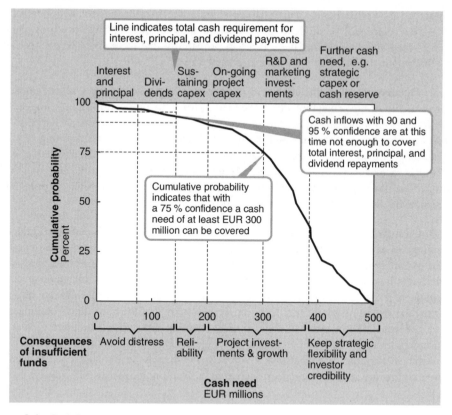

Figure 8.6 Cash flow-at-risk diagram

using permitted but randomly picked parameters, the investors begin to get an accurate estimate of the probability distributions of the project cash flows – accurate, that is, to the extent that the links modeled between the risks and the financial data and probability distribution functions are accurate (there are several easy-to-use software packages available that make this step easier).

The use of Monte Carlo simulations in capital budgeting was first advocated by our colleague David Hertz in 1968.[5] This approach in simulating and quantifying risks for investment evaluation builds on the value-at-risk (VaR) concept. In this concept, probabilities or confidence levels are simulated for financial parameters, e.g. cash flow, so that statements about the probability of the absolute value of the parameter can be made. For example, if 9500 out of 10 000 Monte Carlo simulations result in a cash flow higher than €10 millions, it can be stated that there is a confidence level of 95 % that this amount will be exceeded. If in the same set of simulations, the cash flow limit of €20 million was exceeded only 8000 times, it can be said that the confidence level of this cash flow amount is 80 %, meaning that there is a risk of 20 % that total cash expenditure will exceed the €20 million limit.

Figure 8.6 shows a cash flow-at-risk diagram incorporating the confidence levels for various levels of cash flow. The reader has to keep in mind that this diagram is valid only for a single

---

[5] Hertz, D. (1968).

point in time and that a change in business parameters, or consideration of another period, requires the recalculation of all the data. The diagram shows the confidence level on the y-axis and the amount of available cash on the x-axis (where the cash is distributed according to the typical priorities of a company). In this sense, it is more important that the company has sufficient liquidity to pay back its outstanding interest and principals than to have money available for strategic investments (in this diagram the level of importance decreases from left to right).

The graph in Figure 8.6 is the result of a Monte Carlo simulation entailing 10 000 single scenario calculations. It shows that the company cannot serve its interest payments, principal repayments and dividends at the 95 % level of confidence but that it can do so at a confidence level of about 93 % (the horizontal lines at 95 % and 90 % are typical confidence levels for debt and dividend repayment). It is for the company to judge whether or not this level of confidence is sufficient, or whether additional measures need to be taken to increase its level of security that it will be able to serve the payment of these costs. This decision will be dependent, in part, on the price at which this increased confidence level can be obtained. It has to be kept in mind that the price for increased security decreases the availability of cash for other (lower priority) expenditure.

The graph also shows that the company can have confidence at the 75 % level that it will have €300 million available to finance all its planned, sustained, and ongoing CAPEX projects.

The multiple applications of this cash flow-at-risk calculation allow companies to produce a time series of probability distributions. If the time series covers the entire project period, this will allow the company to derive key financial parameters, such as the project's overall NPV. Making the calculation for different points in time provides two types of information: (a) the development of a discrete financial parameter over time in terms of its probability value, e.g. the confidence level of achieving a €20 million cash flow in each year of the project or, (b) the absolute values for a parameter at constant confidence level, e.g. for cash flows that are available with 80 % confidence during the project period. With type (b) information it is possible to calculate NPVs at different confidence levels.

There are three steps in calculating the project's overall NPV value:[6]

- Use the cash flow-at-risk concept to obtain the range of probabilities for the investment's cash flow at a particular moment in time, for example, the probability distribution of the cash flow after the first year of the project.
- Calculate the same information at different points in time, e.g. the probability distribution for the cash flow at the end of each project year. (When performing such calculations all business plan assumptions and risk parameters must remain unchanged.)
- Extract the cash flow values at the same confidence level from each calculation and determine the overall project NPV obtained from this series.

The solid lines in Figure 8.7 illustrate cash flow curves over the project period, which are based on confidence levels of 90 %, 95 %, and 99 %, respectively. The costs incurred by the company (only those of interest, principal, and dividend payments are considered here) are shown by the dashed line. From Figure 8.7 it becomes clear at what level of confidence the company is able to settle these financial obligations.

---

[6] Other parameters can be calculated similarly, by analogy.

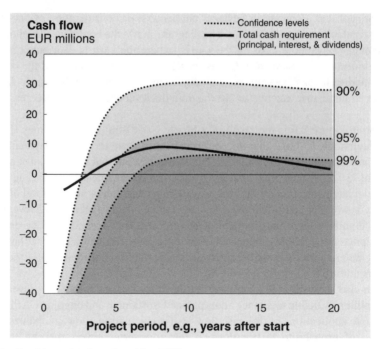

Figure 8.7   Confidence levels and positive NPVs

Though such simulations sometimes might appear to be costly and overly complicated, they do have the advantage that they press the investors to face up to the uncertainties and interdependencies inherent in the project. A detailed Monte Carlo simulation model makes it very clear what could go wrong and the investors can use these calculations to improve their forecasts of future cash flows, thereby making their calculations of the project's NPV more accurate.

The biggest challenge in creating such a model is that it is extremely difficult to estimate the interrelationships between the variables and the underlying probability distributions. For such a simulation to be realistic it will also need to be complex. This task is made all the more challenging by the fact that forecasters are seldom completely impartial, even when trying to be. The probability distributions on which simulations are based therefore tend to be biased in ways that the creator might not even be aware of. Even if the investors outsource this task and the model is constructed by an independent person, the problem doesn't go away completely, for the investors could well end up relying on a model they do not fully understand.

Risk classification

The next step is for the investors to classify all the risks simulated in Step 2 according to the "threat potential" they have quantified for the investment. We define the threat potential as the negative financial consequences caused by risk(s). For example, a fire could cause the closure of an entire production facility. As the fire would have a high negative impact, it has a high threat potential.

Based on the insights from the Monte Carlo simulations in Step 2 (the impact of risks on NPV is shown in Figure 8.5), the investors should develop strategies to mitigate the risks that have a high threat potential and a high probability of occurrence. In our power plant example, the risk of a delay in production does not require extensive measures, as the potential negative impact on the overall project is limited. The risk of contingencies occurring is also very low and, in most cases, the remaining risk exposure could be covered by an insurance policy.

Any changes in power plant utilization cannot, in most cases, be mitigated by the company. The incidence of such risk could include a combination of extreme weather conditions, changes in the economic situation, or changes to the supply situation. The latter, for instance, might include a shortfall in supply due to the temporary shutdown of nuclear power plants or the lower production capacity of hydroelectric power plants during dry periods.

The biggest threat potential, however, is likely to be of changes to the price of natural gas. This threat therefore requires the greatest attention by the company. It would be wise for the company to secure the supply of natural gas for its operations at favorable terms in order to avoid any future financial risk. In this specific example it is clear that "hedging gas prices" long term might be very costly or impossible.

When evaluating the overall level of risk, the investor should not only consider the effects that each risk will have when taken in isolation, but also how the various risks might interact with each other.

Figure 8.8 illustrates the cumulative effect of the risks categories of contingency, delays to production, and changes in utilization. This helps to identify the right amount of capital that is required at each period of time and at a given level of business risk.

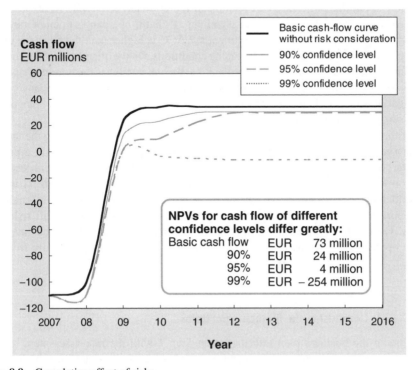

Figure 8.8 Cumulative effect of risks

The results of the risk assessment carried out for the CCGT power plant show that the degree of confidence that the investors can have in the plant's cash flows is significantly lower than that in the basic business plan scenario (this is shown in Figure 8.8 by the solid line and the base line, respectively). The project would, if successful, underperform in terms of the plan's targets, either as a result of attempts to mitigate the high probability of illiquidity, or the over-financing of the project.

The probability of delays to production explains the main difference between the base line and the 90 % confidence line (large dashes). The smaller discrepancies seen at the later stages of the project can be explained by differences in the assumed full-load factors. The 95 % confidence line (small dashes) reflects the fact that there is a 5 % probability that even longer delays in construction could be expected. The assumption of a 1 % contingency risk, with its subsequent plant shutdown, dominates the outline of the 99 % confidence line (mixed dashes). Taking into account all these risks, it is not possible to provide a positive NPV at the confidence level of 99 %.

In consequence, the company will need to raise additional finance, and allow greater flexibility in repayment until 2011 to take account of any potential delays in production or hedge risks (e.g. fire insurance).

In addition to the benefits already described, there is one further advantage for the company in making a thorough risk assessment. Because the results of the assessment will not be fully known outside the company, it will create an information asymmetry that will be to the company's advantage. The company will possess greater detail about the project and its associated risks, including their possible mitigation, than is available to other investors, who will have to resort to assessing the investment based on their previous experience, by comparison to similar projects, or in relation to the company's overall risk exposure. One positive consequence of this information asymmetry from the company's point of view is that, if the company's calculation of the investment's WACC is higher than the bank's estimate, it has the option of accepting the bank's financing conditions. On the other hand, if the company's calculation of the WACC is lower than the bank's estimate, it still has the option of opening up its books to provide the bank with insight into the project's risks and the company's planned risk mitigation strategy. This extra information could enable the company to renegotiate the interest charged by the bank for financing the investment.

This information asymmetry could also have a significant impact in shaping the legal form of the project's realization – whether it should be an integrated business unit, a profit and loss center, or a legally separate company. For example, if the risk assessment leads to the conclusion that the project is riskier than has been estimated by other financial investors, then in all likelihood it should be organized as a business unit. This would enable it to be incorporated into a broader portfolio of projects, diversifying the overall risk for the company. On the other hand, if the investment has been evaluated fairly by investors, it could be operated as a separate legal entity, so that it could benefit potentially from lower overheads.

8.2.3   Step 3: Composing the financing portfolio

By combining the business plan information in Step 1 with the risk assessment results of Step 2, investors can determine the optimum amount of capital required for the investment and the financing structure adequate to meet a given level of confidence.

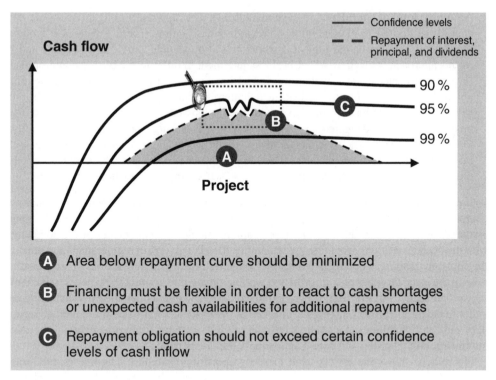

Cash flow

—— Confidence levels

– – Repayment of interest,
   principal, and dividends

90 %

95 %

99 %

Project

Ⓐ Area below repayment curve should be minimized

Ⓑ Financing must be flexible in order to react to cash shortages
   or unexpected cash availabilities for additional repayments

Ⓒ Repayment obligation should not exceed certain confidence
   levels of cash inflow

Figure 8.9   Key criteria for composing financing portfolio

To obtain the best financing solution, most companies use a portfolio of financing instruments in which the composition of a single portfolio element can be fine-tuned in order to obtain the best trade-off between three key criteria:

1. **Low financing costs.** One reason for seeking to optimize the financing is to minimize its cost. The shaded area under the repayment curve in Figure 8.9 represents the overall (integrated) financing costs over the entire project period (the expected opportunity costs are not considered in this illustrative example). As each dollar, euro, or yen has to be repaid with interest, there are two principal levers to positively influence financing costs: the reduction of the absolute amount of capital taken on and the minimization of the level of interest obtained.

2. **High repayment flexibility.** The financing needs to be kept as flexible as possible to enable the company to react to cash shortages or unexpected cash availability (that can be used for additional repayments). The magnifying glass indicates the risk of seasonal or short-term cash shortages that might become a reason for illiquidity and, subsequently, the termination of operations in what is, overall, a profitable business. On the other hand, the financing also needs to allow the potential for decreasing the debt level by extraordinary repayments of principal in periods in which the company has increased cash availability. Another ambition in financing, therefore, is to retain the maximum flexibility in the repayment of debt (both interest and principal), while being aware that each extra degree of flexibility will increase financing costs.

3. **Adequate level of confidence in cash availability.** The repayment obligations should not exceed the desired level of confidence regarding cash inflow. The company will require detailed information on the project in question as, for example, provided by Steps 1 and 2 of this approach, as well as sound business judgment in order to establish the appropriate level of confidence in cash availability. Too optimistic a view (due to incorrect assumptions about the risks) will inevitably lead to misinterpretation of the warning signals, failure to set in place appropriate corrective measures, or missed opportunities. As a result, the business will be endangered by cash shortages and the high probability of illiquidity. On the other hand, risk adversity is always punished by high financing costs that will burden the project's financial success and might become the reason why the project does not meet the company's investment criteria – so scuppering it even before it has set out.

In order to illustrate this trade-off we have developed two different financing portfolios to compare their effects on the CCGT power plant investment case. In Portfolio 1, the following assumptions were made: 30 % of the raised capital belongs to shareholders of the company, with financial institutions providing the remaining 70 % in the form of regular loans and bonds; the company requires a confidence level of 95 % for all financing transactions. This scenario reflects the basic business plan information without taking into account the risk assessment of the second section. In Portfolio 2, we optimized cash demand and avoided overfinancing or underfinancing the project, taking on finance for the exact amount of cash required to repay debt and equity liabilities at a confidence level of 90 % (assuming the same debt-equity-ratio but incorporating leasing and debt from partners into the portfolio).

Figure 8.10 shows the results from these two portfolio examples. The line representing interest + tax + dividend illustrates the total amount of payments required at each point in time. Consequently, the area below this line represents the total financing costs. In Portfolio 1,

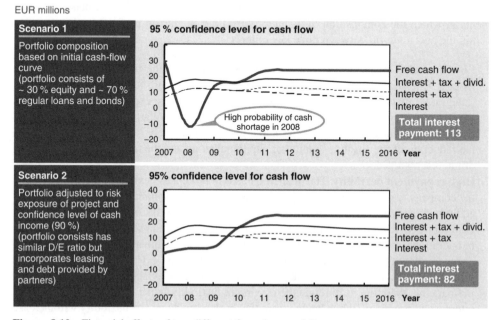

Figure 8.10   Financial effects of two different financing portfolios

where 70 % of the financing is debt, the company is highly leveraged and has little flexibility in terms of its repayments; the only flexibility being that of decreasing or postponing payments to shareholders. The negative free cash flow line in Portfolio 1 indicates the effects of neglecting to pay attention to the risk of delays in production. The missing cash inflow from revenues reduces the power plant's cash reserves, which are necessary to finance its operations during the ramp-up phase. In this scenario, the cash deficit exceeds the company's cash reserves. If no additional cash is raised in 2008, the business would become illiquid. In contrast, in Portfolio 2 there is no period when the company faces negative free cash flow. In this portfolio, the company also has lower overall financing costs compared to Portfolio 1.[7]

8.3 SUMMARY

The described approach based on evaluating the investment's cash flow and assessing investment risks can help companies to compose a better financing portfolio. In particular, the risk assessment is benefical: as the results of the assessment will not be fully known outside the company, it will create an information asymmetry that the company can use to renegotiate the interest charged by the bank for financing the investment.

REFERENCES

Brealey, R. A. and Myers, S. C. (2000) *Principles of Corporate Finance, 6th edition.* McGraw-Hill.

Koller, T., Goedhart, M. and Wessels, D. (2005) *Measuring and Managing the Value of Companies, 4th edition.* John Wiley & Sons Inc.

Hertz, D. (1968) Investment Policies That Pay Off. *Harvard Business Review*, January/February, pp. 96–108.

---

[7] Opportunity costs for equity have not been considered in this example.

Part III

9

Right Allocation: How to Allocate
Money Within the Company

CHAPTER HIGHLIGHTS

Although there is not a one-size-fits-all approach to selecting the right investment portfolio, in this chapter we develop some guidelines to portfolio development based on the "best practices" of successful companies. We illustrate:

- the four characteristics of a successful capital allocation approach: 1) alignment of capital allocation approach to strategy; 2) use of clearly defined metrics and processes; 3) adoption of mechanisms to avoid distortions in decision making; and 4) processes to ensure close collaboration between the corporate centre and the business units;
- why the structure and role of the corporate center in a multi-divisional company should determine its capital allocation approach;
- appropriate capital allocation approaches for "strategic architects", "financial holdings", "operators" and "strategic controllers".

Until now we have talked about when, where and how to invest. In this discussion we have had a single investment in mind. However, in most companies managers face myriad potential investments, even if not all of them are as significant in size as a new power plant or an automotive factory. The main challenge, therefore, is to select the right investments and to create the most promising investment portfolio.

This challenge becomes even more complicated in multi-divisional companies in which several business units are competing for capital from the corporate center. How the company decides on the best allocation of capital among them is of utmost importance, yet many companies struggle with this question. To understand why this is so, let's look at an example of how a particular manufacturing company allocates capital.

This company has five business units, all of which are of varying profitability and different strategic importance. These five businesses are on 40 sites worldwide, 20 of which are used by more than one business unit. The company allocates 70 % of its investment budget based on each site's replacement value. The rationale is that this will enable each business unit to make all the necessary replacement investments. The problem with this approach is that the company doesn't take into account the differing strategic importance of the various business units, nor the degree of importance of any one individual site to the overall site network. Despite the fact that all these sites are treated equally, the company is nonetheless aware that some sites are of much higher importance than others and might need to be expanded, while others are much less important and will need to be closed down. Although this approach is no doubt "quick and easy", the danger with such simplistic solutions is that they are rather arbitrary and not linked to the company's strategy.

Though there is no one-size-fits-all approach to investment allocation as each approach needs to be tailored to the individual company's strategic imperatives, we have distilled a number of guidelines derived from practices of successful companies. In this chapter we outline these practices and present an approach that takes account of the corporate center's role in the capital allocation process.

9.1 KEY REQUIREMENTS FOR CAPITAL ALLOCATION

There are four fundamental practices to effective capital allocation. We will look at each of these key requirements before turning to examine a number of examples of how they are applied in real life.

1. **Align capital allocation and strategy.** Overall, the most important requirement for ensuring efficient capital allocation is that the corporate strategy should be clearly defined. Strategy and capital allocation are inextricably linked: if a company does not know in which businesses it wishes to compete in the short, medium, and long term, then there is little guidance for how it should allocate capital. Although this might seem obvious, all too often companies try to optimize their capital allocation without having a strategy to guide them. Once the strategy is clear, it is fairly easy for the corporate center to allocate money to business units based on the degree of their strategic importance (for example, by establishing a value-based capital allocation index, as we will explain below).[1]

2. **Produce clear and stringent definitions of all performance parameters and processes.** To ensure clarity in the definition of the capital allocation process, the company needs to define the key performance indicators that will be used in the analysis of their potential investments, as well as any corresponding factors necessary in this calculation (e.g. WACC and calculation period). In our experiences, most companies do not rely on a single key performance indicator to assess or rank mutually exclusive investment opportunities; rather they use a combination of up to three financial indicators, for example, net present value, the internal rate of return, and the investment's predicted payback period.[2] Some companies also calculate such measures as the return on investment (ROI) or the return on invested capital (ROIC). However, these metrics are always complementary to the KPIs already mentioned. Most companies also use business unit-specific hurdle rates, rather than applying one hurdle rate for the whole company. In addition, important input parameters, such as the assumptions on factor costs (e.g. future oil prices in the chemicals industry, or gas prices in power generation) need to be standardized, so as to make investment proposals comparable. In our experience this is often not the case.

3. **Avoid bias and keep decision making objective.** During the entire capital allocation process, the corporate center needs to "depoliticize" decision making and detect and counteract

---

[1] When using a capital allocation index, the corporate center also reserves part of the overall investment budget for strategic projects that do not fall under the purview of the business units. It is necessary that the corporate center should ensure that it does not end up in a situation in which the NPV of its strategic projects is always below that of the projects proposed by the business units. If this indeed proved to be the case, the corporate center should then ask itself whether it is actually pursuing the right strategy!

[2] The discussion about the best method for ranking mutually exclusive projects has been long and intensive. For example, the differences between Net Present Value (NPV) and the Internal Rate of Return (IRR) seem to cause everlasting problems. For an overview on this issue please see Vernimmen et al. (2005), p. 315. See also Weber et al. (2006) for an overview of the KPIs used by large German companies.

any conscious and unconscious distortions and biases in order to ensure that decisions are based on objective criteria. In addition to the steps already mentioned, standardizing input data and defining the key performance indicators this needs to include, for example, the involvement of neutral parties (such as external industry experts) in the analysis, evaluation, and selection of the investment alternatives. This evaluation should not rest with the project proposal. Once a major investment has been completed, an audit of its performance in comparison to the predicted KPIs will help establish a fact base and help reduce any bias or distortion in future investment proposals.

4. **Ensure close collaboration between the corporate center and the business unit – this requires appropriate coordination mechanisms and information systems.** No company makes its allocation either at purely a corporate center level or at a business unit level. Typically, both levels interact closely to determine the investment portfolio. In fact, when interviewing 27 business units in six asset-heavy industries, we saw that the high performers (i.e. the top nine companies with a ROIC 20 % above the industry average) seem to prefer a bottom-up capital allocation process to a top-down one (Figure 9.1). The top performers collect investment ideas from all levels of their organizations, and more frequently make use of innovative techniques, such as think tanks, than do other companies. This approach requires a "backbone" of mechanisms to coordinate and align the corporate center and the business units, and information systems to provide the right information to all the participants involved in the decision-making.

We will now look at some examples of how these principles are put into practice.

Specialty chemicals company example: The company has 15 business units that operate in various segments of the chemicals industry. In this company, the corporate center has put in

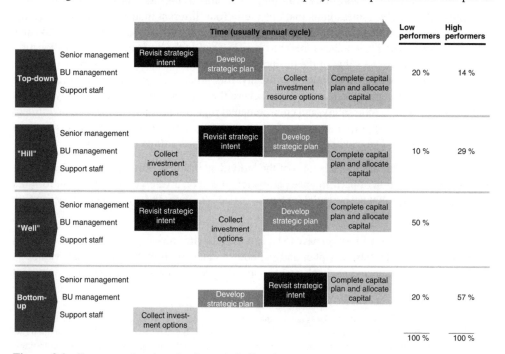

Figure 9.1 Four general options for the capital allocation process

place coordination mechanisms that ensure close collaboration between the corporate center and the business units. First, the corporate center sets the total investment budget (100 %) based on a formula that takes into account the total cash available, the debt-equity ratio, and a benchmarking of the company's peer group. It then distributes a "base budget" (equivalent to 70–75 % of last year's depreciation) to the business units for reinvestments. This is to secure the current status of its assets and to execute the obligatory projects, for instance to comply with health, safety, and environmental regulations. Around 20 % of the total budget is reserved by the board for "strategic investments", e.g. in new business areas. The residual capital (i.e. total budget – base budget – budget for strategic investments) is available for business unit projects. The business units can apply for a share of this residual capital by presenting a business plan for their projects. These plans include the calculation of the net present value of the investments, a strategic assessment and the management's rationale for each investment.

The business plans follow clear and stringent definitions set out by the accounting and control department in order to eliminate biases and to ensure all the proposals are fully comparable in how they are defined. Once the plans have been submitted, the corporate center discusses them with the business units and selects the projects it will support, depending on the available investment budget. This process allows the corporate center to align its capital allocation with the company's strategy and to balance the company's future growth with the needs of its cash-generating businesses.

In order to ensure objectivity in its decision making, the corporate center carries out a "post-completion audit" for major investments to check whether or not the assumptions and figures in the investment proposal were realistic. This approach helps to reduce the level of bias or distortion inherent in the presentation of the investment proposals.

Technology components company example: This company uses a slightly different approach. The company has 20 business units that operate in four different industries. In this company, the corporate center sets the total budget based on a predefined capital expenditure-to-sales ratio and distributes a percentage of this as a "base budget" to the business units. This allocation is made according to the value of the business units' fixed assets, valued at historic costs. As in the case of the specialty chemicals company, this process is designed to ensure that the necessary reinvestment is made, in order to secure the current status of the company's assets and to comply with health, safety, and environmental regulation. A part of the total investment budget is taken by the corporate center for use in strategic projects, such as acquisitions in new business areas. The residual budget is then allocated accordingly, based on:

- the capital expenditure-to-sales ratio of the individual business unit; modified by
- a stringent definition of performance parameters based on a value-based allocation formula that takes into account the potential (a) return, (b) sales growth, and (c) strategic attractiveness of the business.[3]

All investments above € 1 million have to be approved by the corporate center. This assessment is based on the unit's business plan and includes a calculation of the net present value, an assessment of the expected payback period and a detailed explanation of why the investment

---

[3] The formula used by the company is a multi-faceted, value-based capital allocation index, which is designed to ensure the right balance between the business units in the portfolio in terms of growth and cash-generating businesses. The index consists of three main components: (a) return: based on CFROI and relative delta-value contribution (i.e. the return above capital costs); (b) average sales growth, and (c) an index of the strategic attractiveness of the business (based on an assessment of the market characteristics and the business unit's market position).

is of strategic importance. Once the capital is allocated to the business units, they are free to invest their budget without further interference from the corporate center. This approach therefore gives the business units some degree of entrepreneurial freedom.

As with the speciality chemicals company, the technology components company's top-down process reduces biases and distortions. This makes the decision-making more objective since the various business units are not competing for capital solely on the basis of their individual investment proposals.

Power and gas company example: This company does not use a budget formula but follows a "target investment" approach that is based on long-term plans. In this approach, the capital allocation is linked closely to strategy as the capital is allocated to the various business units based on the company's five-year strategy and budgetary plan.

Once the five-year plan has been developed, the business units make their project proposals to take up the budget. The corporate center then evaluates and discusses these proposals with each business unit. This process ensures tight coordination between the business units and the corporate center and usually involves several rounds of discussion. This enables the business units to incorporate any feedback from the corporate center into their proposals.

To ensure that all the investments from the various business units are comparable with each other, the corporate center defines detailed investment guidelines that include investment frameworks, discount rates, etc. During this process, the corporate center clusters all the proposed investments from the various business units into a number of categories (e.g. repair, growth, IT, etc.) and then analyzes the aggregated investment activity accordingly. This enables it to develop an overview of where its money is going. If it sees, for instance, that too little money is being invested in growth projects, it can then take appropriate action.

Multinational petroleum company example: In this company the corporate center first defines the total budget and then assigns preliminary budgets to each segment based on its expectations of the future evolution of the industry over the next 5–10 years (an assessment based on the predicted prices, actions of its competitors, its own portfolio options, etc.). Due to the characteristics of the petroleum industry, a significant share of the capital budget is predetermined as a result of earlier long-term investment decisions. In the second step, this preliminary budget is further divided up and allocated to the various business units. This approach enables the corporate center to act strategically in allocating its capital, without a high level of involvement from the various business units.

The final budgets are set after a series of bilateral opportunity-focused negotiations. During these negotiations each of the business units has to prove that the potential return of their investment is likely to be among the most rewarding for the company: only the most beneficial will receive funding. While the rates of return are largely consistent throughout the entire company, they may differ somewhat by segment in order to allow for future potential. In this approach, the petroleum company focuses on measuring the most important performance parameters, including the return on capital employed, the funding and development costs per barrel, and cash flow (these parameters are supported by the use of more traditional performance indicators, such as IRR, NPV, and investment payback). This approach allows a high degree of flexibility in capital allocation, keeping the company focused on the best-available options for capital usage, and thereby maintaining a high level of return on its capital.

These examples illustrate the different approaches companies can take to allocate money. Each approach depends to a large extent on each company's industry environment as well as the role each company's corporate center takes in the allocation process (e.g., the degree of freedom it leaves to the business units for allocating money to individual projects).

9.2 FOUR MODELS OF THE CORPORATE CENTER ROLE IN SHAPING THE INVESTMENT PORTFOLIO

The role the corporate center plays in shaping the investment portfolio will largely determine the approach the company takes to capital allocation. We distinguish between four corporate center roles, depending on the level of intervention and business integration, ranging from a low level of intervention (a financial holding structure) to a high level (corporate center as operator) (Figure 9.2).

1. **Financial holding.** Corporate centers that work within a financial holding structure monitor the performance of the companies within the business portfolio and shape the portfolio's overall evolution. Typically, the corporate center seeks to add businesses to its investment portfolio that previously have been undervalued and then turn them around. In this structure, the corporate center only intervenes in a business in exceptional cases as, for instance, in order to ensure that the business unit meets its target, or to sell a business at an optimum time or price.
2. **Strategic architect.** Where the corporate center takes the role of strategic architect it will determine the overall strategic framework within which the business units operate. In this structure the corporate center will not only seek to shape the portfolio but will intervene in individual businesses to check the business logic and suggest further initiatives.

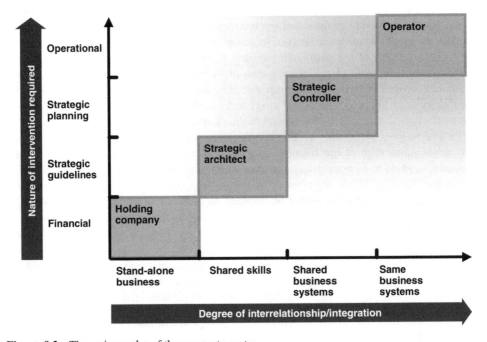

Figure 9.2   The various roles of the corporate center

3. **Strategic controller.** The corporate center in the role of strategic controller is more integrated into the day-to-day operations of the business units, providing them with functional support. It will intervene to ensure coordination between the businesses and to achieve the potential synergies.
4. **Operator.** The corporate center which acts as operator closely manages all the company's business activities. The operator initiates and leads most investment decisions, including all the key ones, and all improvement programs. It will intervene on a monthly basis to review all its businesses' financial and operational parameters. This structure provides little managerial freedom to the business units heads.

Each of these structures has specific characteristics in terms of how they manage capital allocation. Operators and strategic controllers show a high involvement in their businesses: they have a good understanding of each business unit's specific environment and challenges, for example, in terms of the market situation, emerging technologies, trends, competitors, and operations. Based on this knowledge they are able to make trade-offs between the business units and play an active role in the capital allocation process. In contrast, the corporate centers that take the role of a strategic architect or operate within a financial holding structure usually have only limited knowledge of their business units' markets and show a relatively low level of day-to-day involvement. They are often not able or willing to make trade-offs between business units. This role is reflected in their approach to capital allocation.

We believe that if a corporate center is to allocate capital efficiently it needs to have a fairly detailed understanding of each of the business units under its purview. Capital allocation in multi-divisional companies works well only if the corporate center has a clearly defined strategic masterplan and an adequate in-depth understanding of the environments in which each of its business units operate (e.g. in terms of markets, technologies, and competitors). Only with this level of understanding is the corporate center able to make the necessary trade-offs between its business units.

TECHNICAL INSERT

Investment metrics for evaluating individual investment opportunities

The metrics used in evaluating and comparing individual investment opportunities can be classified into three different categories, depending on their level of sophistication: static metrics, dynamic metrics and relative metrics.

Static metrics: These are the simplest and easiest to understand, but have the disadvantage that they do not discount future cash flows to their present values. Well-known examples of static metrics are "net cash flows" (the sum of all cash inflows and outflows during an investment's lifetime) and "payback time".

The calculation of an investment's payback time is comparable to the calculation of the break-even point, in that the analysis determines the amount of time that is required for an investment's net cash inflows to "repay" the original cash outflow. Although this calculation is very simple and highly intuitive, it is of limited suitability for capital investments as it ignores changes in monetary value over time.

Dynamic metrics: These are more sophisticated than static metrics, as they use discounting to adjust future cash flows to their present monetary value. However, they are not suitable for comparing investments of different sizes or durations. The most frequently-used dynamic metrics are Net Present Value (NPV) and Internal Rate of Return (IRR).

NPV is the sum of all the present values of an investment's future net cash flows (i.e. each cash inflow or outflow is discounted at today's monetary value) minus the initial investment outlay. If the result is positive, the investment is expected to add value to the company. Despite its widespread use, NPV is not suitable for comparing investments of different sizes or project durations.

IRR is the discount rate that would result where the NPV is zero. The use of IRR is very popular among managers as it seems to produce a very intuitive result (as a percentage yield). However, IRR is rather complex to calculate (sometimes there is no single correct mathematical solution), and is potentially misleading, especially when comparing projects of different sizes or durations.

Relative metrics: These are an enhancement of the dynamic metrics discussed above. In addition to the basic dynamic calculation, they also consider the relative magnitude of the benefits compared to the initial investment size.

Net Return on Investment (NROI) is thus highly suitable for measuring capital investments. NROI is the NPV of an investment's future net cash flows relative to the amount of money invested, i.e. divided by the present value of all investment cash outflows (NROI is also known as PV/I, i.e. present value over investment). This evaluation technique takes into account both the present monetary value and the amount that is invested, thus enabling the comparisons of the relative consequences of various different investments.

Figure 9.3 summarizes the strengths and weaknesses of the various metrics discussed here and their suitability for evaluating capital investment opportunities.

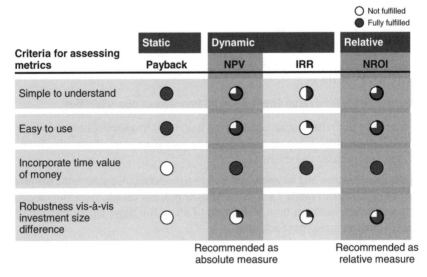

Figure 9.3   Strengths and weaknesses of investment metrics

Figure 9.4 shows a snapshot of metrics used by different companies in various industries. As mentioned earlier, most companies use a combination of several financial indicators, e.g. net present value, payback period and internal rate of return. Projects are then usually assessed versus business unit-specific hurdle rates to take into account the different risk-return-profiles of the various businesses.

Company	Hurdle rate BU specific	Hurdle rate Company	Metrics used NPV	Metrics used Payback	Metrics used IRR	Examples of other metrics
Petroleum	✓	–	✓	✓	✓	ROCE, F&D per barrel
Technology	✓	–	✓	✓	–	Value-based metrics
Chemicals	✓	–	✓	✓	✓	Return on capital employed
Chemicals	–	✓	✓	–	–	Value-at-Risk
Chemicals	✓	–	✓	✓	✓	Capacity utilization
Utility	✓	–	✓	✓	–	Risk-adjusted beta
Industr. conglom.	✓	–	✓	✓	✓	Total return to shareholders
Pharma	✓	–	✓	✓	–	ROI, option values
Pharma	✓	–	✓	–	–	ROI, option values
Software	✓	–	✓	✓	✓	Option values, market shares
Utility	✓	–	✓	✓	✓	ROI, ROIC
Petroleum	✓	–	✓	✓	✓	Value-investment-ratio

Source: Interviews; analysis of case examples; McKinsey

Figure 9.4   Metrics used by various companies

From our perspective, companies should complement metrics like NPV or IRR with a relative metric like Net Return on Investment (NROI) when measuring returns on capital investments. NROI is fairly easy to understand and use and takes into account both the change in monetary values over time and the different sizes of the various investment opportunities. However, no metric is perfect and each has its drawbacks. When evaluating capital investment projects, therefore, one should never rely on a single metric but take into consideration all the relevant aspects and use additional metrics wherever they are appropriate.

We will now look in more detail at the different capital allocation approaches, first examining the approach appropriate for operators and strategic controllers, before looking at that suitable for strategic architects and financial holding structures.

9.3   CAPITAL ALLOCATION APPROACH FOR OPERATORS AND STRATEGIC CONTROLLERS

We propose a four-step approach to capital allocation for those corporate centres which are structured as operators or strategic controllers (Figure 9.5).

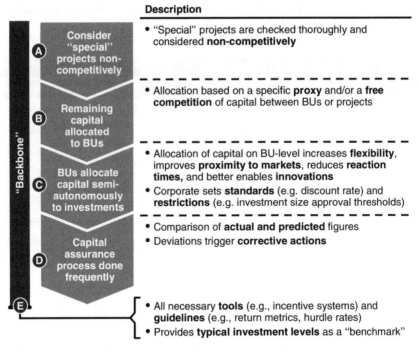

Figure 9.5   4-step capital allocation approach for strategic controllers and operators

In this approach, we assume that the corporate center defines the size of the total investment budget and withdraws all money from the business units into a corporate fund. This money is then redistributed to the business units based on the following logic.[4]

9.3.1   Step 1: Treat special projects as high priority

In the first step, special projects are considered separately without reference to other projects. Special projects are either (a) defined by a set of clear criteria drawn up by the corporate center in collaboration with the business units, or (b) identified by the business units and submitted to the corporate center as investment proposals. The special projects submitted by the business units are checked by the corporate center to establish whether they should benefit from the label of special status or not. Special projects are given priority ahead of all other projects.

Three types of project can be labelled as special projects: obligatory projects, new business projects, and strategic projects.

Obligatory projects: Certain obligations arise because of regulatory intervention (e.g. resulting from new health and safety regulation). Projects should only be given this status if

---

[4] We assume in the following description that the capital allocation process is done once a year. However, there are companies where the corporate center reserves a certain amount of the overall investment budget for ad hoc projects that arise during the year.

they fulfill regulatory obligations (i.e. they are not replacement investments, which are not obligatory). Such projects have to be considered as high priority, as they are essential for the company's continued operation in the market. Each business unit needs to submit a full list of such obligatory projects, along with the required investment. To reduce the potential for abuse of the high-level priority conferred by obligatory status, the corporate center should scrutinize all such projects above a certain size, as well as a random sample of the smaller ones.

Projects in new business areas: This category covers all investments in areas of business in which the company is otherwise not yet active. Again, such projects should have high priority if they are of strategic importance. This status is not applicable to projects that involve the expansion of existing business areas (though these might be treated as large, strategic projects).

Large, strategic projects: Large-scale investments of high strategic importance, e.g. substantial individual investments or the expansion of existing business areas, should also be given high priority due to their importance to the company's future prosperity. A single business unit cannot be held solely responsible for such a project due to the higher-than-normal level of risk such investments often entail. The challenge for the corporate center is to establish a clear set of criteria that defines which projects are eligible for this status.

9.3.2   Step 2: Allocate remaining capital to business units

In Step 2, the remaining capital is allocated to the various business units. This allocation is made either according to a specific formula or as a result of free competition between the business units (or projects) for the available capital. Taking into account company-specific requirements, the allocation can be made using a two-category approach or a three-category one (Table 9.1).

Overall, the two-category approach is less sophisticated than the three-category one but is easier to administer. The main challenge in the two-category approach is to determine the basis for allocation (whether this is to be done by proxy or through competition). The main challenges in the three-category approach are to determine the size of each category and to set effectual criteria for the competition for capital.

Table 9.1   Categories for allocating capital to business units

Option 1 Two-category approach	Option 2 Three-category approach
Special projects category Money for special projects identified in Step 1	**Special projects category** Money for special projects identified in Step 1
Business unit category Money allocated to the business units for all other projects (both medium and small investments)	**Competition for capital category** Capital allocated to all other projects based on free competition for capital (at the project level)
Allocation based on proxy or competition for capital (at the business unit level)	**Small investments category** Remaining (usually smaller) investments allocated to BUs based on one or more proxies (e.g. BU capital efficiency).

The competitive element of the three-category approach increases the level of entrepreneurship and, potentially, overall business performance. On the other hand, it also increases the degree of complexity in the allocation of capital and, therefore, the demand on corporate resources.

The two-category approach treats all the projects of each business unit as a single entity, whereas the three-category approach looks at each project individually. As a result, even when a competitive element is introduced into the two-category approach, it is fairly simple to administer, as each business unit competes solely with the others at the unit level and not at the project level, as is the case in the three-category approach. Similarly, the two-category approach does not allocate capital to individual projects but only to the business unit as a whole (in the three-category approach, this is only the case in the "small investments" category).

We will examine how each of the categories is defined, as there are considerable differences between the two approaches. As already discussed, the special projects category is used only for the special projects identified in Step 1.

Business unit category: Within the two-category approach, this is used for all the projects other than the special projects. The money is first distributed to the individual business units and they are then responsible for making the allocation to the individual projects. The distribution to the business units is based on one or several proxies (for instance, the business unit's rate of return), or following competition between the business units for the available capital.

Competition for capital category: Within the three-category approach, this is used for all large and medium-sized projects other than special projects. The available capital is awarded following the results of a competition between the various eligible projects and the capital can only be utilized by the winners. Each project is evaluated along a set of clearly-defined criteria, e.g. their strategic fit and Net Present Value or Internal Rate of Return.

Small investments category: This is used in the three-category approach for all the projects that are not in the special projects category and which are not large enough to enter the competition category. As in the case of business unit category, in the small investments category the money is allocated to a business unit as a whole and not to specific projects, the distribution being based on one or more proxies at the business unit level (e.g. the return of the business unit). The business units are then responsible for making the capital allocation to the individual projects. The capital distribution in this category also has to take into account the allocation made in the other categories, so as to ensure that each business unit meets its required minimum level of investment.

We have observed two different approaches for determining the overall size of the small investments category. Certain companies set aside a specified proportion of the total investment budget (e.g. 30 %) and then allocate this to the business units, based solely on a proxy. Others allocate the main part of the investment budget to the business units based on a proxy (e.g. 70 % of depreciation) and then use the remainder for other purposes, such as strategic projects. The specific requirements of the individual company tend to determine which approach is used.

Table 9.2 Examples of proxies for allocating capital to business units

Capital allocation is based on ...	Advantages	Disadvantages
Business unit's depreciation Business unit's asset replacement value Last year's budget	Easy-to-understand approach with readily available base figures.	Mainly consolidates the status quo; does not take into account future needs and developments.
Judgment of top-level management	Takes into account abilities and experience of senior management who also decide the strategy (thereby ensuring a close linkage).	Subjective and non-standardized approach, often without sufficient fact base; discourages entrepreneurship at the business unit level.
Return measure (e.g. EVA or ROIC)	Standardized, fact-based, objective approach.	Includes only past results and focuses on too few aspects; does not reveal the entire picture.

It is noticeable that the size of each investment category varies considerably between companies, depending on the industry concerned. For example, process-driven industries, such as chemicals, require significant reinvestments to ensure that their assets are maintained in a reliable state. This has a significant influence in increasing the relative size of the business unit category (for example, the budget of one particular chemicals company allocates 75 % of its annual depreciation to replacement investments for its business units).

The corporate center has the option of using one of several proxies for allocating capital to the business units in the business unit category or small investments category (see Table 9.2). These proxies are only the starting point for efficient capital allocation and are often adjusted during the capital assurance process (which we describe below).

9.3.3 Step 3: Business units distribute capital to individual investments

In Step 3, each business unit acts fairly autonomously in distributing the capital they have been allocated to their individual investments. This gives the business unit management the freedom to make the necessary trade-offs between the various investments without involving the corporate center. These tradeoffs can be due to technical necessities (e.g. the replacement of assets) or for strategic reasons (e.g. the acquisition of new production assets, or an increase in the sales force in order to penetrate new markets). This approach increases management flexibility and improves responsiveness by keeping decision-making in as close proximity as possible to the markets, and encourages innovation and entrepreneurship.

The corporate center only interferes in this process by setting standards (e.g. return metrics, discount and hurdle rates), by placing overall restrictions (e.g. by imposing an investment size approval threshold), and by ensuring that the synergies of a multi-divisional company are realized in the investment (e.g. in terms of economies of scale). The corporate center also takes care to ensure that investments which have been rejected in Step 1 are not carried out in Step 3.

TECHNICAL INSERT

Project selection: prioritizing individual investment opportunities

One of the more challenging tasks for an investment manager is to prioritize one investment over another. We follow a six-step approach to help managers select the best individual investments from a large pool of opportunities.

The approach is by definition based on the assumption that the total investment level is restricted because of budget limitations. All the investment options are also assumed to be within the same market or business area. Therefore, we can evaluate all projects against the same hurdle rate (as shown in the previous technical insert, most companies apply business unit-specific hurdle rates. This can easily be implemented in the project ranking by taking the excess return above hurdle rate as ranking criteria). Furthermore, we assume that all the investments are independent of each other, i.e. none of the investments are mutually exclusive, nor are there any portfolio effects or interdependencies between the projects. (At the end of this section we will describe briefly how it is possible to modify these assumptions.[5])

Step 1: Define the criteria that the investment projects will need to fulfill and that will be used in their subsequent evaluation. These criteria should include all the necessary minimum requirements. They can be quantitative, for example, in terms of the maximum project duration or minimum effect on revenues, and/or qualitative, for example, in fulfilling specific regional criteria or quality-related prerequisites. This list should also include one key decision criterion (e.g. the Net Return on Investment), including its "hurdle rate" (below which the investment is unacceptable), if this is applicable.

Step 2: Identify all the individual investment opportunities. All the opportunities should be recorded in a standardized manner, e.g. in a central investment proposal database. In order to ensure that all the various opportunities are fully comparable, all the fields (i.e. the basic project information and the criteria identified in Step 1) should be defined clearly. This requires precise rules about how the data is to be gathered or generated and how the metrics should be calculated.

Step 3: Evaluate each the investment opportunities according to all of the criteria defined in Step 1. Depending on the nature of these criteria, the result could either be a simple yes or no (for example, regarding whether a project fulfills the quality-related prerequisites) or a number (e.g. the Net Return on Investment). The qualitative criteria could, potentially, include a brief annotation or qualification in their assessment, if this is useful.

Step 4: Group each investment opportunity into one of three categories, depending on their nature and level of their fulfillment of the criteria:

- **A-projects:** This group comprises a limited number of special projects (see above) that have overarching relevance and which are essential to the company's future prospects. These can either be obligatory (e.g. for legal or regulatory reasons) or highly critical from a strategic perspective.

---

[5]Readers should treat this approach only as a guideline. A company's approach will need to be tailored to the specific requirements and circumstances of the individual company. Furthermore, when evaluating investment opportunities it is, of course, important to also take into consideration all the strategic and operational aspects of the business, and not just the purely financial ones.

- **B-projects:** This comprises all the investment proposals that fulfill or exceed all the defined criteria and requirements.
- **C-projects:** All the investment opportunities that do not fulfill all the defined criteria, i.e. they do not meet all the minimum requirements or are below the key criterion hurdle rate. These projects are immediately discarded.

Step 5: Rank all the A and B projects within their individual groups, according to the key criterion. They might be ranked, for instance, in descending order of Net Return on Investment (Figure 9.6).

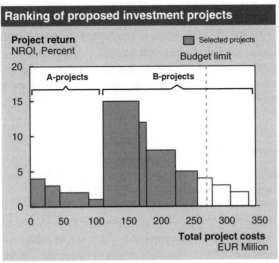

Figure 9.6   Ranking of investment opportunities

Step 6: Determine the portfolio of investment opportunities. This is done by including all the A-projects and then subsequently selecting each of the top B-projects in order from the list, until the point where the budgetary limit has been reached. The remaining B-projects will not be implemented and will either be deferred to a later date or cancelled. Alternatively they may be executed if additional financing can be made available as they fulfill all investment criteria.

As pointed out, this approach assumes that the investments are not mutually exclusive and that there are no interdependencies between the various projects. However, if mutually exclusive investment opportunities do exist (i.e. only one of two options can be implemented, for example for technical reasons), in general, the lower-ranked alternative can simply be eliminated after Step 5 in favor of the superior investment opportunity.

9.3.4   Step 4: Implement a capital assurance process

"Capital assurance" is the process for checking how the proposed investment has actually been spent. This ensures that the investment has achieved the expected return. From our perspective, the implementation of an appropriate capital assurance process is an essential part of capital allocation and ensures that the process is conducted on a rational basis.

An effective capital assurance process needs to have direct feedback loops to the capital allocation process. In this process, the estimated figures (i.e. the figures that were submitted in the initial investment proposal) are compared to the actual figures during the investment phase and for the completed project. The causes of deviations from the predicted figures are then analyzed (this process is similar to that in the "post completion audit" described in our chemicals example above).

Capital assurance should, therefore, follow a simple three-step process: (1) measure the gap between promised returns and actual returns; (2) identify the root causes of the gap; and (3) take action to close the gap.

The capital assurance process enables an organization to learn from the success or failure of past allocation decisions. It also enables management to quickly recognize any adjustments that might be necessary in their current projects. Because the capital assurance process provides a direct feedback loop to the capital allocation process, it forms the basis for making ongoing improvements to capital allocation. This helps create a positive loop for improving both the efficiency of the process itself and for improving management performance – and thus helps to minimize unwanted behaviors.

Capital assurance process types

Depending on the project type and the number of projects involved, the actual design of the capital assurance process can vary considerably (see Table 9.3).

Detailed deviation analysis: this makes a comparison of the notional values in the business plan with the actual outcomes. This comparison is made across a large number of parameters (including industry-specific KPIs). The department responsible for the detailed deviation analysis (e.g. the corporate controlling department) also conducts analyses to determine the root causes of any major deviation.

Time-and-money approach: the unit responsible for carrying out the analysis examines whether the various projects are within the expected parameters in terms of time and money, i.e. whether their costs and ramp-up time are in accordance with the original proposal. The unit responsible also randomly selects a limited number of projects for more detailed examination (in a similar manner to that of the detailed deviation analysis).

Table 9.3   Investment types and corresponding capital assurance process types

No. of projects	Few projects		Many projects
Capital assurance process type	Detailed deviation analysis	Time and money	Business unit performance
Investment types	• Strategic investments • Large obligatory investments • Investments in new business areas • Investments selected through the competition for capital	• Medium-sized obligatory investments • Small obligatory investments	• Medium-sized investments • Small investments • Other investments

Business unit performance approach: in this approach the investment of the business unit is evaluated as a whole, rather than at the level of individual projects. The department responsible for the evaluation will use mid- to long-term averages (e.g. 3- and 5-year averages) to avoid too great a focus on the short term. The business unit's investment performance will be adjusted for extraordinary effects, such as windfall profits or extraordinary losses.

As no single measurement can provide all the information that is required in developing an effective capital assurance process, a combination of parameters is normally used, including industry-specific key performance indicators. For example, in the petroleum industry, in addition to the standard financial indicators (such as net present value or cash flow) and strategy and operational indicators (such as market share or volume growth), petroleum companies also make use of industry-specific metrics for capital efficiency (such as the capital efficiency of reserve-adding capital expenditure or capacity-adding capital expenditure, and the capital efficiency of front-end engineering or facilities upgrades), as well as metrics of comparative costs (e.g. the cost of exploration and recovery per barrel). The customization of such industry-specific parameters is an essential part of developing a successful approach to capital assurance.

9.3.5   Improving the "capital allocation key"

In case the corporate center uses a proxy for allocating capital to its business units, the feedback loop of the capital assurance process provides input to the regular update and improvement of this proxy. This ensures that the "allocation key" becomes more and more accurate over time (Figure 9.7).

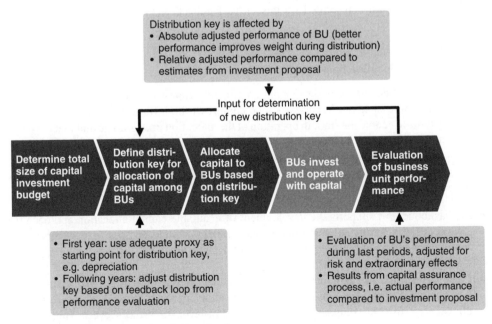

Figure 9.7   Improving the capital allocation key

In the first year, a provisional proxy (e.g. depreciation) is used as the initial distribution key. In the following years, the key is adjusted to take account of the feedback from the assurance evaluation. The distribution key is affected by two factors in the assurance evaluation: (1) the absolute, adjusted performance of the business unit (better performance will increase the unit's weight in the capital allocation process); and, (2) its performance relative to the estimates of the investment proposal. The absolute, adjusted performance takes account of the risks and any extraordinary effects.

One further advantage brought about by the implementation of the capital assurance process is that the feedback loops help reduce any potential unwanted "gaming" behavior of business unit managers. Whereas, for instance, a business unit manager might otherwise be rewarded by deliberately overstating the expected benefits from an investment project (for instance, so that his or her unit obtains a higher share of the available capital), once the feedback loops are in place, if the investment performs worse than stated in the proposal, this deviation will be detected and fed back in the next capital allocation round. As a result, the business unit might well receive less capital in the next allocation. On the other hand, if a business unit manager were to do the opposite and deliberately understate the expected benefits from an investment project (for instance, gaming, so that the unit might exceed the plan handsomely and, therefore, receive more capital during the next capital allocation round), if the project is in the competition for capital category there is no guarantee that this would indeed be the case. Indeed, stating too low a benefit could ensure that the business unit fails to receive any capital in the first round (i.e. because its return is too low compared to that of other projects in the competition).

The capital assurance process, therefore, incites business unit managers to state the expected returns correctly: overstatement or understatement both lead to negative consequences for them individually and for their business unit as a whole. In contrast, the business unit manager who states the expected returns according to the extent of their knowledge receives an appropriate amount of capital and is rewarded for this in the feedback of the next round of the capital assurance process.

9.3.6   Capital allocation backbone

The final element necessary in developing an effective approach to capital allocation is the "capital allocation backbone". The backbone comprises the infrastructure that provides the necessary tools to enable the smooth operation of the allocation process. The unit that develops and maintains this backbone is usually located in the corporate center controlling department. Although the particular set-up and tasks of the backbone vary somewhat, depending on company specifics and the company's capital allocation approach, all capital allocation backbones have several characteristics in common:

- The backbone unit supports the development of a suitable capital allocation approach. In general, it helps to decide which options and variants should be used (e.g. whether they should have a competitive element or not) and designs the details of the chosen approach (e.g. in terms of the size of each category).
- It also defines the key parameters (e.g. the various metrics of returns) and assumptions (e.g. on factor costs) used in the capital allocation approach as well as the respective reference group (i.e. company-level, business unit-level, or project-level). This ensures

that all the various business units use the same methods and assumptions in their calculations.

- The backbone unit also implements mechanisms for coordination (e.g. to support the division of labor between the corporate center and the business units) and the information systems (to ensure that the right information is available at the right time to the right people).
- It designs guidelines for the preparation, analysis, and evaluation of the obligatory projects (e.g. in order to check whether a project is truly "obligatory" or not, as well as to track implementation).
- The unit also sets clearly defined, transparent conditions and requirements for the preparation, analysis and assessment of investment project business plans (e.g. for "large strategic" and "competitive" projects).
- It develops and provides appropriate incentive systems (e.g. to reward wanted behavior and reduce deliberate distortions).
- In addition, it provides guidelines on typical investment levels in various categories of investment that can be used as benchmarks by the corporate center's controlling department.

TECHNICAL INSERT

Illustrative example of capital allocation approach

The company in the following example is active in three business areas: adhesives (AD), automotive supplies (AU) and high-viscosity lubricants (LU). We will use this example to illustrate how our capital allocation approach will work in a multi-division company.

The three business units differ considerably in size (illustrated by their annual sales volume in € millions) and in the performance of the business units (characterized by their risk-adjusted return margins as a percentage of sales). The company has a total capital fund of €70 million available for investments during the year. It has traditionally allocated this capital based on depreciation. Table 9.4 summarizes the information.

Table 9.4   Information for capital allocation approach – current situation

	ADHESIVES	AUTOMOTIVE	LUBRICANTS
Sales volume p.a. [€ millions]	150	250	100
Risk-adjusted return margins [Percentage of sales]	16 %	12 %	14 %
Allocation of total funds [€ millions]	21 (30 %)	35 (50 %)	14 (20 %)

However, the management is unsure about whether the current process leads to optimal results, so it has adopted our approach to capital allocation.

Table 9.5 provides an overview of the categories and process assumptions used by the company in its new approach.

Table 9.5   Overview of classifications and process assumptions

Classifications and key assumptions	Rationale

Size thresholds for obligatory projects:
  > €100 000: check each project
  < €100 000: random check on sample of
  10 %
	Important to avoid "slack" in obligatory project list (e.g. overstating costs, incorrect categorization as "obligatory project", etc.). Need to find balance between workload and control.

Classification of non-obligatory investments:
  > €2 million: large strategic project
  > €0.5–€2 million: competition for capital
  < €0.5 million: small investments
	Projects differ considerably in terms of how they have to be submitted, analyzed, selected, and controlled. Each type has clearly defined, transparent specifications for preparing the investment proposal and its analysis.

Size of small investments category: 60 % of total available investment volume.	Options range from 0 % (corporate chooses every investment) to nearly 100 % (BUs choose every investment). The chosen level of 60 % gives BUs sufficient flexibility and encourages entrepreneurship, but still ensures adequate level of corporate control.
Guidelines for preparation, analysis, and evaluation of obligatory projects: check foundation for obligatory status and translation of obligation into costs.	Corporate center checks whether the project has rightfully been given the obligatory status, and if this obligation is implemented in the most cost-efficient manner.
Guidelines for preparation, analysis, and evaluation of large strategic projects: detailed business plan.	Mixture of clearly defined metrics to give balanced view of investment: quantitative metrics (ROI, cash flows, scenario analysis, etc.), qualitative metrics (effect on customers, market, etc.), strategic metrics (fit with corporate and BU strategy), and formal metrics (compliance with corporate rules, e.g. hurdle rate, growth assumptions, etc.).
Guidelines for preparation, analysis, and evaluation of competition for capital projects: each business plan is scored and ranked along predefined dimensions.	Each project is scored along several dimensions (e.g. ROI, strategic fit, time-to-launch, scenario sensitivity, success probability) and ranked.

Step 1: Treat special projects as high priority (section 9.3.1)

Description of situation: In total, the business units have classified 73 projects as obligatory. These require a total investment of €4.4 million: 70 of these projects (totalling €3.6 million), spread equally among all three business units, are below €100 000; three projects are above €100 000. The business units have proposed four large strategic investments requiring a total investment of €14 million. All four projects are above €2 million in cost (Table 9.6). The company currently has no intention of entering any new business areas.

Table 9.6   Obligatory and large strategic investments

€ millions	AD	AU	LU
Obligatory projects ≤ 0.1	1.2	1.2	1.2
Obligatory projects > 0.1			
• OBLIGATORY 1	0.4		
• OBLIGATORY 2	0.2		
• OBLIGATORY 3			0.2
Large strategic investments ≥ 2.0			
• LARGE 1: Geographic expansion in Thailand	4.0		
• LARGE 2: Production facility enlargement		5.0	
• LARGE 3: Improved sales force structure		2.0	
• LARGE 4: Low-scale production facility			3.0

Resulting activities and outcome: The corporate center checks the obligatory projects OBLIGATORY 1, OBLIGATORY 2, and OBLIGATORY 3, as well as seven other projects (a random sample totalling 10 % of each business unit's smaller obligatory projects), to establish whether they meet the criteria for obligatory status. All the projects so checked are found to have been defined rightly as obligatory. However, an analysis of the business plans (to check the cost of meeting the regulatory requirements) of the 10 obligatory projects reveals that OBLIGATORY 1 could achieve the same legislative objective using a different setup and thereby save €100 000.

All the obligatory projects are accepted by the corporate center, resulting in a total investment of €4.3 million (Table 9.7).

Table 9.7   Allocation to special projects

€ millions	AD	AU	LU
Obligatory projects	1.7	1.2	1.4
Large strategic investments		7.0	3.0
Total	**1.7**	**8.2**	**4.4**

The business plans for large strategic investments are analyzed thoroughly along four dimensions: quantitative (ROI, cash flows, scenario analysis, etc.); qualitative (customers, market, etc.); strategic (fit with corporate and BU strategy); formal (compliance with corporate rules, e.g. hurdle rate, growth assumptions, etc.).

LARGE 1 is rejected due to insufficient strategic fit and the high level of instability in the scenario analysis; while LARGE 2, LARGE 3, and LARGE 4 are accepted largely as proposed (LARGE 3 requires minor, nonfinancial adjustments). The total investment for all special projects is €14.3 million (Table 9.7).

Step 2: Allocate remaining capital to business units (section 9.3.2)

Description of situation: The company uses the three-category approach to allocate the remaining capital. This includes both a competitive category and a small investments category. Its small investments category totals 60 % of the total investment volume (i.e. €42 million). The competition for capital category totals €13.7 million (€70 million − €14.3 million − €42 million). The size of this category helps to maintain entrepreneurship within the company but still provides the corporate center with a good level of control over its investments.

In total, 16 medium-sized investments were submitted in the competition for capital (each between €0.5–2.0 million), requiring a total expenditure of €24 million. In the small investments category, each business unit submitted proposals equivalent to about 10 % of their sales (Table 9.8).

Table 9.8   Medium-sized and small investments

€ millions	AD	AU	LU
Medium-sized investments submitted for competition of capital	7.0 (5 projects)	11.0 (7 projects)	6.0 (4 projects)
Proposals for small investments	15.0	25.0	10.0

Resulting activities and outcome: Each evaluator in the competition committee scored each of the medium-sized projects along several dimensions (ROI, strategic fit, time-to-launch, scenario sensitivity, probability of success, etc.), assigned an overall score, and ranked all the projects. The aggregation of all the evaluators' analyses produced an overall competitive ranking. Based on this ranking, the capital was then allocated to the projects in the resulting order, until the money allotted to the competition for capital category had been used up.

Based on the competition for capital's budget of €13.7 million, ADHESIVES was awarded four projects totalling €5.5 million, AUTOMOTIVE three projects totalling €3.9 million, and LUBRICANTS three projects totalling €4.3 million.

The business units' proposed small projects totalled €50 million in investment: this is above the category's budget of €42 million. The company therefore decided to allocate the available capital based on a simple measure of the risk-adjusted business unit return (risk-adjusted sales margin) and business unit size (sales), multiplying both metrics together (ADHESIVES 16 % × 150 = 24; AUTOMOTIVE 12 % × 250 = 30; LUBRICANTS 14 % × 100 = 14).

Following this formula, the corporate center made the following capital allocation: €14.8 million to ADHESIVES, [€42 million × 24/(24 + 30 + 14)] €18.5 million to AUTOMOTIVE, and €8.7 million to LUBRICANTS (Table 9.9).

Table 9.9   Allocation from competition for capital and small investments categories

€ millions	AD	AU	LU
Allocation from competition for capital category	5.5	3.9	4.3
Allocation from small investments category	14.8	18.5	8.7
Total	**20.3**	**22.4**	**13.0**

Step 3: Business units allocate capital to investments (section 9.3.3)

While the capital allocated in the categories of large strategic projects, obligatory projects, and competition for capital can only be used in the manner specified, that allocated in the small investments category can be distributed as each business unit sees fit. However, the business units have to take into account four limitations on this distribution that are set by the corporate center:

- **Approval size threshold:** Each project's costs need to be less than €500 000; above this size, all projects have to be submitted in the competition for capital category. Once they are rejected in this category, the business units are not allowed to pursue them further.
- **Corporate calculation standards:** The project's calculation should be made according to corporate specifications (e.g. at a discount rate of 8 %, using fixed growth rates for each country, in terms of risk treatment, etc.).
- **Minimum performance standards:** All the projects must achieve an ROI of at least 10 %.
- **Sign off:** All projects above €100 000 need to be signed off by the corporate center. The corporate center also selects at random a further 10 % of small investments (a minimum of three projects per business unit) for a more detailed examination.

Step 4: Implement capital assurance process (section 9.3.4)

The company has decided to use three levels of analysis in its capital assurance process. The required data will be provided by the business units and analyzed by a joint capital assurance team.

Firstly, the team will carry out a detailed deviation analysis for all the large strategic investments (i.e. LARGE 2, LARGE 3, and LARGE 4) and all its investments in the competition of capital category (i.e. 10 projects above €500 000). A range of suitable metrics, including industry-specific KPIs (the appropriateness of which has already been established by the company) will be used to analyze any deviations from the proposed values. The capital assurance team will seek to establish the underlying root causes of these deviations.

Secondly, the corporate center will conduct a time-and-money analysis for all the obligatory projects to check that total costs and ramp-up times are in accordance with the original proposals. Deviations of more than 10 % will be analyzed in more detail.

Thirdly, it will carry out a business unit performance analysis for the small investments category, i.e. an evaluation of each business unit's risk-adjusted performance (excluding extraordinary effects).

While the deviation analysis and the time-and-money analysis are carried out semi-annually, the business unit performance analysis is performed once a year.

Outcome of new allocation process

As Table 9.10 shows, the revised approach to capital allocation has resulted in a significantly different outcome compared to the old approach. While ADHESIVES and LUBRICANTS benefit from the new approach (+ 4.8 % and + 24.3 % respectively), AUTOMOTIVE receives less money (−12.6 %). This new allocation better reflects the company's strategic considerations, opportunities, and performance.

Table 9.10   Overview of results from new capital allocation approach

€ millions	Capital allocation				
Allocation categories	AD	AU	LU	$\sum$	Comments
Special projects category					
– Obligatory projects	1.7	1.2	1.4	4.3	All obligatory projects accepted (one with reduced amount)
– New business areas	–	–	–	–	No entry in new business areas planned
– Large strategic investments	–	7.0	3.0	10.0	One project of BU$_A$ rejected (insufficient strategic fit; instability of scenarios)
Competition for capital category	5.5	3.9	4.3	13.7	10 out of 16 projects (with original volume of €24 million) selected
Small investments category	14.8	18.5	8.7	42.0	Allocation to BUs based on risk-adjusted BU return and size
Total (new approach)	**22.0**	**30.6**	**17.4**	**70.0**	New approach takes into account BU situation and specialties
Old allocation approach	21.0	35.0	14.0	70.0	
Deviation (%)	4.8	−12.6	24.3		

9.4   CAPITAL ALLOCATION APPROACH FOR STRATEGIC ARCHITECTS AND FINANCIAL HOLDING STRUCTURES

The capital allocation process described above requires the corporate center to possess a certain minimum level of working knowledge and involvement in the day-to-day running of the company, especially in terms of being able to make trade-offs between the business units when making investments. In the case of a strategic architect or a financial holding structure, the corporate center is often not sufficiently involved in such issues to have the depth of understanding necessary to make such trade-offs. When the corporate center operates within such structures, therefore, it requires an approach that is less dependent on in-depth knowledge.

The approach to capital assurance proposed for this situation includes five steps based on benchmarking present performance and future expectations. The benchmarking is supported by in-depth analysis where necessary. This approach should provide the corporate center, when it is not involved in operations, with a good starting point for making its capital allocation (Figure 9.8).

Step 1: The first step is to define appropriate key performance indicators (it is feasible to obtain these from other companies). The KPIs should reflect the level of capital investment

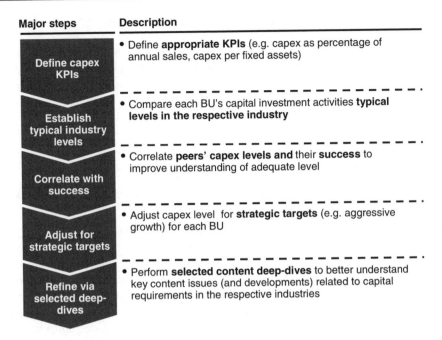

Major steps	Description
Define capex KPIs	• Define **appropriate KPIs** (e.g. capex as percentage of annual sales, capex per fixed assets)
Establish typical industry levels	• Compare each BU's capital investment activities **typical levels in the respective industry**
Correlate with success	• Correlate **peers' capex levels and** their **success** to improve understanding of adequate level
Adjust for strategic targets	• Adjust capex level for **strategic targets** (e.g. aggressive growth) for each BU
Refine via selected deep-dives	• Perform **selected content deep-dives** to better understand key content issues (and developments) related to capital requirements in the respective industries

Figure 9.8   Approach for strategic architects and financial holding structures

deemed necessary in the industry, e.g. in terms of capital expenditure as a percentage of sales, or capital expenditure per fixed asset.

Step 2: Using the KPIs selected in the first step, each business unit's capital investment activities are then compared to the levels typical for their industry. This will provide a first indication of the likely distribution of capital between the business units.

Step 3: A correlation analysis of peers' capital expenditure levels and performance (e.g. based on an outside-in analysis of financial statements, analyst reports, and press research) will help refine the estimate developed in Step 2. This analysis will also help produce a better understanding of the alternative capital allocation strategies used by other companies, and which of them has been more successful. [6]

Step 4: The preliminary capital expenditure budget should then be adjusted to take account of the company's strategic targets for each business unit (e.g. its aspiration for aggressive growth). Certain companies use scoring models to achieve this. Such models are based on a mixture of financial KPIs (e.g. CFROI and sales growth) and the strategic attractiveness of each business (e.g. based on a score that evaluates the opportunity offered by the market and the business unit's position in that market).

Step 5: In order to further refine and challenge the preliminary capital investment levels and their allocation, the corporate center performs in-depth analysis of certain selected

---

[6] This is not to suggest that there is a direct link between capital expenditure levels and financial performance as investments need time to have an effect on the company's performance and investments are only one among several factors that influence performance.

industries and markets in order to gain a better understanding of their key issues and potential developments.

Companies that use a benchmarking-based approach usually also retain a base budget in addition to the benchmarking-based capital budget that is used for any necessary reinvestments. The base budget is usually allocated to the business units based on a proxy (e.g. the business unit's depreciation or its replacement value). As described earlier, the suitability of a specific proxy will depend on a range of company-specific factors.

TECHNICAL INSERT

Illustrative example of benchmark-based approach

We will illustrate how this benchmark-based approach works using a simplified example of a conglomerate that employs just a single KPI (Table 9.11).

Description of situation: Our hypothetical company has four business units: AUTOMO-TIVE, SEMICONDUCTORS, CHEMICALS and ENERGY. All the business units are of roughly the same size (€100 million sales) and have approximately the same level of annual depreciation. Currently, the total capital of €100 million is allocated yearly, based on the annual depreciation, i.e. every business unit gets the same amount of capital: €25 million. The company has decided to increase its activities and now wishes to grow aggressively in ENERGY while retaining its position in SEMICONDUCTORS (i.e. defending its market albeit with reduced investment).

Resulting activities and outcome: Capital allocation is based on a combination of industry-specific benchmarks of capital expenditure per sales and strategic targets. An analysis of the company's major competitors shows that the typical levels of capital expenditure (as a percentage of sales in each industry) are as follows: AUTOMOTIVE, 15 %; SEMICON-DUCTORS, 20 %; CHEMICALS, 30 %; ENERGY, 35 %. The interim allocation of capital to each business unit is based on these levels. The allocation is then adjusted in accordance with the company's strategic priorities. As a result, ENERGY receives more capital than the industry average (to aid its aggressive growth) and SEMICONDUCTORS less (as it is expected merely to defend its position). The resulting capital allocation differs consider-ably from the original distribution and better reflects industry standards and the company's strategic priorities and targets (Table 9.11).

Table 9.11   Illustrative example of benchmark-based approach

Calculation metrics (€ millions)	AUTOMOTIVE	SEMI-CONDUCTORS	CHEMICALS	ENERGY
Current capital allocation	25	25	25	25
Typical level of capital expenditure per sales in each industry (%)	15	20	30	35
Sales	100	100	100	100
Interim capital allocation	15	20	30	35
Effect of strategic targets on allocation	0	−10	0	+10
New capital allocation	15	10	30	45

9.5   SUMMARY

The allocation of money to the right business opportunities and the compilation of the right investment portfolio are two of the most important tasks facing top management. To a large extent, the success or failure of these tasks determines the company's potential for future value creation. As mentioned at the outset, there is no one-size-fits-all approach to capital allocation, as each approach needs to be tailored to the individual company's strategic imperatives. We hope, nevertheless, that the guidelines presented here and the approaches we have described will help the reader to design the capital allocation approach that is best suited to his or her company.

REFERENCES

Vernimmen, P. Quiry, P. Dallocchio, M., Le Fur, Y. and Salvi, A. (2005) *Corporate Finance: Theory and Practice*. John Wiley and Sons Ltd.

Weber, J., Meyer, M., and Birl, H. (2006) *Investitionscontrolling in Deutschen Großunternehmen. Ergebnisse einer Benchmarking-Studie*. Wiley-VCH.

Index